DeFi

by Seoyoung Kim, PhD

DeFi For Dummies®

Published by: **John Wiley & Sons, Inc.,** 111 River Street, Hoboken, NJ 07030-5774, www.wiley.com

For general information on our other products and services, please contact our Customer Care Department within the U.S. at 877-762-2974, outside the U.S. at 317-572-3993, or fax 317-572-4002. For technical support, please visit https://hub.wiley.com/community/support/dummies.

Wiley publishes in a variety of print and electronic formats and by print-on-demand. Some material included with standard print versions of this book may not be included in e-books or in print-on-demand. If this book refers to media such as a CD or DVD that is not included in the version you purchased, you may download this material at http://booksupport.wiley.com. For more information about Wiley products, visit www.wiley.com.

Library of Congress Control Number: 2022948456

ISBN: 978-1-119-90680-3; ISBN 978-1-119-90681-0 (ebk);
ISBN 978-1-119-90682-7 (ebk)

SKY10038191_110922

Contents at a Glance

Table of Contents

Introduction

Welcome to *DeFi For Dummies*! Whether you are simply curious to learn the decentralized finance (DeFi) lingo, are interested in trying out a DeFi application, or have a burning desire to code and deploy your own DeFi protocol, this book is for you!

In this book, you'll find helpful information and advice for exploring the world of DeFi. You'll also find useful step-by-step guides along the way that will teach you how to set up a Web3 wallet, how to navigate DeFi platforms, and even how to develop your very own DeFi application.

DeFi is a rich and multidisciplinary field, drawing from math, cryptography, computer science, contract theory, and economics. Although I incorporate these elements throughout the book, you don't need a background in these areas to understand the concepts presented or to follow the hands-on instructional guides provided.

About This Book

This book provides a holistic treatment of the rapidly evolving DeFi space — its evolution, applications, and underlying technology.

Keep in mind, though, that this book intends to provide a customizable journey for all audiences — whether you work in tech or finance or simply want to be a more interesting conversationalist at happy hour. (In other words, rest assured that you don't have to read the book in its entirety to understand the separate topics!)

Foolish Assumptions

The most important assumption that I make about you is that you are interested in learning about DeFi! That said, I do make additional assumptions in writing the step-by-step instructional guides that are peppered throughout this book. Although I don't assume any prior knowledge or experience in programming or Web3 applications, I do assume the following:

- You have a computer and access to the internet.
- You know the basics of navigating your computer and the internet, and you know how to download, install, and run programs.
- You understand that, because of formatting and space constraints, some web addresses or long hashes may be split across two lines of text. Keep in mind that these web addresses and large numbers should be copied verbatim as though the line break doesn't exist.
- You understand that DeFi is a rapidly evolving space. In fact, many protocols and systems were in active updating or were anticipating migration at the time of writing. Keep in mind that some of my illustrated guides may no longer represent ongoing conditions on the ground by the time you read this book.

  For instance, as of September 15, 2022, Ethereum completed its long-awaited Merge, shifting from a consensus protocol that was based on proof of work (PoW) to one based on proof of stake (PoS). Although this shift doesn't impact the step-by-step guides provided throughout this book, it does impact some of the descriptions regarding block times and the process by which blocks are added to the Ethereum blockchain.

  Moreover, the Ropsten test network, which historically operated as a PoW-based blockchain that most closely followed the protocol of the Ethereum Mainnet, may be deprecated by the time you get to the step-by-step guides. Thus, you may prefer to use a different test network, such as Goerli, when following the instructional portions of this book. The instructions remain the same, but you'll need to keep in mind that my instructional figures and steps refer to the Ropsten test network rather than, say, the Goerli test network. Moreover, you'll need to get the appropriate test ETH for the test network that you select. For instance, you can simply Google "Goerli test faucet" to find free test ETH for the Goerli test network. These reminders are also peppered throughout the book.

Finally, I assume you know that I do not provide legal or investment advice. The protocols I describe and the step-by-step guides I provide to borrow, lend, or trade on DeFi platforms are designed to be demonstrative and didactic.

Icons Used in This Book

I use the following icons throughout this book to guide your expectations or to highlight certain pieces of information.

TIP

The Tip icon draws your attention to potential shortcuts or easy adaptations that can be made without breaking an entire system.

REMEMBER

The Remember icon highlights information that is particularly important to know or to later recall to clear up possible confusion.

TECHNICAL STUFF

The Technical Stuff icon is used to direct your attention away from (if you are a non-techie) or to draw your attention to (if you are an aspiring techie) technical details that aren't required to understand the main points.

WARNING

The Warning icon tells you to watch out! It marks important information that may save your time, sanity, tokens, or even friendships.

Beyond the Book

In addition to the material in the hard copy or e-book you're reading right now, you can also find this book's Cheat Sheet by going to `www.dummies.com` and entering *DeFi For Dummies* in the search field. The Cheat Sheet offers useful terminology and quick tips on how to start dabbling in the world of DeFi. You can also access up-to-date code and supplementary files at `https://www.seoyoungkim.com/defifdcode.html`.

Where to Go from Here

I've written this book in a way that allows you to craft your own journey based on whether you are more interested in applications, high-level ideas, or technical development. You don't have to read the entire book to successfully execute the step-by-step guides, and I carefully guide you through certain sections or chapters that require actions or knowledge from a prior section or chapter in the book.

That said, I highly recommend that you begin with Chapter 1 to place your DeFi journey in context.

1 Getting Started with DeFi

IN THIS PART . . .

Discover the world of decentralized finance.

Learn the DeFi lingo.

Execute your first DeFi transactions.

IN THIS CHAPTER

» Defining decentralized finance

» Comparing CeFi and DeFi processes

» Considering the cons of a DeFi world

» Exploring promising DeFi implementations

Chapter 1
Introducing Decentralized Finance

The modern *decentralized finance* (DeFi) era truly began with Bitcoin, the first widespread implementation of a decentralized method of recordkeeping that is permissionless yet reliable and secure. Bitcoin effectively provides a currency that doesn't rely on the stability of a central authority.

The implications of such a technology are huge for developing economies where faith in central government is low and bank runs are a serious risk, if not a reality. Moreover, much of the world's population is, at most, one generation removed from being forcibly chased from their homes. Just 70 years ago, Seoul, the capital of Korea, was captured and recaptured four times, and families were permanently separated in a war that ultimately resulted in two separate nations. The fall of Saigon 50 years ago resulted in a mass exodus of Vietnamese refugees seeking asylum; and more recently, the fall of Kabul (2021) and the Russian invasion of Ukraine earlier this year (2022) led to more waves of emigrants who found themselves in sudden exile.

But aside from more dire circumstances — like the collapse of a banking system or the fall of your government — it's natural to question what true value Bitcoin's underlying technology adds in a stable and wealthy nation. After all, I trust that Bank of America won't maliciously siphon funds from my account, and despite the infamous Wells Fargo fake account scandal (for which it was ultimately fined $3 billion), I would even entrust my money to a Wells Fargo checking account. Nonetheless, reliable economies still have submarkets that are inherently rife with distrust of the central operator, with dark pools (securities exchanges in which participants can trade anonymously and with less transparency) being a case in point. (Try Googling "dark pool lawsuit"!) This trust issue naturally goes away if there is no central operator to distrust, and with the advent of Bitcoin, a proven technology now exists to implement modern DeFi processes across many use cases in finance.

This book isn't about touting the next big cryptocurrency or NFT. It's about the promise of the underlying technology, and where and how that technology can be elegantly applied in ways that truly add value to the situation at hand.

Demystifying DeFi

The idea of decentralized processes is certainly not new. After all, before *centralized finance* (CeFi) arose to establish trusted intermediaries, primitive DeFi was the status quo. Transactions were all peer-to-peer, and you were constrained by your local neighborhood to gain access to capital and to obtain goods by bartering one item for another. Recordkeeping was minimal, and ownership was determined by physical possession.

In modern markets, transactions require confidence in the validity of the agreement, which is provided by reliable and secure recordkeeping systems. After all, when you sell your car, you are really transferring the legal right to access the car. Without a reliable recordkeeping system in place, chaos would ensue. (Imagine the return of Finders Keepers as a rule of law!)

What's truly exciting now is the distributed-ledger technology that provides a reliable and secure method of recordkeeping that is not maintained by a trusted intermediary, such as Bank of America or the DMV. Behold the dawn of the modern DeFi era!

From autonomous collectives to trillion-dollar DAOs

Well-functioning, leaderless communities are all around us, and in each circumstance, an inherent governance mechanism incentivizes and gels the group to act in concert — all without an elected official to assign roles and lead the process. From homework teams to neighborhoods to informal potlucks, small groups can effectively and efficiently self-govern when there are grades to maintain, property prices to protect, or reputational concerns at stake.

These small-scale examples probably feel reasonable and natural. But what if I told you that a trillion-dollar organization could autonomously validate, execute, secure, and provide ongoing updates to an entire system without an elected leader to assign tasks? The concept sounds naïve at best, and possibly crazy.

And yet, Bitcoin has provided a battle-tested case in point for the underlying technology that enables it to function in a decentralized and autonomous fashion. Yes, Bitcoin is indeed a trillion-dollar *decentralized autonomous organization* (DAO)! Of course, at this scale and with the value at stake, a DAO can't rely solely on simple mechanisms like reputational concerns to incentivize participants to behave honestly and in a way that upholds the values of the system. Instead, the underlying protocol must be foolproofed against malicious players who may work hard to cheat the system. I explain these protocols in greater depth in Chapter 9, "DeFi Building Blocks."

Transacting in DeFi versus CeFi

By this point in the chapter, DeFi may still seem rather abstract. Comparing examples of DeFi versus CeFi processes for certain types of transactions can help to demystify the distinction.

Borrowing assets

Suppose you want to borrow money. How would this transaction be implemented in primitive DeFi versus modern CeFi versus modern DeFi?

- **Under a primitive DeFi process:** You hit up everyone you know within reasonable geographic proximity — a neighbor, a friend, a family member — and hope that someone will lend you something that you can barter with at your local marketplace.
- **Under a modern CeFi process:** People have checking accounts, savings accounts, CDs, and so on with the bank, which means that all these people have lent money to the bank. In turn, the bank lends some of this money to you.
- **Under a modern DeFi process:** People lock up funds in a *smart-contract account*, which is a software program on a public blockchain that automatically enforces and executes the rules in the smart-contract code. This smart-contract account is programmed to function as a lending pool from which you can borrow funds. (See Chapter 7 for details on how decentralized loans work.)

Selling assets

Suppose that instead of borrowing assets, you have assets that you want to sell. Comparing the three types of processes again, here's how this transaction would be implemented:

- **Under a primitive DeFi process:** You again hit up everyone you know within reasonable geographic proximity — a neighbor, friend, family member — and attempt to barter by trial and error.
- **Under a modern CeFi process:** Liquidity providers stand by, waiting to buy the asset from those who want to sell

and to sell the asset to those who want to buy. These liquidity providers commit to buy and sell a certain quantity of assets at varying prices on designated exchanges that serve as official marketplaces for the assets in question. In turn, you place an order to sell the asset through your brokerage firm (who has custody of the asset).

» **Under a modern DeFi process:** Liquidity providers lock up assets and funds in a smart-contract account. This smart-contract account serves as a liquidity pool and is programmed to function as an *automated market maker.* (See Chapter 6 for details on how automated market makers work.) In turn, you can swap your assets for funds from this smart-contract account.

Check out Chapter 4, "Making Your First DeFi Transactions," for a quick, hands-on tutorial if you want to get your hands dirty without learning the technical underpinnings.

Dispelling harmful DeFi myths

REMEMBER

Of course, both the CeFi and DeFi worlds have some bad actors, but DeFi activity is *not* synonymous with illicit activity. The misconception that DeFi applications primarily facilitate or promote criminal activity is untrue and harmful to the DeFi community.

In contrast to cash transactions, which typically aren't recorded, crypto transactions (such as in bitcoins or ether) are memorialized for all time on a public recordkeeping system known as a *blockchain.* In fact, any legitimate entity that touches crypto must employ the services of at least one blockchain analytics firm (such as Chainalysis) to credibly convey that it is serious about adhering to anti-money laundering (AML) provisions.

As the lowest-hanging fruit, blacklisted accounts (such as those associated with ransomware attacks or on the OFAC list) are barred from transacting with legitimate institutions. From there, blockchain analytics firms assign risk scores to graylisted accounts based on suspicious activity that suggests a possible connection to other graylisted or blacklisted accounts. Chapter 9, "DeFi Building Blocks," introduces you to tracing activity on a block explorer, and Chapter 11, "Launching a Smart Contract on Ethereum," delves more deeply into this process.

Just as it's (nearly) impossible to spend $10 million in ill-gotten cash (you can't show up with suitcases of cash to buy a home), it's (nearly) impossible to spend $10 million in ill-gotten crypto.

Going Full Circle: The DeFi-CeFi Infinity Loop

A large part of DeFi activity really entails learning (or relearning) why CeFi arose in the first place and is so critically important. The following sections explain how primitive DeFi processes were made more efficient by CeFi processes, which were then challenged by modern DeFi processes (but which, in turn, demonstrated weaknesses of their own, highlighting again the value of CeFi and perpetuating the DeFi-CeFi infinity loop).

Safeguarding wealth

Suppose you want to save assets and keep them safe. How would this process be improved from primitive DeFi to modern CeFi to modern DeFi (and then back to modern CeFi)?

- **Starting with a primitive DeFi process:** Perhaps you keep your money (or gold or diamonds) under your mattress (or in a hole) and hope that no one finds it (but also that you don't forget where you stored it). Given the danger and other obvious flaws in trying to safeguard your money, trusted institutions arise to take over this function.
- **Transitioning to a modern CeFi process:** You entrust your money to a bank. But then Bitcoin emerges, and perhaps traditional banking seems boring (or maybe you're in a country with a precarious banking system or volatile political climate).
- **Trying out a modern DeFi process:** You keep your private crypto key (a sequence of numbers) in a safe place, or you split your private key and store it across multiple safe places (maybe under your mattress or in a hole, and again, hope that no one finds it but also that you don't forget where you stored it). But then you remember that you're

bad at being your own bank. You may forget where you hid your keys, or someone may steal them, or they may become damaged in a fire. You decide to entrust your crypto wealth to a vault service, and now you're back to modern CeFi!

Transferring funds

Now suppose you want to transfer funds to another party. Comparing the evolution of processes again, here's how this transaction might be attempted and improved across iterations:

- **Starting with a primitive DeFi process:** You physically hand over the money (or gold or diamonds) and hope that no one robs you along the way. Given the danger and other obvious flaws (you can't send money to someone far away), trusted institutions arise to take over this function.
- **Transitioning to a modern CeFi process:** You write a check or request your bank to wire money to another account. But this process can be slow and expensive, especially for international wire transfers.
- **Trying out a modern DeFi process:** You use a noncustodial wallet service, such as MetaMask, to send crypto to another account. But then you realize that you sent the funds to the wrong account! Sadly, there's no one to call and no one who can halt or reverse the process. So then you decide to go back to writing checks or wiring money through your trusted bank.

Continuing the cycle

As the preceding examples show, the need to have a way to track transactions and troubleshoot problems while finding cost savings causes people to go full circle, from DeFi to CeFi and back again. Overall, we really aren't good at being our own banks, and we benefit from well-defined property rights. Intermediaries naturally arose to provide legitimacy, protection, order, and reliable recordkeeping. Sadly, these intermediaries became complacent and charged more than they should, and the particularly accelerated pace of technological development in the last 10–15 years brought on the *financial technology* (FinTech) movement. With that movement came the aggressive push to *disintermediate* — that is, to cut out the middleman and democratize the system for smaller players.

However, truly decentralized platforms can be clunky and frustrating, with bad UI/UX (user interface/user experience) and little to no customer support, and updates take a long time to coordinate in leaderless organizations (*and* we are bad at being our own banks). So then a defined group or elected leader steps in again to provide a better and more streamlined experience, and the DeFi-CeFi infinity loop goes on . . . .

Deciding to DeFi or Not to DeFi

As you've likely gathered from the previous sections, a large part of the DeFi thought process is learning and relearning the efficiencies and deficiencies of both CeFi and DeFi. In the fervor to embrace DeFi, it's important to remain mindful of CeFi market mechanisms in place and why those mechanisms may be important.

So before you explore the remaining chapters that expound on all the wonderful things you can do with modern DeFi, such as trading on decentralized exchanges (see Chapter 6) or taking on a decentralized loan (see Chapter 7), the following sections offer some important caveats.

Acknowledging inherent deficiencies in DeFi

Decentralized processes have some built-in problems that are difficult to avoid or resolve. They are fraught with inefficiencies and coordination issues, which is why identifiable entities with elected leaders naturally arise. After all, Microsoft would achieve far less if it lacked centralized leadership and all shareholders had to be consulted before any decision can be implemented.

Societal costs to individuals arising from coordination issues are particularly tangible when you consider commercial banks and other types of lending institutions. When you walk into Bank of America to borrow money, an entire back-end process with its investment-banking arm is involved. This back-end process is critical to your ability to get the loan in the first place. The process entails pooling and securitizing the bank's loans so that they can be sold to other financial institutions (such as funds and other asset management firms). If Bank of America can't sell the loans to get them off of its balance sheet, it will issue fewer loans. Without integrating this critical back-end process, decentralized lending volume will remain constrained, as evidenced by the thousands of small community banks that don't issue as many loans or even certain types of loans because they lack coordinated access to sell off the loans.

Overall, complete reliance on decentralized, peer-to-peer lending would have the perverse effect of making capital less accessible to smaller players.

Recognizing CeFi problems that migrate into DeFi

Simply taking CeFi processes and slapping them onto a blockchain can't magically wave away problems from the CeFi world.

For example, improperly structured and insufficiently backed assets are as toxic in the DeFi world as they are in the CeFi world. A recent debacle with the so-called stablecoin, TerraUSD (UST), saw its value plummet from its dollar peg to just a few cents on the dollar, creating a situation reminiscent of the Financial Crisis of 2007–2008, also known as the Great Recession. This crisis etched the terms *mortgage-backed securities* (MBS) and *collateralized debt obligations* (CDOs) into the minds of the general public, who until that point had been blissfully unaware of the shadow banking system and structured products.

Moreover, securities laws must be followed in the DeFi world as well as in the CeFi world, and problems with enforcing ownership rights of physical assets aren't solved by simply storing ownership records on a public blockchain. Overall, DeFi is not the answer to all of CeFi's problems.

Identifying hurdles to adoption

Even for truly amazing and value-adding DeFi applications, the hurdles to adoption remain high for the general population. Most tutorials leave much to be desired because they are either out of date, overly simplified, or far too complicated, and navigating DeFi protocols is far from intuitive. (You can get your first taste in Chapters 3 and 4.) Overall, when it comes to DeFi processes, the user experience is relatively unfriendly compared to that of CeFi processes that have better production teams, user interfaces, and help desks.

For instance, consider the process of obtaining bitcoins from a Bitcoin ATM (BTM), as shown in Figure 1-1. This transaction should be one of the easiest and friendliest entry points into the DeFi ecosystem. However, the process still confuses many users, who are ill equipped to know what to do with the paper wallet that materializes after the BTM has swallowed their cash.

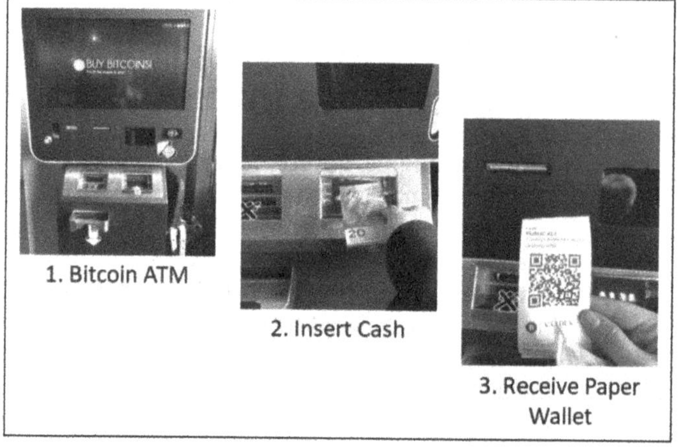

FIGURE 1-1: Bitcoin ATM (BTM) in Zurich.

DeFi also still suffers from the *crypto horn* effect, which refers to the negative impressions of crypto that spill over into anything even tangentially related to crypto (the opposite of a *halo* effect). With extreme price swings generating instant millionaires and overnight paupers, crypto hasn't been placed in the most favorable light. Because no way to meaningfully talk about true, modern DeFi exists without embedding crypto into the conversation, the DeFi movement sadly suffers from the ensuing misunderstandings and even disdain that plagues crypto.

Contemplating the Future of DeFi

The most exciting prospects for DeFi relate to projects that provide a practical pathway toward solving issues of distrust in modern financial markets. This umbrella extends to projects that provide access to financial services and concessions (such as delayed settlements, covered in Chapter 7) that, so far, have been available only to large institutions.

For example, to solve issues of distrust, perhaps a decentralized exchange will soon materialize as a registered *alternative trading system* (ATS) on which to trade tokenized securities. Imagine a decentralized dark pool free from concerns that a central operator may be illegally soliciting and placing orders ahead of a large trade that was placed first! Automated market makers are currently far from being able to handle the magnitude of volume required by institutional trades, but current implementations (explained in Chapter 6) provide a promising starting point.

Another promising development in DeFi is the ongoing empowerment of smaller (non-institutional) players. One of my favorite DeFi applications is Aave's flash loan protocol (detailed in Chapter 7), which democratizes delayed settlements and reduces up-front capital requirements for small retail traders. Perhaps the next phase in decentralized trading could entail decentralized clearing corporations!

The potential amazingness of seemingly unimportant applications

Practical considerations aside for a moment, implementing a DeFi process for its own sake can provide interesting puzzles and thought experiments, and I'm hugely in favor of creating DeFi implementations just for DeFi's sake. After all, *RSA encryption* technology, which for decades provided an effective method for secure data transmission, was born from a subfield within *number theory*, which is a branch of *pure mathematics* — a discipline focused purely on mathematics for its artistic merits and without consideration for external applications. Sometimes creative problem solving simply for the sake of creative problem solving yields the most practical applications of all!

In a similar vein, it's exciting to watch how DeFi processes are being implemented and improved in decentralized *metaverses* (discussed further in Chapter 8). Gamified analogues can highlight real-world use cases and pave the way for real-world implementations, as evidenced by how the addictive aspects of video games have shaped motivational processes in the real world. The prevalence of dashboards and gamified progress reports across professional and educational settings shows that life does indeed take lessons from art. Likewise, if million-dollar plots of virtual land in decentralized metaverses can be secured as ERC-721 non-fungible tokens (NFTs) on the Ethereum blockchain, perhaps developing nations with less reliable recordkeeping systems can follow suit.

Less than one-third of the world's population enjoys secure property rights — a problem identified by the World Bank as fundamental to reducing poverty and fostering growth. Imagine, for example, if such governments were to commit to well-defined and well-protected property rights. Transparent and reliable records of ownerships and transfers could be implemented as NFTs on a well-established public blockchain, and automated lending protocols could allow borrowers to access funds by posting their NFT-ized land titles as collateral. Such an endeavor could help to forge the path toward creating digital records of substantial non-fungible assets in economies fraught with poor recordkeeping systems.

The ERC-721 NFT standard began with CryptoKitties, an overwhelmingly successful digital collectible (like a digital, blockchain-based analogue of Beanie Babies) that was launched on the Ethereum blockchain in 2017. Perhaps the world needs more adorable cats and creepy apes (such as the famous Mutant Ape Yacht Club NFTs) to be unnecessarily slapped onto a public blockchain to demonstrate the feasibility of greater concepts.

Can we completely replace CeFi?

Once upon a time, the world ran on primitive DeFi, so it's certainly possible to replace CeFi with decentralized processes, complemented by modern technology where possible. However, the real question to ask is *should* we? This chapter covers some serious drawbacks to DeFi. Some of these drawbacks are largely cosmetic issues that can be overcome, but others point to unavoidable problems inherent in decentralized processes.

As it stands, there's still much value to be extracted from the DeFi movement — and I see a world with CeFi and DeFi processes humming along at some point in (possibly symbiotic) coexistence.

Proceeding on Your DeFi Journey

I hope this book is an enjoyable and insightful journey into a modified way of thinking (and possibly a new way of life!).

Along the way, I hope to spark ideas, dispel harmful misconceptions, and encourage creative development. I wish you a fulfilling and productive experience as you go on to select your next chapter. Cheers!

IN THIS CHAPTER

» Knowing the DeFi keywords

» Distinguishing frequently conflated topics

Chapter 2

Discovering the DeFi Lingo

From trustless systems to layer 2 scaling solutions, the rapidly developing world of modern DeFi is full of new and esoteric terms that make it difficult for newcomers to get started. This chapter acquaints you with a host of common DeFi terms and clarifies some common misconceptions relating to measures of DeFi activity and how DeFi versus CeFi processes are implemented.

I don't go into too many technical details in this chapter. The purpose here is to get you started with key DeFi concepts so that you can meaningfully navigate the subsequent chapters as well as confidently flex some DeFi street cred at your next cocktail party or family gathering.

Introducing Key DeFi Terms

This section covers some commonly used language and concepts that are now deeply embedded in the DeFi vernacular.

Moving into the Web3 era

Web3 refers to a vision for a decentralized web, built on blockchain technology and token-based economics, with the view to shift power and data ownership from tech companies back to individual users.

Although people use the terms Web3 and Web 3.0 interchangeably, *Web 3.0* originally and more often refers to the next generation of a smarter World Wide Web. Unlike Web3, the original coining of Web 3.0 (also known as the *Semantic Web*) doesn't focus on decentralization as a core tenet. Instead, Web 3.0 is the next natural extension of the web as we experience it today. *Web 1.0* focused on static content delivery, and *Web 2.0* offered greater interconnectivity and was more participatory, especially with the rise of social media and platforms conducive to a creator economy. Now, Web 3.0 aims to promote even greater interconnectivity through the use of machine learning and other artificial intelligence mechanisms.

Going the way of a DAO

A *decentralized autonomous organization* (DAO) is a leaderless community where anyone is free to enter and exit as they please, without permission, and can participate as little or as much as they wish. A DAO (pronounced *dow*, similar to *the Tao* of ancient philosophy) typically has its own *native token* that serves as the currency of the community. The main goal of this self-governed community is to maintain a reliable system that stores information, facilitates transactions, and provides a public record of all community members and their respective activity in the system.

Note that referring to "a DAO" is not the same as referring to "The DAO," where the latter specifically references a (now defunct) decentralized fund that was implemented by way of a nexus of smart contracts on the Ethereum blockchain. The DAO was famously hacked within months of launching, and the fallout led to a major rift in the Ethereum community. (For more details on the aftermath of this security breach, see Chapter 10.)

Characterizing blockchains and consensus protocols

The public and permissionless recordkeeping system that secures transaction records and account balances of crypto assets such as Bitcoin is known as a *blockchain-based distributed ledger.* Also referred to as a *public blockchain,* this system organizes transaction records into blocks that are cryptographically linked.

Unlike a private ledger, such as one kept by a bank or a brokerage firm, public blockchains are

- **Permissionless:** Anyone can read or write to the blockchain (yes, anyone!). Of course, there are carefully crafted rules in place, known as the *consensus protocol* (or *consensus mechanism*), to ensure that only legitimate transactions are recorded and that past records are not maliciously altered.
- **Distributed:** Replicated copies of the blockchain are shared across all participants.
- **Trustless:** Public blockchains do not require a trusted authority. Despite being permissionless, the records are reliable and tamper-proof (without the need to entrust the recordkeeping to a central bookkeeper).
- **Autonomous:** Transactions are recorded and the ledger is continuously maintained without a designated leader overseeing the process.

Chapter 9, "DeFi Building Blocks," goes into greater detail on the underlying mechanics of public blockchains and the consensus protocols — *proof of work* (PoW) versus *proof of stake* (PoS) — that ensure the trustless security of these public blockchains (even if some of the participants are careless or outright dishonest!).

Describing cryptocurrencies and NFTs

A *cryptocurrency* is a fungible crypto asset whose ownership and transaction records are secured on a public blockchain. Fungible tokens are like dollar bills: You don't care which dollar bills you receive as long as you receive the correct quantity.

A *non-fungible token* (NFT) is also a crypto asset secured on a public blockchain. However, unlike cryptocurrencies, NFTs are designed to keep a record of non-fungible items. Non-fungible tokens are like concert tickets: You care which specific concert tickets you receive, because one ticket may put you in the front row whereas another may place you all the way in the back of the venue.

Chapter 5, "Decentralized Assets," provides an overview of common categories and use cases of crypto assets.

Defining smart contracts and dApps

A *smart contract* is a software program — a set of code and data built on a public blockchain — that enforces a set of well-defined rules that are automatically executed when called.

A *decentralized application* (dApp) combines a front-end user interface with back-end smart contracts, using a public blockchain for data storage.

Chapters 11 and 12 walk you through how to deploy a smart contract, and Chapter 13 walks you through how to implement a full-blown dApp.

Getting acquainted with L1, L2, and the EVM

Layer 1 (L1) refers to the base (main) blockchain where transactions are ultimately secured. Bitcoin and Ethereum are examples of L1 platforms.

Layer 2 (L2) refers to a platform that piggybacks off a base blockchain for security. L2 platforms are designed to speed up the processing of transactions, which are ultimately reconciled and secured on a base blockchain.

The *Ethereum Virtual Machine* (EVM) refers to the computational environment that defines how instructions are specified and state transitions are processed on Ethereum. *EVM-compatible* platforms mimic the EVM — which is really a fancy way of saying that a smart contract developed for Ethereum can easily be deployed on another EVM-compatible platform.

Chapter 10 goes into greater detail describing various L1 and L2 platforms. Chapter 12 demonstrates the ease of deploying smart contracts on EVM-compatible platforms after you've done so on Ethereum (in Chapter 11).

Grasping important metrics: Market cap, volume, and TVL

A token's *market capitalization* (market cap) refers to its total market value, calculated as the price per token times the total circulating supply. A token's *volume*, typically captured over a 24-hour period, refers to its total trading volume (how many times the token was bought and sold, and how much value changed hands in the previous day). Figure 2-1 provides a snapshot from CoinMarketCap, accessed at `https://coinmarketcap.com/`, presenting these metrics for the top five tokens by market cap.

Name	Price	Market Cap	Volume(24h)	Circulating Supply
Bitcoin BTC Buy	$20,163.48	$385,679,748,066	$32,048,661,257 1,590,148 BTC	19,136,150 BTC
Ethereum ETH Buy	$1,530.51	$186,903,819,141	$17,416,872,142 11,384,131 ETH	122,165,314 ETH
Tether USDT Buy	$1.00	$67,553,870,148	$44,726,513,938 44,723,795,392 USDT	67,549,764,120 USDT
USD Coin USDC Buy	$1	$52,287,297,076	$7,995,740,395 7,995,655,435 USDC	52,286,741,488 USDC
BNB BNB Buy	$285.73	$46,113,572,381	$988,421,537 3,458,184 BNB	161,337,261 BNB

FIGURE 2-1: Snapshot from CoinMarketCap, taken on August 29, 2022.

Although market cap and volume are widely publicized and important metrics, they don't provide a good sense of how active a given protocol is. When it comes to crypto, most holders are not actually using the associated platforms; they are simply purchasing the crypto to hold and sell at a later time (hopefully at a profit). For instance, consider concert tickets. Some people buy the tickets intending to attend the concert (they will actually use these tickets), whereas others buy the tickets hoping to later resell them at a higher price.

Total value locked (TVL) provides a better idea of the actual usage of a given platform or specific protocol for DeFi activity. TVL is determined as follows:

- For a given DeFi application (a nexus of smart contracts built on a public blockchain to provide some sort of DeFi service), the protocol's TVL is calculated by taking the sum of the tokens locked across the smart-contract accounts powering the protocol.
- The TVL for a given blockchain, such as Ethereum, is calculated by taking the sum of the TVLs of each of the protocols on the network.

Figure 2-2 provides a snapshot from DefiLlama, accessed at `https://defillama.com/`, presenting the top five DeFi applications by TVL, and Figure 2-3 shows a snapshot from DefiLlama presenting the top five blockchains by TVL.

Name		TVL
1	MakerDAO (MKR)	$7.92b
2	Lido (LDO)	$6.76b
3	AAVE	$6.08b
4	Curve (CRV)	$5.8b
5	Uniswap (UNI)	$5.6b

FIGURE 2-2: Snapshot from DefiLlama of top DeFi applications by TVL, taken on August 29, 2022.

Chapter 14, "The Top Ten DeFi Applications," provides more information on these DeFi protocols, and Chapter 15, "The Top Ten Smart-Contract Platforms," tells you more about these networks for DeFi activity.

Name	Protocols	TVL
1 Ethereum (ETH)	542	$34.26b
2 Tron (TRON)	10	$5.76b
3 BSC (BNB)	449	$5.37b
4 Avalanche (AVAX)	249	$1.87b
5 Polygon (MATIC)	295	$1.83b

FIGURE 2-3: Snapshot from DefiLlama of top blockchains by TVL, taken on August 29, 2022.

Knowing Important Distinctions

Finally, I round out this chapter with a couple of important differences between CeFi and DeFi implementations.

Custodial versus noncustodial

Custodial describes processes and marketplaces where a trusted intermediary takes custody of your assets, securing and trading them on your behalf.

Noncustodial describes processes and marketplaces where you maintain custody of your assets until you've sold or otherwise disposed of them.

For instance, in a noncustodial marketplace like eBay, you retain control of your goods until you've sold them. In contrast, consignment markets tend to be custodial: You submit your secondhand luxury goods to the custody of a trusted consignment shop that will sell the items on your behalf.

Custodial marketplaces are inherently CeFi, whereas noncustodial marketplaces may be CeFi or DeFi, depending on how the marketplace is implemented. Chapter 6, "Decentralized Exchanges and Marketplaces," offers greater color and context concerning this distinction as it pertains to stock markets and crypto exchanges.

On-chain versus off-chain

On-chain transactions are recorded on a public blockchain as they are executed, whereas *off-chain* transactions are tracked separately (typically for convenience, privacy, or speed), with final state changes ultimately being recorded on a public blockchain.

Custodial crypto exchanges, such as Coinbase, keep an off-chain account of ownership records and transactions made on the exchange (that is, these transactions are not recorded to a public blockchain). When you move your crypto assets from your custodial Coincase.com wallet to a noncustodial wallet, such as MetaMask, this transaction will be recorded on-chain. Any subsequent transactions you make from your account via the MetaMask wallet service also occur on-chain.

Chapter 3, "Dabbling in DeFi," walks you through installing the MetaMask browser extension and setting up your MetaMask wallet.

IN THIS CHAPTER

» Introducing the MetaMask browser extension

» Connecting to the Ethereum blockchain

» Funding your account with ETH (or test ETH)

Chapter 3

Dabbling in DeFi: Getting Your Hands Dirty

To meaningfully navigate the DeFi-verse, you first need to set up a Web3 wallet that can submit transactions and access smart contracts on a public blockchain (see Chapter 2 for key DeFi terms and concepts). Because so much of the DeFi ecosystem has been built on Ethereum, this chapter shows you how to get started with MetaMask, an application that connects you to the Ethereum blockchain. I don't dive into all the bells and whistles in this chapter. My main purpose here is to get you up and running so that you can make your first DeFi transactions as quickly as possible.

TIP

If you already have the MetaMask browser extension installed and connected to a funded account (with ETH and/or test ETH), you can skip straight ahead to Chapter 4 to begin making your first DeFi transactions.

Setting Up Your Wallet

This section shows you how to install and set up a Web3 wallet. I focus on MetaMask, which is one of the most well-known and widely supported noncustodial crypto wallets connecting you to the Ethereum blockchain. Other popular contenders include WalletConnect and the Coinbase Wallet (not to be confused with the custodial Coinbase.com wallet).

Unmasking MetaMask

MetaMask is an amazingly simple yet powerful application that allows you to manage your Ethereum accounts and to interact with the Ethereum network. With this wallet app, you can create new accounts, import existing accounts, and submit transactions. In addition to handling ether (ETH), the token native to Ethereum, this wallet application is also compatible with ERC-20 fungible tokens and ERC-721 non-fungible tokens (NFTs).

TECHNICAL STUFF

MetaMask operates as a browser extension, which makes it easy for you to connect to web-based Ethereum dApps (decentralized applications), the vast majority of which have integrated MetaMask functionality in their websites. More ambitious readers may be glad to discover in Chapter 11 that Remix — a web-based integrated development environment (IDE) — is integrated with MetaMask to allow you to seamlessly launch smart contracts on Ethereum without having to download additional software or run a full node on your computer (something I explain further in Chapter 9).

WARNING

Exercise caution when interacting with dApps, just as you would when engaging with any application coming from an unknown or untrusted source.

Installing MetaMask

MetaMask currently supports the Chrome, Firefox, Brave, and Edge browsers. I've chosen to proceed in Chrome because it's the most commonly used desktop internet browser in the U.S.

BRAVING THE BRAVE BROWSER

Brave provides a privacy-focused browser whose default setting is configured to automatically block cookies and other web trackers. By default, Brave also automatically blocks online advertisements, instead allowing users to opt-in and earn Basic Attention Tokens (BATs). By integrating BATs into the Brave browsing experience, creators can be compensated for their content and viewers can be compensated for their attention.

In addition to serving as a Clearnet browser to access the World Wide Web, Brave has integrated the InterPlanetary File System (IPFS) to allow users to quickly and easily access the distributed peer-to-peer network, which is part of a group of networks colloquially known as the darknet or dark web. This decentralized file-sharing network depends on a vast network of participants who store and share duplicate information in a way that doesn't depend on a central server to host the content.

Thus, in true DeFi fashion, Brave is working to bring a new, distributed vision of Web3 to the masses along with a democratized reboot of the web-based advertising ecosystem!

TIP

If you're feeling a bit adventurous and want a full DeFi immersion, I recommend getting comfortable with the Brave browser, which you can download from `https://www.brave.com`.

REMEMBER

Keep in mind that your visual and textual prompts may differ slightly from what's shown in the following steps, depending on your chosen browser. You can use these steps to download and install the MetaMask browser extension:

1. **Go to `www.metamask.io` and click the Download Now button, as shown in Figure 3-1.**
2. **Click the Install MetaMask for Chrome button, as shown in Figure 3-2.**

   You're rerouted to the MetaMask page of the Chrome web store, as shown in Figure 3-3.

FIGURE 3-1: The MetaMask main page.

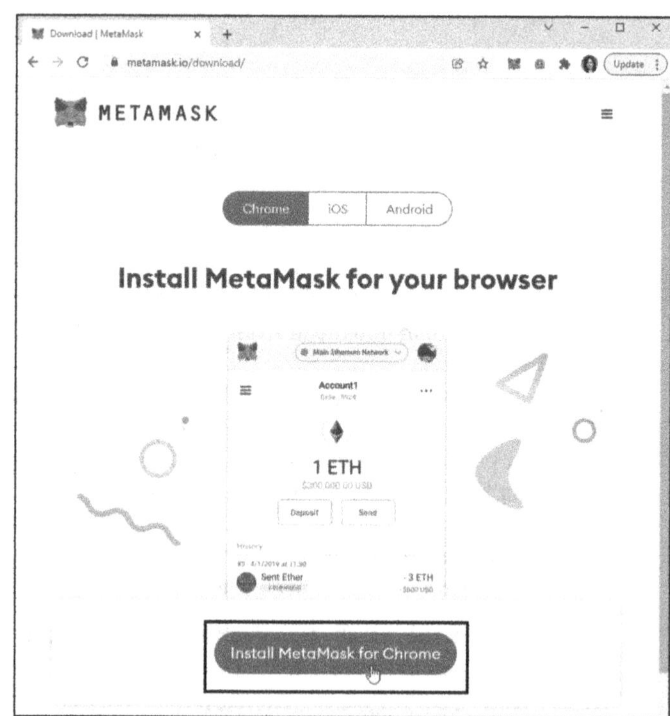

FIGURE 3-2: Installing MetaMask on the Chrome browser.

FIGURE 3-3: The MetaMask page within the Chrome web store.

REMEMBER

Of course, if you're using a different browser, the prompts will look slightly different, as shown in Figure 3-4.

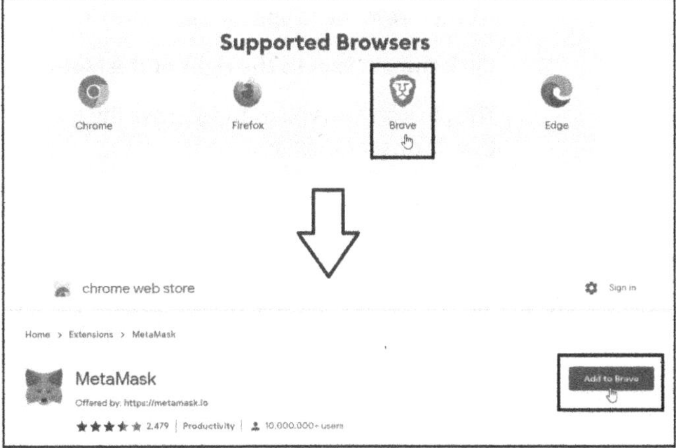

FIGURE 3-4: Installing MetaMask on the Brave browser.

3. **Click the Add to Chrome button.**

   A pop-up window appears, as shown in Figure 3-5.

4. **Click the Add Extension button.**

   After the installation is complete, a pop-up window momentarily appears to inform you that MetaMask has been added to your browser.

   You should now see a small fox icon in the upper-right corner of your browser window (to the right of the address bar), as shown in Figure 3-6.

   If the fox icon doesn't automatically appear in your browser's toolbar, follow these additional steps:

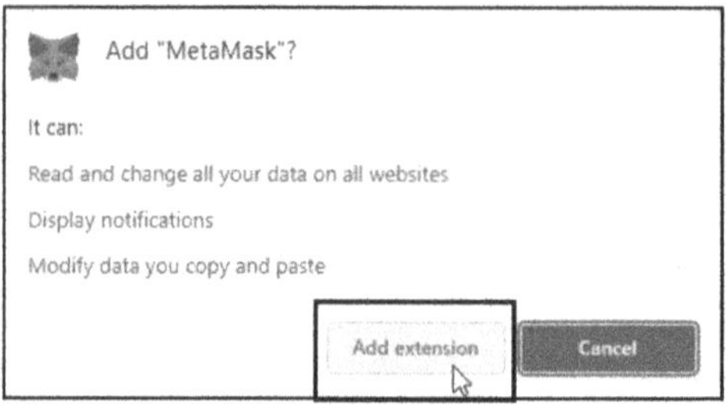

FIGURE 3-5: Pop-up window to add MetaMask browser extension.

5. **Click the puzzle-piece-shaped icon in the upper-right corner of your browser window (to the right of the address bar).**

   A drop-down menu appears, as shown in Figure 3-7.

6. **Click the pin icon to the right of the MetaMask fox icon.**

   The pin icon turns blue, and you see the fox icon pinned to your browser's toolbar.

Yay, you're now ready to set up your MetaMask wallet!

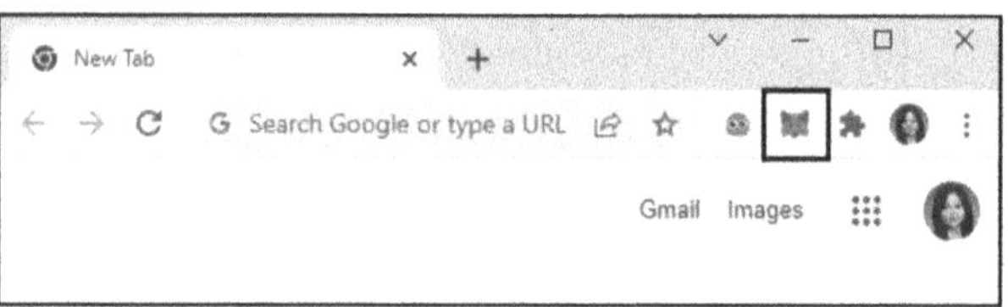

FIGURE 3-6: The MetaMask fox icon in the browser toolbar.

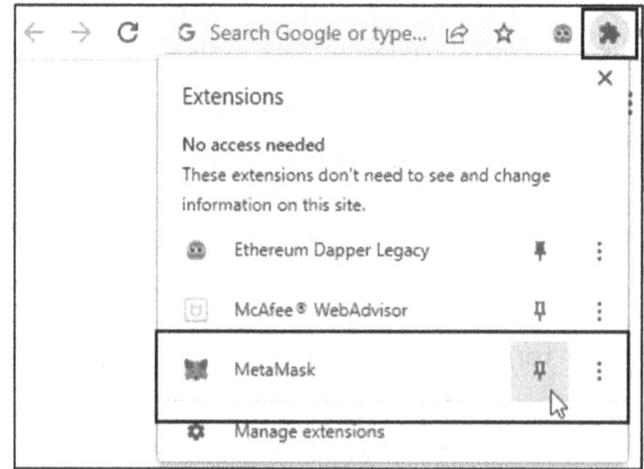

FIGURE 3-7: The browser extensions drop-down menu.

Setting up MetaMask

After you've successfully installed the MetaMask browser extension, you can follow these steps to set up your wallet:

1. **Click the MetaMask fox icon in your browser's toolbar.** (In my case, I am continuing to use the Chrome browser.)

   A new browser window appears, with a Get Started button displayed at the bottom of the page.

2. **Click the Get Started button.**

   The page that opens shows an Import Wallet and a Create a Wallet button, as shown in Figure 3-8. The Import Wallet button on this page is what you'll use if you ever need to reinstall MetaMask and recover a MetaMask wallet that you've already set up.

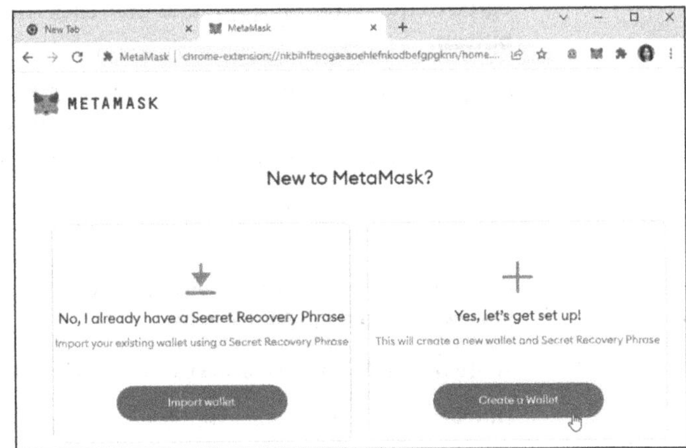

FIGURE 3-8: Creating a new MetaMask wallet.

3. **Click the Create a Wallet button.**

   On the Help Us Improve MetaMask page that opens, you can click either the No Thanks or I Agree button, depending on whether you want to share your usage data with the MetaMask development team.

   The next page opens, prompting you to create a password, as shown in Figure 3-9.

4. **Create and confirm your new password.**

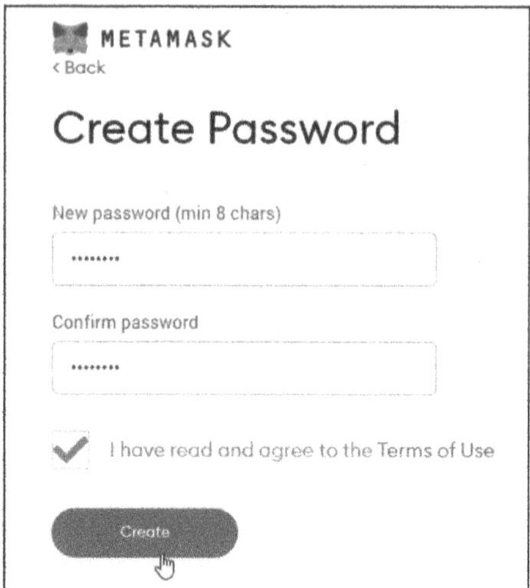

FIGURE 3-9: Setting your MetaMask wallet password.

5. **Click the check box to confirm that you've read and agree to the terms of usage, and then click the Create button.**

   A page appears that features instructions and a brief video explaining the importance of your Secret Recovery Phrase. Watch this video and read the instructions carefully.

   When you're ready, click the Next button, which takes you to your Secret Recovery Phrase.

6. **Click the lock icon to reveal your private 12-word phrase, as shown in Figure 3-10.**
7. **Write down this phrase and store it for safe keeping.**

   This Secret Recovery Phrase represents the digital keys that provide access to your crypto wallet and its contents. Do *not* share this phrase with anyone.

WARNING

Do not skip this critical step! You'll need your Secret Recovery Phrase if you ever need to reinstall the MetaMask browser extension or if you want to access your MetaMask wallet on a different browser or different computer.

In fact, even the MetaMask Support team cannot recover your MetaMask account for you. Specifically, MetaMask's "Basic Safety and Security Tips" state that:

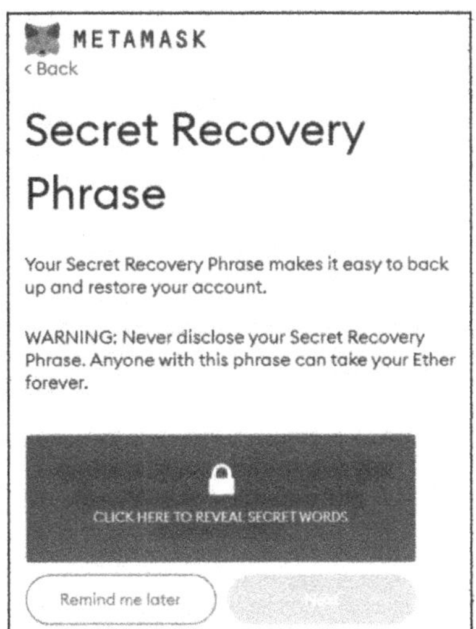

FIGURE 3-10: Obtaining your MetaMask Secret Recovery Phrase.

"MetaMask is not a cloud-based solution. If your device breaks, is lost, or has data corruption, there is no way for the MetaMask Support Team to recover this for you. **This Secret Recovery Phrase is the only way to recover your MetaMask accounts.**" (See `https://metamask.zendesk.com/hc/en-us/articles/4404722782107-User-guide-Secret-Recovery-Phrase-password-and-private-keys` for more details).

8. **After you've secured your Secret Recovery Phrase, click the Next button.**

The next page requires you to confirm your Secret Recovery Phrase by selecting the correct words in the correct order, as shown in Figure 3-11.

WARNING

Do not share this unordered word matrix with anyone, as I've (foolishly!) done here for demonstrative purposes.

TECHNICAL STUFF

Using this word matrix, a hacker can easily create a program to regenerate my Secret Recovery Phrase. In fact, this hypothetical hacker could guess my secret phrase within `12! = 12 x 11 x 10 x .... X 2 x 1 =` **`479,001,600`** attempts, which represents the total number of possible permutations of the words presented in Figure 3-11. Although 479,001,600 distinct guesses would be quite onerous to attempt manually, a computerized algorithm can glide through this guessing game.

FIGURE 3-11: Confirming Your Secret Recovery Phrase.

9. **After you've clicked each word in the correct order to produce the correct word sequence, click the Confirm button.**

   Congratulations! Your browser takes you to your initial MetaMask Account 1 Page, as shown in Figure 3-12.

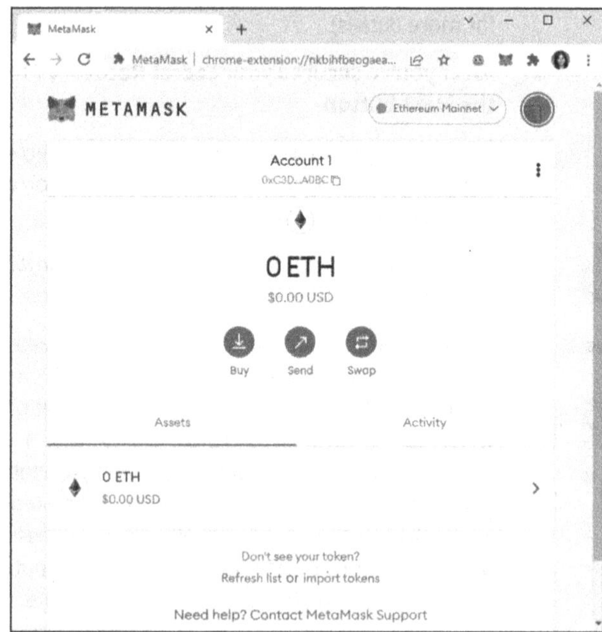

FIGURE 3-12: A newly initiated MetaMask wallet.

REMEMBER

Going forward, you can simply access your MetaMask wallet by clicking the MetaMask fox icon in your browser's toolbar, which reveals a drop-down window, as shown in Figure 3-13. (Revisit Steps 5 and 6 from the previous "Installing MetaMask" section if you need to re-pin the MetaMask fox icon to your browser's toolbar.)

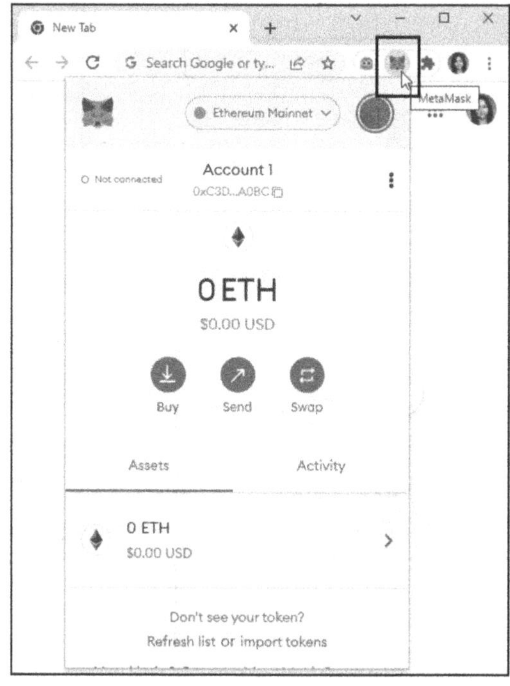

FIGURE 3-13: Accessing the MetaMask wallet drop-down window from your browser's toolbar.

Renaming your account

If you'd like to rename your account, proceed as follows:

1. **From the MetaMask drop-down window, click the vertical ellipsis to the right of the account name and public address, as shown in Figure 3-14.**
2. **From the drop-down menu that appears, select Account Details.**

   A new window appears with the account name above a QR code that contains your public address, as shown in Figure 3-15.

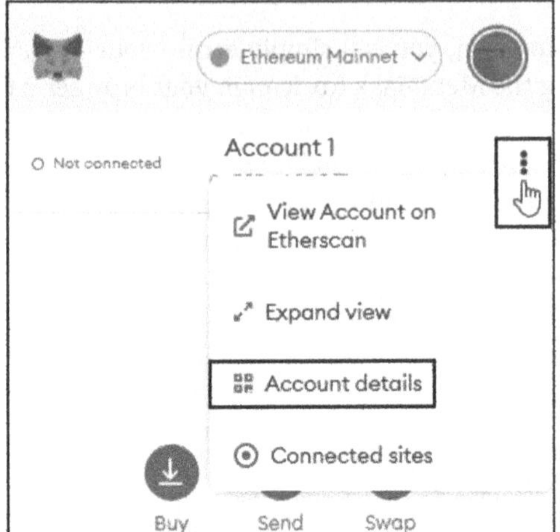

FIGURE 3-14: Navigating account options on MetaMask.

FIGURE 3-15: Account-specific details on MetaMask.

3. **Click the pencil icon next to the account name.**

   A text input box appears, as shown in Figure 3-16.

4. **Rename the account as you see fit, and then click the check box to the right of the text input box to confirm the change.**

FIGURE 3-16: Renaming an account in your MetaMask wallet.

TIP

Great, now you're ready to fund your account! Feel free to skip the following section, "Working with MetaMask on your mobile device," if you're eager to keep the momentum going.

Working with MetaMask on your mobile device

For added mobility, MetaMask is also available on iOS and Android devices. Much of what I demonstrate throughout the rest of this chapter can also be executed from MetaMask's in-app browser on a smartphone or other mobile device, such as an iPad. However, if you plan to ultimately deploy a smart contract on Ethereum (described in Chapter 11), you'll still need to have the MetaMask browser extension on your desktop machine.

Installing MetaMask on your mobile device

Follow these steps to download and install the MetaMask app on your iOS or Android device.

REMEMBER

As before, keep in mind that your visual and textual prompts may differ slightly from what I present below depending on your chosen mobile device.

1. **From your phone's browser, go to** `https://metamask.io`**.**
2. **Follow the series of prompts to ultimately download and install the MetaMask app, as shown in Figure 3-17.**

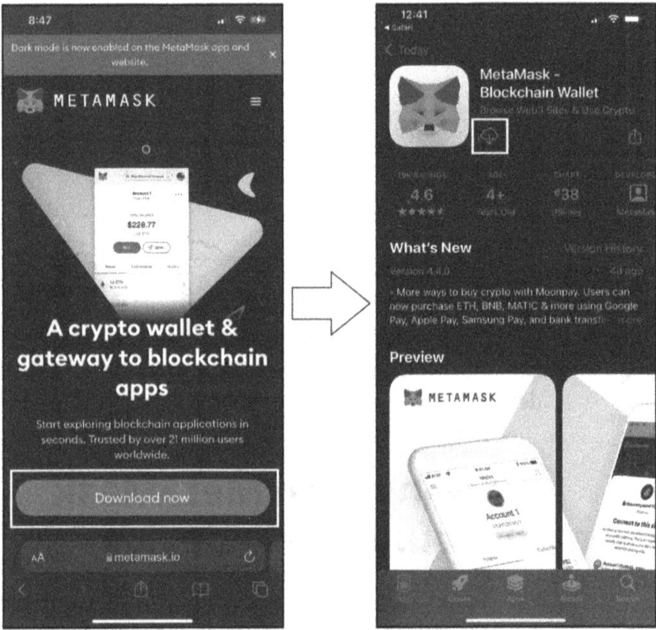

FIGURE 3-17: Installing the MetaMask app on your mobile device.

3. **From the MetaMask app, tap the Get Started button; then select the Import Using Secret Recovery Phrase option.**

   On the Help Us Improve MetaMask page that opens, you can click either the No Thanks or I Agree button, depending on whether you want to share your usage data with the MetaMask development team.

   A new screen appears prompting you for your Secret Recovery Phrase, as shown in Figure 3-18.

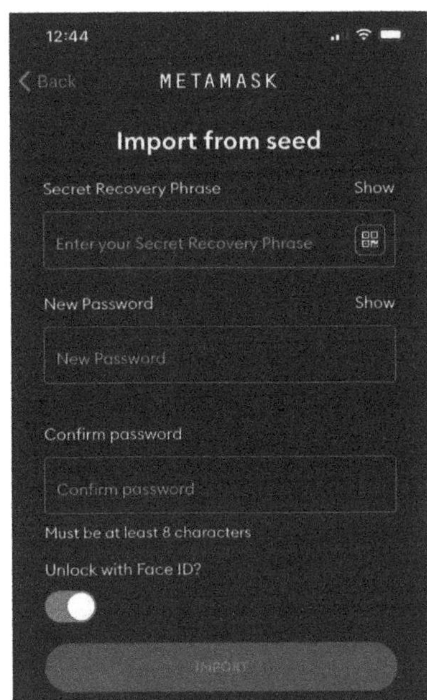

FIGURE 3-18: Importing your wallet from the MetaMask mobile app.

4. **Enter the Secret Recovery Phrase you saved from Steps 6 and 7 of the earlier section, "Setting up MetaMask"; then select and confirm your new password and then tap the Import button.**

   The screen that appears displays your imported wallet, as shown in Figure 3-19. Notice that the public address here — located below the account name — matches the public address shown previously in Figure 3-13.

   Also notice that the new account name you specified in the earlier section "Renaming your account" doesn't get carried over in the import process.

5. **Long-press the account name to rename your account.**

   I've renamed mine to "DeFi For Dummies," as shown in Figure 3-20, to remain consistent with how I named this same account from the MetaMask desktop browser extension in the previous "Renaming your account" section.

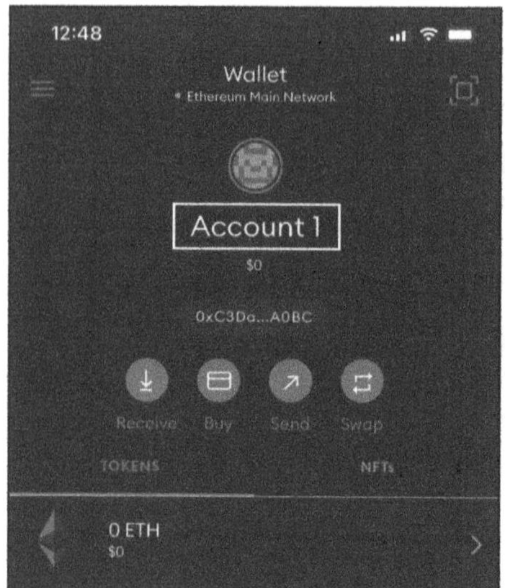

FIGURE 3-19: MetaMask on your mobile device.

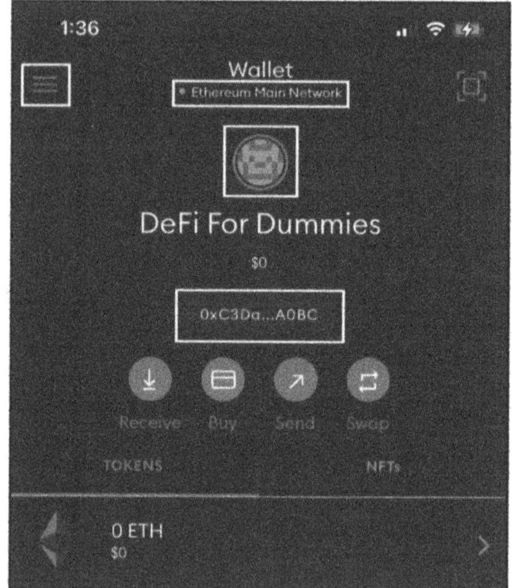

FIGURE 3-20: My renamed account in the MetaMask mobile app.

Getting around in MetaMask on your mobile device

TIP

Here are a few tips for navigating the MetaMask app features from your mobile device:

» To copy the public address, tap the partial address located below the account name and balance.

- To switch accounts or create new ones, tap the colorful orb above the account name.
- To toggle networks, tap the option that currently reads as Ethereum Main Network (located above the colorful orb).
- For additional options, tap the menu icon in the upper-left corner. A drop-down menu appears, as shown in Figure 3-21.

  This drop-down menu allows you to toggle between the wallet and the in-app browser, and enables you to connect to web-based dApps.

The remaining instructions and figures in this chapter apply to the MetaMask browser extension installed on a desktop.

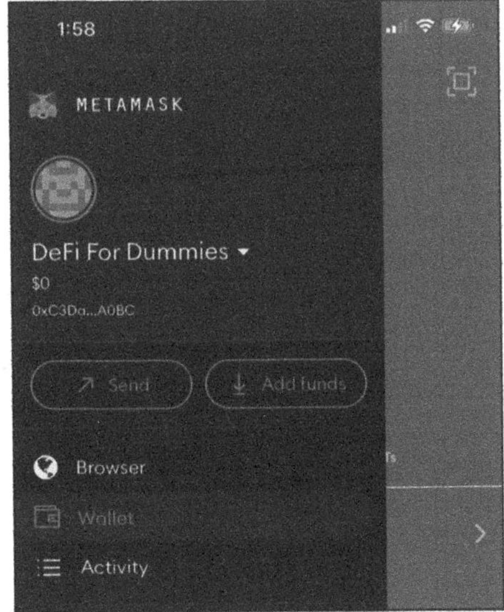

FIGURE 3-21: The MetaMask mobile app drop-down menu.

Funding Your Account

To transact within the Ethereum network, also known as Mainnet, you need some ETH, which is Ethereum's native token. However, you can also use public *testnets*, which are test networks that provide a practice environment designed to mimic the Ethereum Mainnet. Test networks allow you to play around and make transactions as you would on Mainnet without having to spend actual (expensive!) ETH. After you're comfortable with how certain transactions work on a testnet, you can confidently execute those transactions on Mainnet.

TIP

So unless you're really antsy to throw down some actual money, you can skip ahead to a later section, "Getting test ETH," to prepare to practice on a test network first.

Getting (Real) ETH

You can easily buy some ETH via the MetaMask wallet by clicking the Buy button from the MetaMask drop-down window, as shown in Figure 3-22. A new window appears, as shown in Figure 3-23, providing options to buy ETH via Wyre or Transak (if you scroll down).

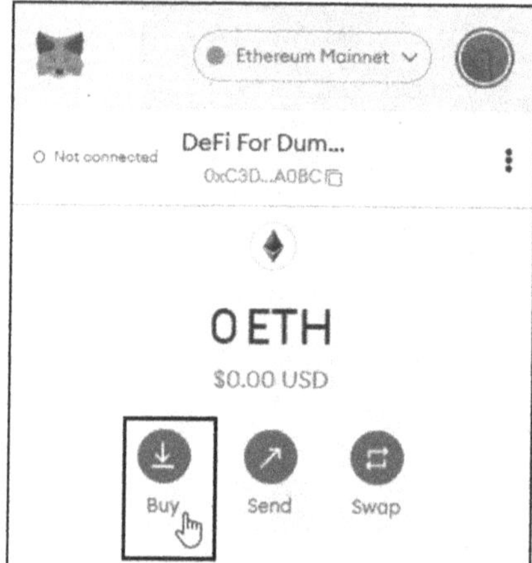

FIGURE 3-22: Buying ETH via the MetaMask wallet.

With these options, you can use your debit card to quickly purchase up to $1,000 and $1,500 worth of ETH, respectively, without providing additional information to satisfy requirements for KYC (know your customer) compliance. If you don't mind the extra steps, you can set up an account on one of the following reputable, U.S.-based crypto exchanges:

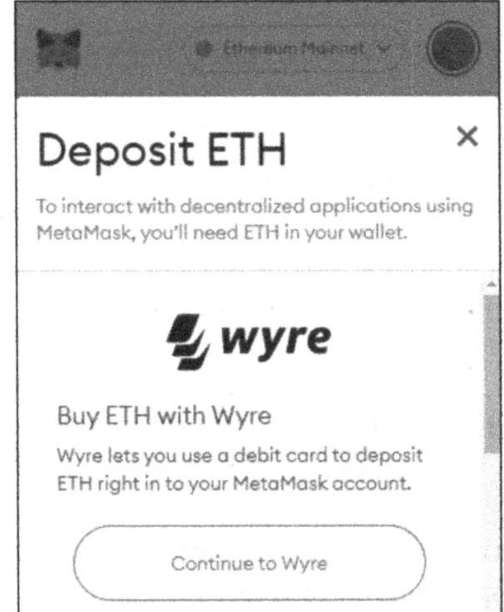

FIGURE 3-23: Quick options for buying ETH for your account.

- » Coinbase, at `www.coinbase.com`
- » Gemini, at `www.gemini.com`
- » Kraken, at `www.kraken.com`

After you've purchased ETH through one of these exchanges, you can transfer it to the account you set up in your MetaMask wallet in the prior section.

Getting test ETH

Just as you need ETH to transact on Mainnet, you need test ETH to transact on a test network. Thankfully, plenty of sources provide free test ETH for you to play around on any of the Ethereum testnets. In general, testnet *faucets* serve to provide test tokens that allow developers and curious dabblers to play around before spending any real money.

In this book, I focus on the Ropsten test network, which has historically operated as a public proof-of-work (PoW)–based blockchain that most closely follows the protocol of the Ethereum Mainnet. In anticipation of The Merge, Ethereum's long-anticipated move from PoW to proof-of-stake (PoS), the Ropsten test network underwent a *merge* of its own to PoS in June 2022.

For more details on PoW, PoS, and other consensus protocols, see Chapter 9.

WARNING

Keep in mind that the Ropsten test network may be deprecated by the time you read this book. All the provided instructions remain the same, but you may prefer to use a different test network, and accordingly, access different test faucets. Refer to the Introduction for more details.

First, follow these steps to connect to the Ropsten test network:

1. **From the main MetaMask drop-down window, click the central drop-down menu, shown in Figure 3-24.**

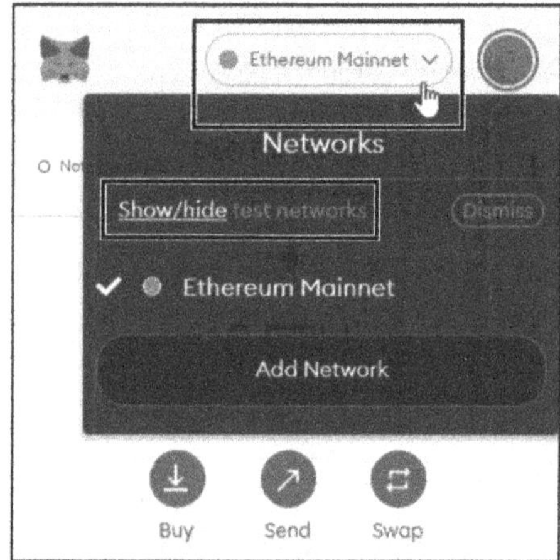

FIGURE 3-24: Networks drop-down menu on MetaMask.

2. **From the Networks drop-down menu, click the Show/ Hide link.**

   A new menu of Advanced options appears, as shown in Figure 3-25.

3. **Toggle the button under Show Test Networks from Off to On.**
4. **Click the Networks drop-down menu again.**

   The drop-down menu now lists the test networks, as shown in Figure 3-26.

5. **Select the Ropsten Test Network.**

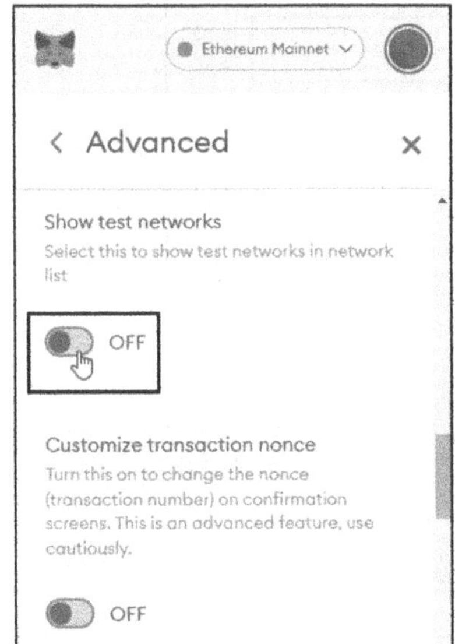

FIGURE 3-25: Advanced options on MetaMask.

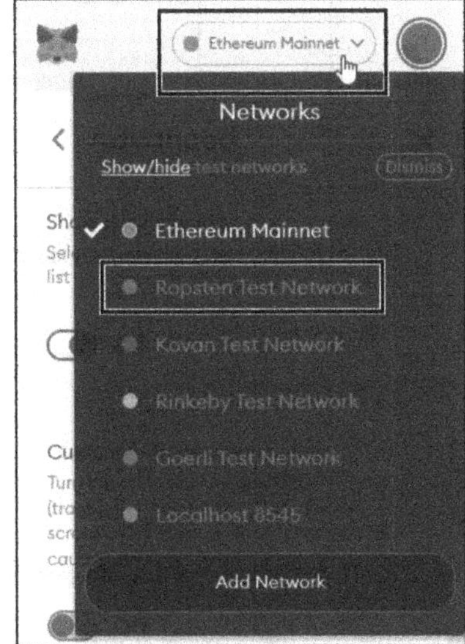

FIGURE 3-26: The Networks drop-down menu on MetaMask now includes test networks.

Now that you've enabled and toggled to the Ropsten Testnet, follow these steps to get some rETH for your account:

1. **From the main window, click the Buy button, as shown in Figure 3-27.**

   A new scroll-down menu appears, as shown in Figure 3-28.

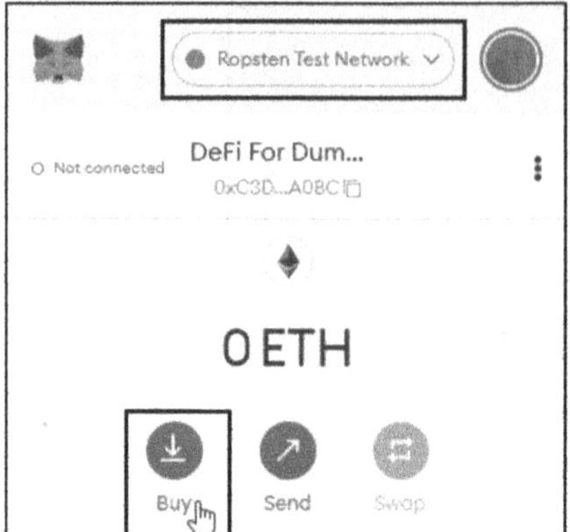

FIGURE 3-27: The MetaMask main window, now under the Ropsten test network.

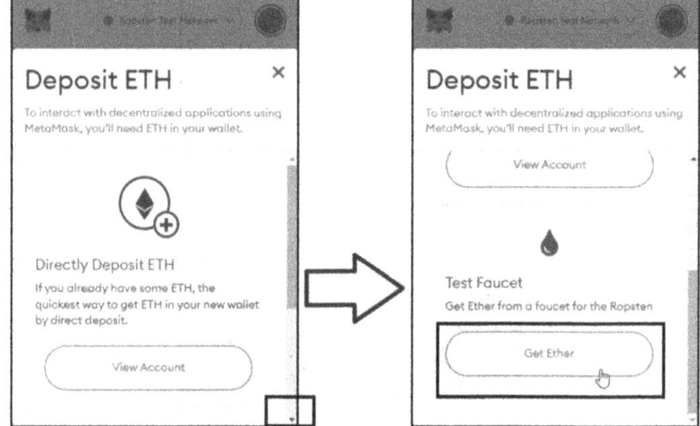

FIGURE 3-28: The Deposit ETH scroll-down menu under the Ropsten test network.

2. **Scroll to the bottom and then click the Get Ether button.**

   You're taken to the MetaMask Ether Faucet site, accessed at `faucet.metamask.io`, as shown in Figure 3-29.

3. **Click the green Request 1 Ether from Faucet button.**

   A MetaMask Notification pops up, as shown in Figure 3-30.

   REMEMBER

   If the pop-up doesn't automatically appear, click the fox icon in your browser toolbar to follow the steps to connect.

4. **Click the Next button followed by the Connect button to connect your account with the faucet site.**

FIGURE 3-29: The MetaMask Ether Faucet.

FIGURE 3-30: Connecting an account to a site with MetaMask.

5. **Wait approximately 1 minute.**

WARNING

Be patient — the process might complete within 15 seconds or, in rare instances of high network congestion, could take around 30 minutes. Repeatedly clicking the button to request rETH will only result in a rate-limit error.

Test faucets typically rate limit requests based on your IP address, account address, and account balance. Most faucets require a 24- to 48-hour cooling period between requests, and don't provide funds to accounts above a certain balance.

REMEMBER

Keep in mind that test faucets may dry out over time. Thankfully, alternative test faucets can easily be found. Simply point your browser to `www.google.com`, and type in **ropsten faucet**.

6. **Check your account balance on MetaMask, as shown in Figure 3-31.**

REMEMBER

If you've waited longer than 30 minutes and still don't see the rETH in your account, make sure you're on the Ropsten test network within your MetaMask wallet.

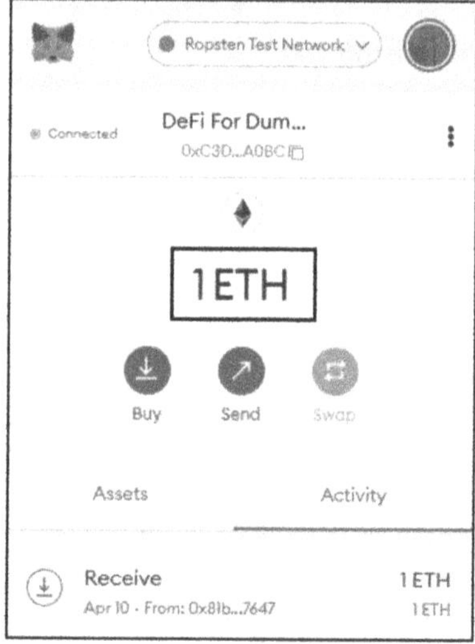

FIGURE 3-31: The Ropsten test ETH (rETH) balance.

Congratulations! You are now the proud owner of 1 rETH and ready to make your first DeFi transactions on the Ropsten test network.

TIP

Although 1 rETH is plenty to complete the next set of exercises in Chapter 4, if you desire more rETH, you can run a quick Google search to find plenty of other test faucets to draw from.

REMEMBER

Finally, keep in mind that your wallet won't reflect your rETH balance when you toggle to different networks, as demonstrated in Figure 3-32, where I've temporarily toggled back to Ethereum Mainnet for demonstrative purposes.

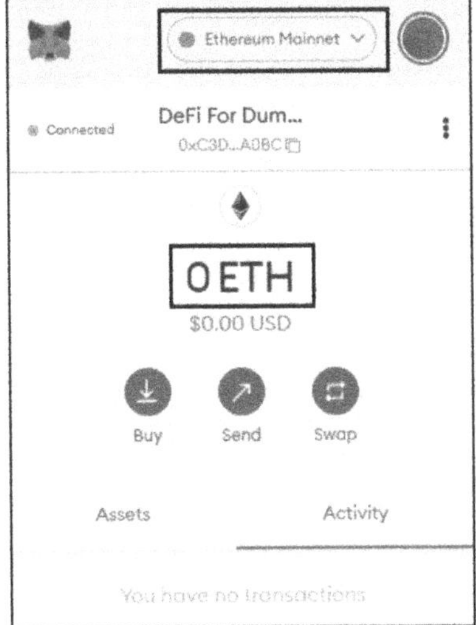

FIGURE 3-32: "Disappearing" rETH balance when toggling to other networks.

IN THIS CHAPTER

» Making a decentralized loan

» Borrowing against your collateral

» Executing a trade on a decentralized exchange

Chapter 4

Making Your First DeFi Transactions

This chapter walks you through the steps to lend, borrow, and execute a trade, all without relying on a CeFi intermediary such as Coinbase (www.coinbase.com) or Gemini (www.gemini.com). Specifically, I show you how to use the Compound and Uniswap DeFi protocols developed on the Ethereum blockchain. Both protocols are available on the Ropsten Testnet in addition to the Ethereum Mainnet. I don't dive into too many details as to how decentralized lending or borrowing (via Compound) or decentralized trading (via Uniswap) actually works. The point is to get your hands dirty with some initial DeFi experience, so I defer more detailed discussions of the underlying mechanics until Chapter 6 and Chapter 7, respectively.

To work through this chapter, you need to have installed the MetaMask browser extension (see "Setting Up Your Wallet" in Chapter 3) and set up your wallet with a funded account (see "Funding Your Account" in Chapter 3).

TIP

The step-by-step instructions run more smoothly if you are logged into MetaMask and connected to your desired network (a testnet or Mainnet) before you begin the instructional guides. For the DeFi transactions I demonstrate in this section, I've chosen to proceed on the Ropsten Testnet from my desktop machine. For the purposes of this chapter, I assume you're also logged in to your MetaMask browser extension, connected to Ropsten, and have some rETH (see "Getting Test ETH" in Chapter 3).

You can choose to proceed on Mainnet if you don't mind using (and wasting!) some actual ETH as you play around. You can also try out these protocols from your mobile device if you've installed MetaMask there also (see "Working with MetaMask on your mobile device" in Chapter 3). The same instructions apply, but the visual and textual prompts may differ.

REMEMBER

Keep in mind, though, that the market conditions you may observe on the Ropsten Testnet (or any testnet for that matter) are not indicative of what may be available on the actual Ethereum Mainnet. For instance, the token supply and liquidity can differ dramatically from what you observe on a test network, as can the quoted rates charged for borrowing capital and the quoted yields proffered for lending capital.

REMEMBER

Also keep in mind that the Ropsten test network may be deprecated by the time you read this book. All the provided instructions remain the same, but you may prefer to use a different test network. Refer to the Introduction for more details.

Time to get started!

Decentralized Lending

Follow these steps to make a decentralized loan:

1. **Point your browser to** `https://app.compound.finance`.

   A pop-up window appears with wallet options, as shown in Figure 4-1.

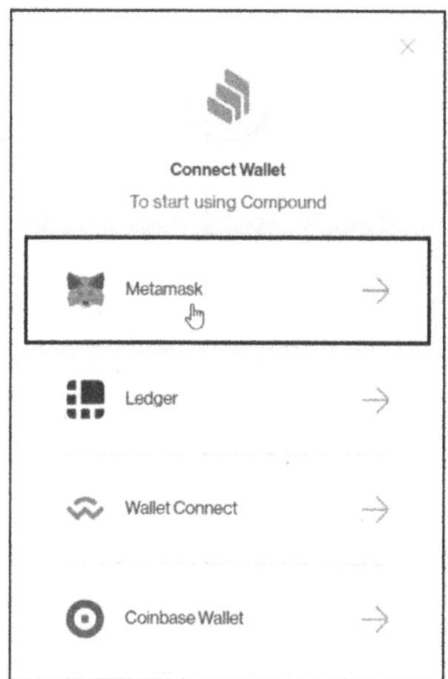

FIGURE 4-1: The pop-up window to connect Compound with MetaMask.

2. **Select the MetaMask option.**
3. **Follow the pop-up window prompts, as shown in Figure 4-2.**

REMEMBER

If the pop-up doesn't automatically appear, click the fox icon in your browser toolbar and follow the steps to connect.

After the connection is established, your screen displays a dashboard, as shown in Figure 4-3.

TIP

If your browser has difficulty in stabilizing, simply click the Refresh button to the left of the browser's input bar.

1. **From the "Supply Markets" side, click to toggle the collateral button for Ether from off to on (see Figure 4-3).**

   The Enable as Collateral pop-up window appears, as shown in Figure 4-4.

2. **Follow the prompts to allow Compound to access the ETH in your account as collateral.**

   Wait for the permissions to be granted.

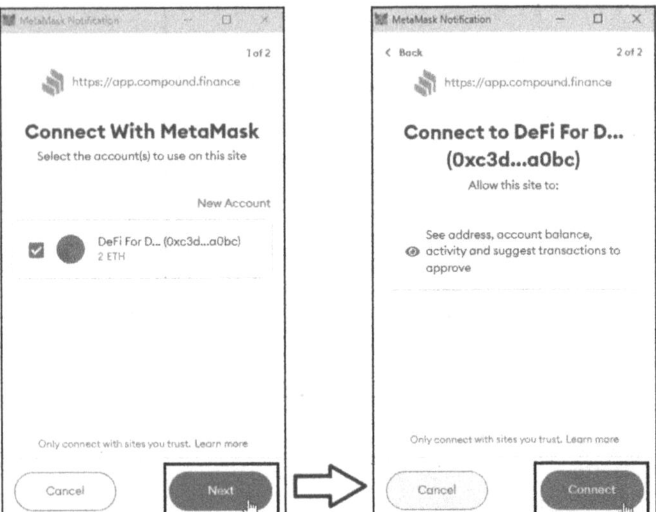

FIGURE 4-2: Connecting to Compound with MetaMask.

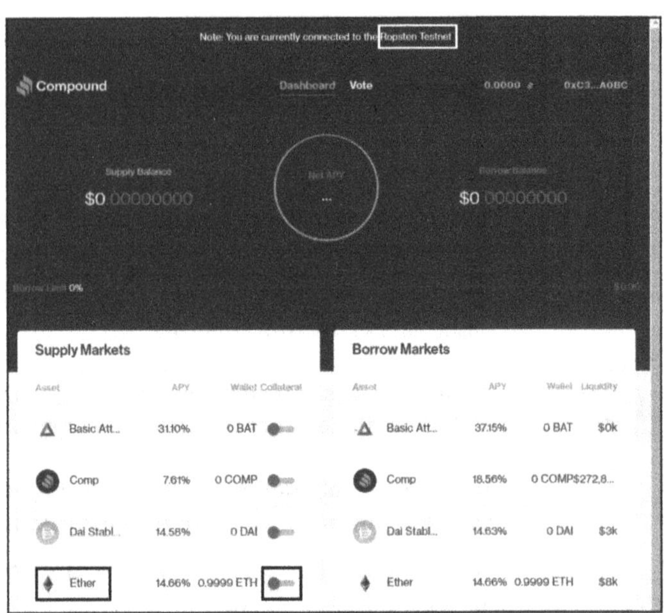

FIGURE 4-3: The Compound main dashboard.

3. **Back at the main Compound dashboard, click the Ether icon located on the "Supply Markets" side (refer to Figure 4-3).**

   The Ether pop-up window appears, as shown in Figure 4-5.

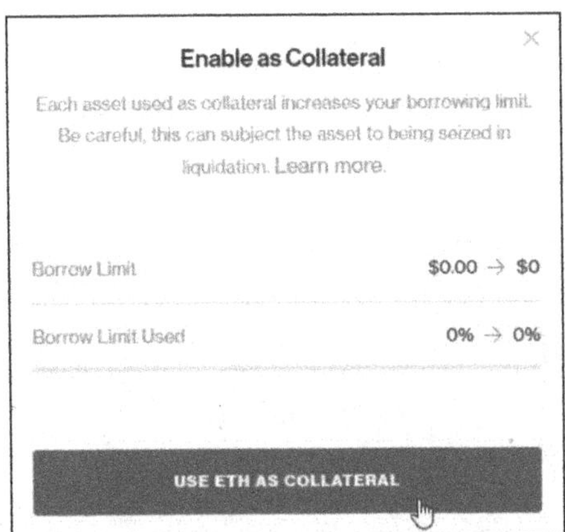

FIGURE 4-4: Allowing Compound to access the ETH in your account.

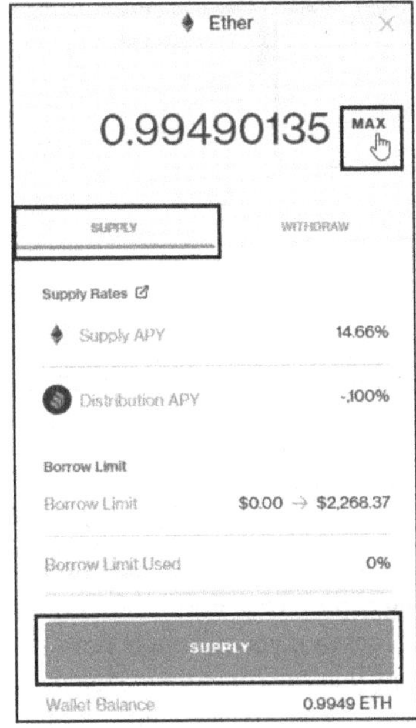

FIGURE 4-5: Supplying ETH to the Ether lending pool on Compound.

4. **Staying on the Supply tab of the Ether pop-up window (refer to Figure 4-5), click MAX to supply all ETH in your account, and then click the Supply button at the bottom.**

5. **Follow the subsequent MetaMask pop-up prompts to confirm the request.**

   Keep in mind that you may need to scroll down to get to the Confirm button on the pop-up prompts.

After the transaction completes, you'll notice an updated Compound dashboard reflecting this change, as shown in Figure 4-6.

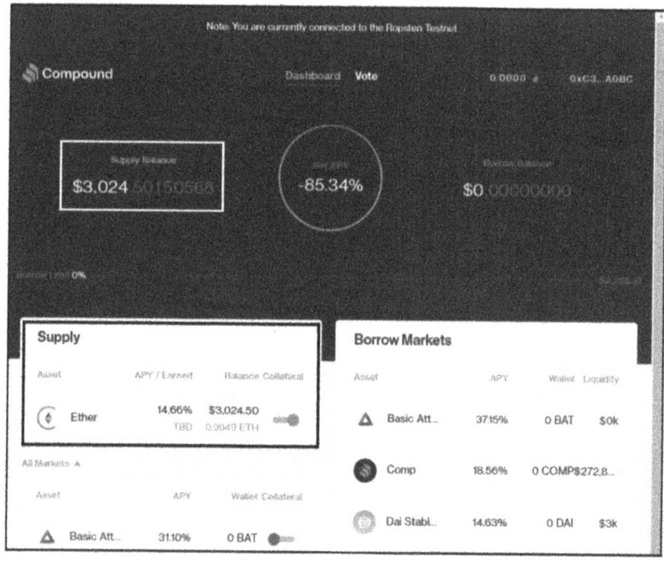

FIGURE 4-6: The updated Compound dashboard with lending supply.

Congratulations, you have now officially contributed ETH to a decentralized lending pool!

A few things to keep in mind:

- **Your ETH is now locked in a smart-contract account to provide lending capital to others who may wish to borrow ETH.** This means you no longer have the ETH in your account (and you can check your account balance from the MetaMask wallet to verify this).
- **In exchange, you earn the quoted APY,** which stands for annual percentage yield, on the amount of ETH locked for the duration you keep it in the lending pool.
- **You can withdraw your ETH from the lending pool at any time (assuming the entire lending pool isn't locked up in outstanding loans).** This means the ETH will be returned to your account, and you will no longer earn a yield on your ETH balance.

For now, keep your ETH locked in the lending pool so that you can proceed to borrow against it. Notice that the Compound platform supports numerous assets, each forming their own distinct lending pools. Thus, you can contribute ETH to the Ether lending pool and use that collateral to borrow, say, DAI from the DAI lending pool! (For more information on DAI, see details about stablecoins in Chapter 5 and the section about DAI and collateralized loans in Chapter 7.)

Decentralized Borrowing

After contributing to a lending pool, as explained in the preceding section, you can tap into other collateral pools on Compound to borrow funds. Follow these steps to borrow against your locked collateral:

1. **From the main Compound dashboard, click the Dai Stablecoin icon located on the Borrow Markets side (refer to Figure 4-6).**

   The Dai Stablecoin pop-up window appears, as shown in Figure 4-7.

   You may need to select another asset to borrow, based on the available liquidity in each of the lending pools at the time you implement this step.

   Refer to Figure 4-6 and note the right-most Liquidity field of each asset under the Borrow Markets side. I chose DAI because at the time I created this example, there was sufficient liquidity in the DAI lending pool for me to borrow from.

2. **Staying on the Borrow tab of the "Dai Stablecoin" pop-up window (see Figure 4-7), click the 80% LIMIT option; then click the Borrow button at the bottom.**

   The 80% Limit option calculates 80 percent of the maximum possible DAI you can borrow based on what your collateral is worth at the time you attempt to borrow.

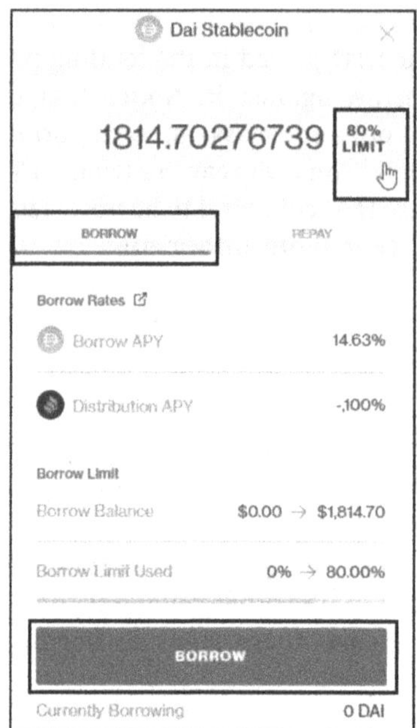

FIGURE 4-7: Borrowing DAI from the DAI lending pool on Compound.

3. **Follow the subsequent MetaMask pop-up prompts to confirm the request.**

   After the transaction completes, you'll notice an updated Compound dashboard reflecting this change, as shown in Figure 4-8.

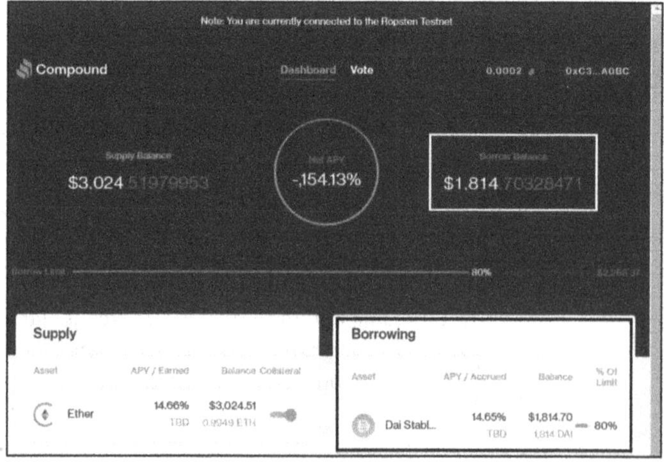

FIGURE 4-8: The updated Compound dashboard with lending supply and loan balance.

Great work! You've now borrowed DAI against your locked ETH collateral.

TECHNICAL STUFF

Notice that the Borrow Limit meter on your Compound dashboard has jumped from 0% (see Figure 4-6) to 80% (see Figure 4-8). To ensure repayment, Compound limits your borrowing based on the value and type of collateral you've locked across all lending pools on Compound. You'll need to monitor your Borrow Limit, because this meter fluctuates with the value of your collateral relative to the value of your borrowed assets. If your meter reaches 100%, your collateral will be automatically liquidated at a discount to repay your loan. (See "Understanding the Compound lending protocol" in Chapter 7 for more details on how overcollateralized DeFi loans work.)

The next section shows you how to use that borrowed DAI to get more ETH.

Executing a Trade on a Decentralized Exchange

Now, armed with borrowed DAI or another borrowed token (from the preceding "Decentralized Borrowing" section), you can exchange your tokens for other tokens on a decentralized exchange (DEX).

Follow these steps to execute a trade on Uniswap, a popular DEX:

1. **Point your browser to** `https://app.uniswap.org`.
2. **Click the Connect Wallet button in the upper-right corner, as shown in Figure 4-9.**
3. **Follow the pop-up window prompts to select and connect MetaMask with Uniswap, as shown in Figure 4-10.**

   Wait for the connection to be established. The pop-up window disappears, and you're back (or, more accurately, still) at the main Uniswap page.

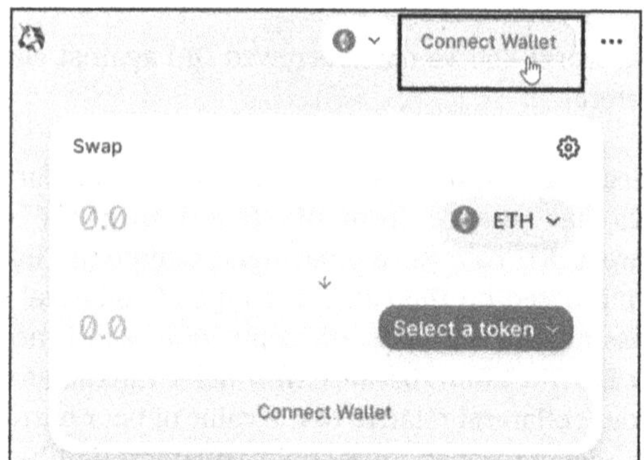

FIGURE 4-9: The Uniswap DEX main page.

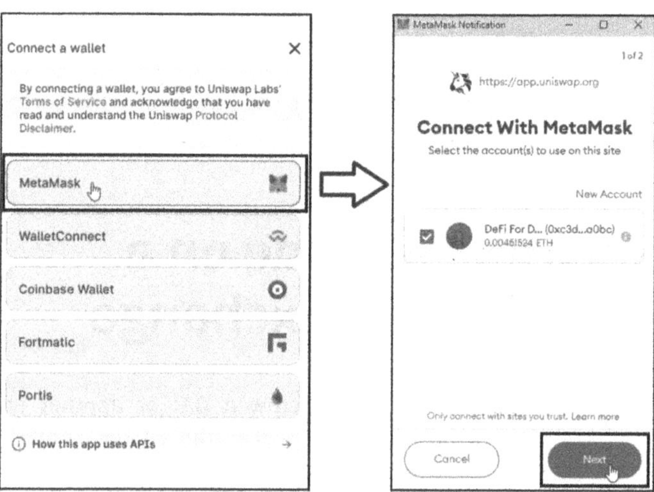

FIGURE 4-10: Connecting Uniswap with MetaMask.

4. **From the main Uniswap page, click the drop-down menu (which initially says "ETH") in the top half of the Swap box, as shown in Figure 4-11.**

   A pop-up window appears that allows you to select a token to trade, as shown in Figure 4-12.

WARNING

If you're on a testnet (instead of Mainnet), Steps 5 and 6 are absolutely critical to ensure that you select the correct token type, even if you see what appears to be your desired token type. For instance, Figure 4-12 shows DAI on the left side as a possible token to proffer. Nonetheless, it's critical to continue onto the (seemingly silly!) search in the next step.

5. **In the Search text prompt, type** DAI.

   Additional DAI-related options automatically appear below your search prompt (see Figure 4-12).

6. **Click the Import button next to the Dai Stablecoin option that's accompanied by the yellow DAI icon (refer to Figure 4-12).**

   The "via Compound" subscript displayed below this option indicates that this selection corresponds to Compound-compatible DAI on your chosen testnet.

7. **Confirm your input request on the pop-up window that follows, as shown in Figure 4-13.**

   The pop-up window disappears, and you're back (or, more accurately, still) at the main Uniswap page.

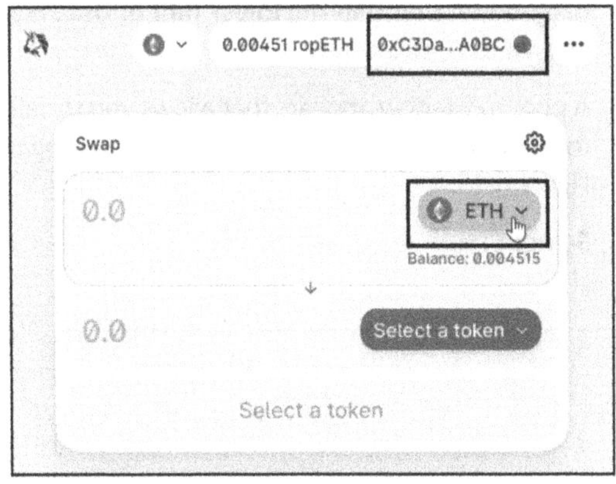

FIGURE 4-11: The Uniswap DEX, now connected to account.

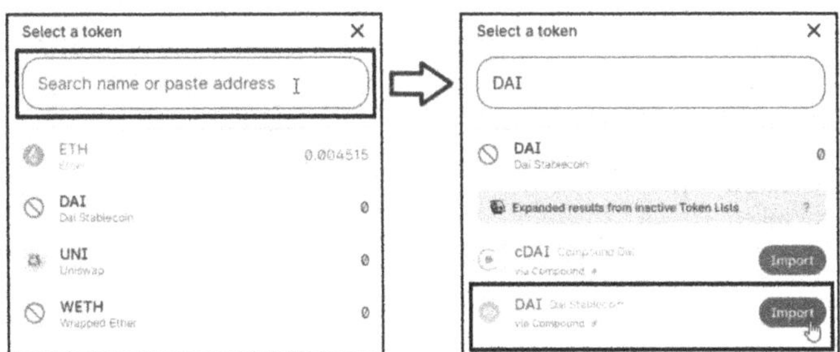

FIGURE 4-12: Adding a token to the Uniswap trading options.

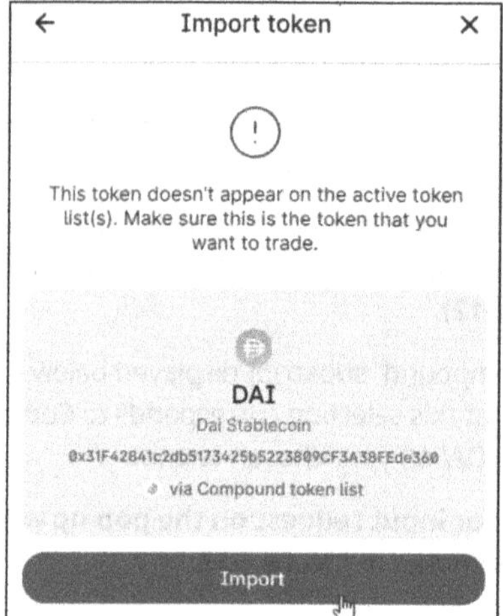

FIGURE 4-13: Importing a token to trade on the Uniswap DEX.

8. **From the main Uniswap page, click the Select a Token drop-down menu in the lower half of the Swap box, as shown in Figure 4-14.**

   A pop-up window appears that allows you to select the token you want to receive in exchange, as shown in Figure 4-15.

9. **Select ETH.**

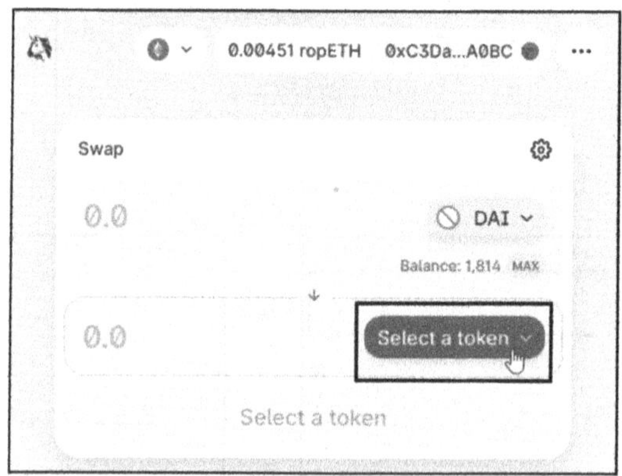

FIGURE 4-14: Selecting a target token on Uniswap.

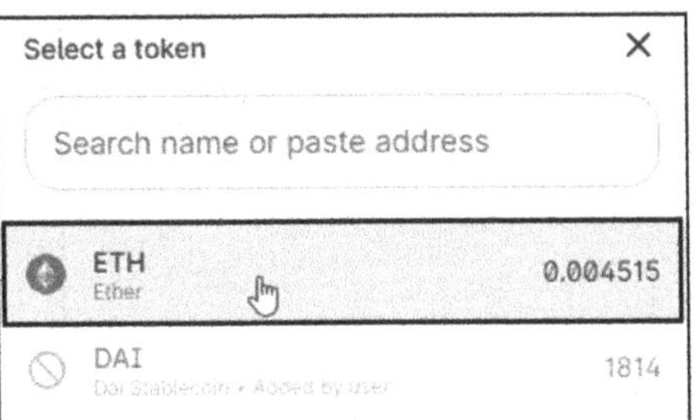

FIGURE 4-15: Selecting ETH as the target token on Uniswap.

10. **Back at the main Uniswap page, enter the quantity** 50 **in the top half of the Swap box (to trade in 50 DAI), as shown in Figure 4-16.**

11. **Click the Allow the Uniswap Protocol to Use Your DAI button that appears (refer to Figure 4-16).**

12. **Follow the MetaMask pop-up prompts to give Uniswap permission to access your DAI.**

    You'll notice a Pending status circle as you wait for the permissions to be granted, as shown in Figure 4-17.

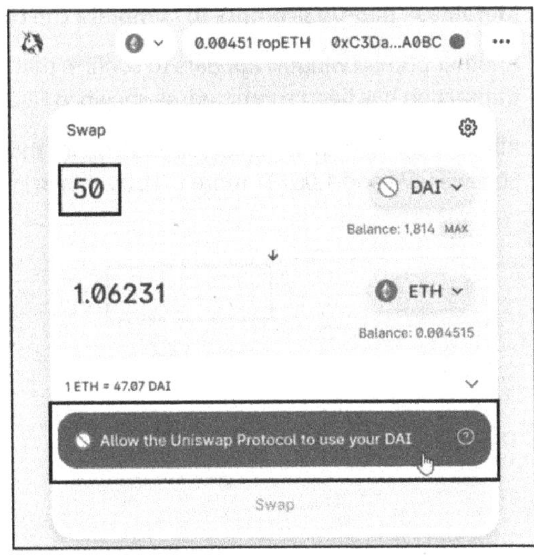

FIGURE 4-16: Allowing Uniswap to access the DAI in your account.

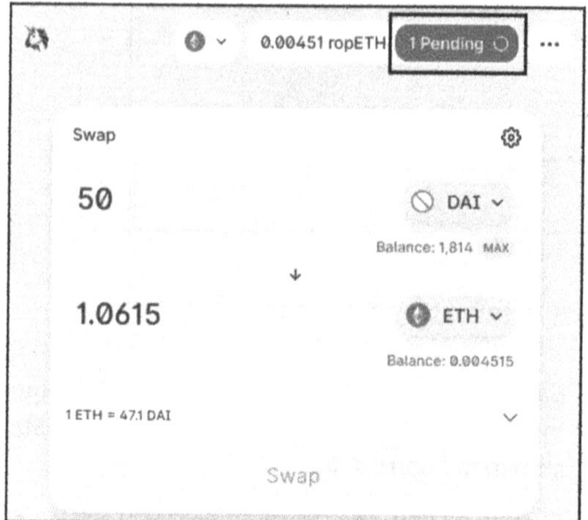

FIGURE 4-17: Waiting for Uniswap's access permission to be granted.

13. **After Uniswap is allowed access to your DAI, click the Swap button, as shown in Figure 4-18.**

    A pop-up window appears to confirm your request, as shown in Figure 4-19.

14. **Click the Confirm Swap button and then follow the MetaMask pop-up prompts to complete the transaction.**

    Another pop-up window appears to confirm that your transaction has been submitted, as shown in Figure 4-20.

    After the transaction is complete, you'll notice that you have 50 fewer DAI and 1.06231 more ETH, as shown in Figure 4-21.

FIGURE 4-18: Trading DAI for ETH on Uniswap.

FIGURE 4-19: Confirming the request to trade DAI for ETH on Uniswap.

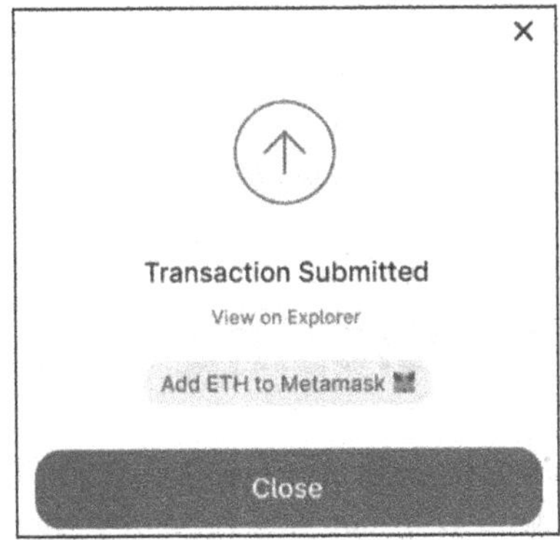

FIGURE 4-20: The pop-up window confirming the transaction in progress.

REMEMBER

Don't focus too much on the (quite low!) DAI/ETH exchange rate here. As mentioned earlier, market conditions on the Ropsten Testnet are not indicative of what you would see on the actual Ethereum Mainnet. The important part is that the same instructions apply whether you're on a testnet or on Mainnet itself.

At this point, you can imagine how this sequence of steps can be repeated to ramp up a leveraged position in ETH. Specifically, using the ETH you just purchased on Uniswap with your borrowed DAI, you can return to the Compound protocol and proceed to lock up this ETH to borrow more DAI, and then return to the Uniswap protocol to buy more ETH, and so on.

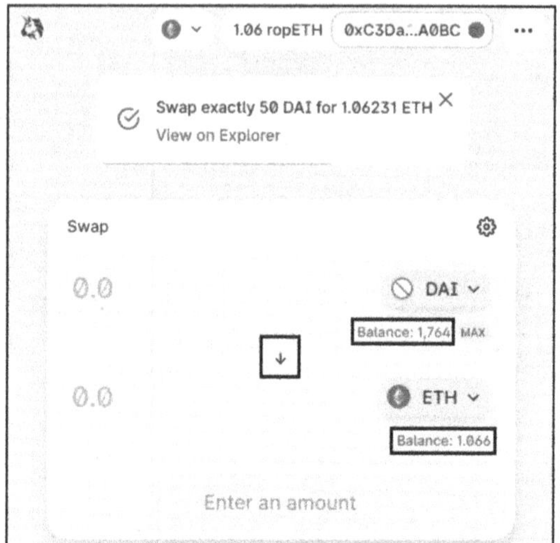

FIGURE 4-21: The Uniswap main page after completion of the trade.

For now, you can practice how to close out your open positions. Recall that you have outstanding debt as well as locked collateral (from the earlier "Decentralized Borrowing" section). The next section provides instructions on how to reverse and unwind.

Unwinding and Closing Out

Continue these steps to swap back your ETH for DAI (on Uniswap) and then repay your DAI loan and reclaim your ETH collateral (on Compound).

1. **Back at the main Uniswap page, click the downward arrow in the Swap box to switch the direction of the trade (refer to Figure 4-21).**

   You'll notice that ETH is now in the top portion of the Swap box and DAI is in the bottom portion, as shown in Figure 4-22.

2. **Click the MAX option in the top portion of the Swap box to trade all ETH in your account (refer to Figure 4-22).**

   Uniswap calculates and presents the amount of DAI you can receive for your ETH, as shown in Figure 4-23.

3. **Click the Swap button that appears at the bottom, and follow the MetaMask pop-up prompts to complete the transaction.**

   Now that you have (most of) your DAI back, you can head back to the Compound protocol.

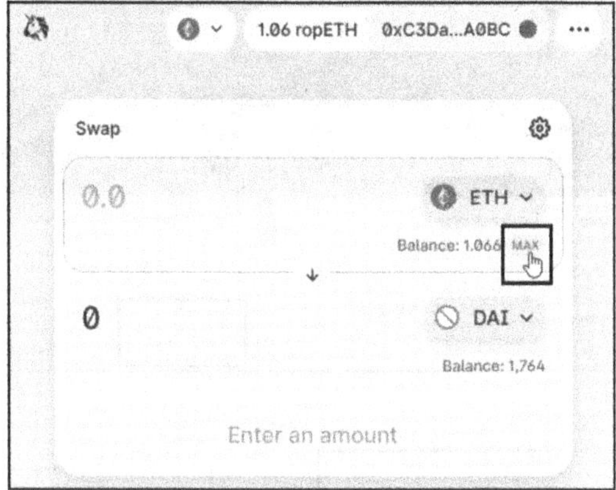

FIGURE 4-22: Trading ETH for DAI on Uniswap.

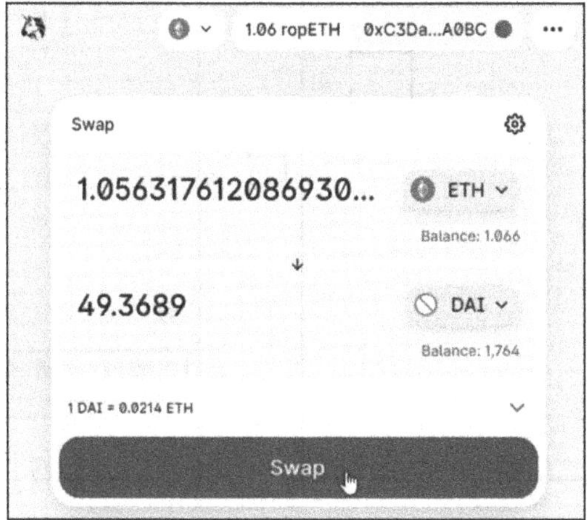

FIGURE 4-23: Requesting ETH to DAI trade on Uniswap.

4. **Return to** `app.compound.finance`**, as shown in Figure 4-24.**
5. **Click the Dai Stablecoin icon under the Borrowing box on the right side.**

   The Dai Stablecoin pop-up window appears, as shown in Figure 4-25.

6. **Select the Repay tab and then click the Enable button (refer to Figure 4-25).**

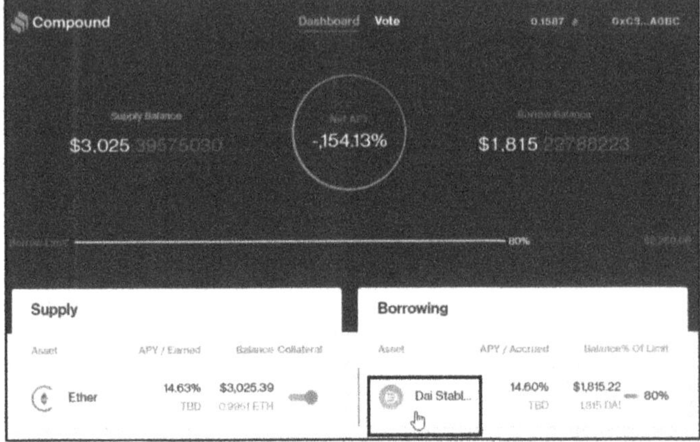

FIGURE 4-24: Returning to the Compound dashboard.

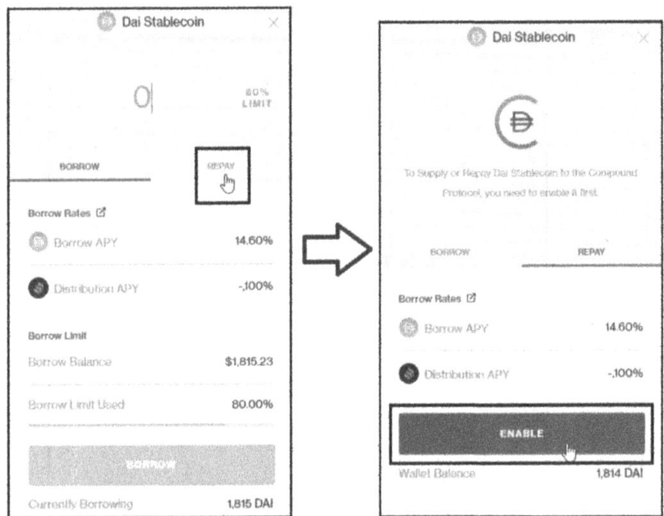

FIGURE 4-25: Allowing Compound to access the DAI in your account.

7. **Follow the MetaMask pop-up prompts to confirm and allow Compound to access the DAI in your account.**

   Wait for the permissions to be granted.

8. **After Compound is allowed to access your DAI, stay on the Repay tab and click the MAX option; then click the Repay button, as shown in Figure 4-26.**

9. **Follow the MetaMask pop-up prompts to confirm, and wait patiently. After the transaction is complete, click the *X* in the upper-right corner to close out the Dai Stablecoin pop-up window.**

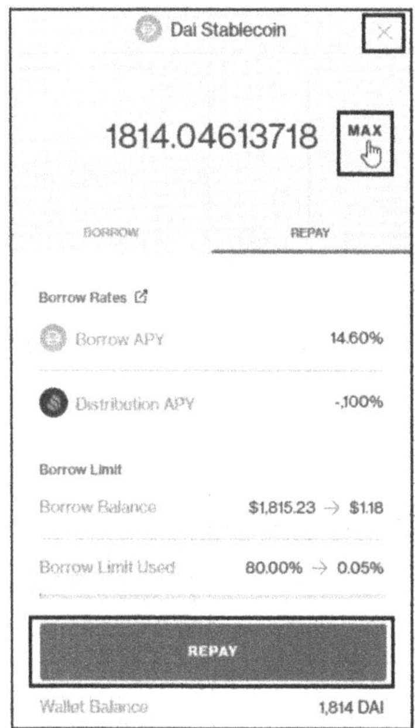

FIGURE 4-26: Repaying a DAI loan on Compound.

10. **Back at the main Compound dashboard, click the Ether icon under the Supply box on the left side, as shown in Figure 4-27.**

    The Ether pop-up window appears, as shown in Figure 4-28.

11. **Select the Withdraw tab, click the 80% LIMIT option, and then click the Withdraw button (refer to Figure 4-28).**

12. **Follow the MetaMask pop-up prompts to confirm, and wait patiently. After the transaction is complete, click the *X* in the upper-right corner to close out the Ether pop-up window.**

    Congrats! Except for some slippage and transaction fees along the way, you've now successfully opened and closed out your DeFi positions. As a final step:

13. **Click the MetaMask fox icon in your browser toolbar to review the final rETH balance back in your control.**

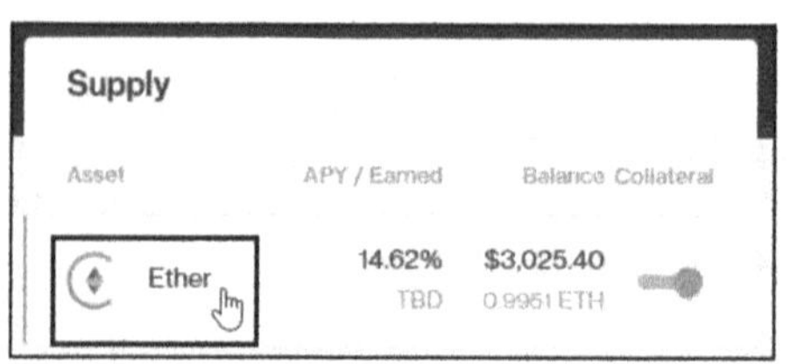

FIGURE 4-27: Assets locked and supplied on Compound.

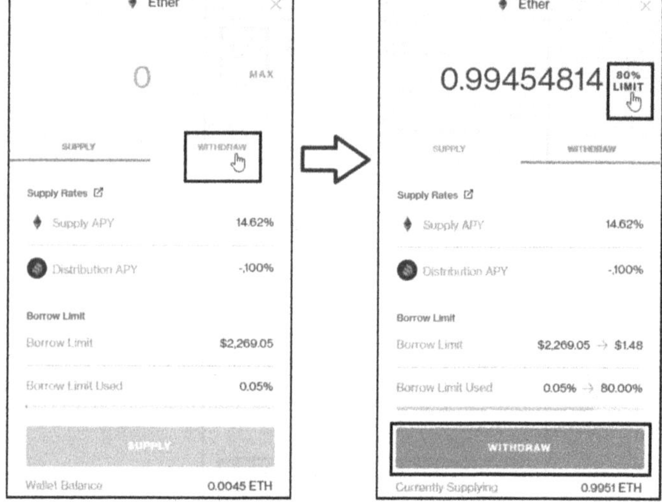

FIGURE 4-28: Unlocking and withdrawing loan collateral on Compound.

2 Diving into the Burgeoning DeFi Space

IN THIS PART . . .

Explore the many different types and uses of crypto assets.

Learn how decentralized exchanges and automated market makers work.

Delve into decentralized lending protocols.

Discover decentralized metaverses.

IN THIS CHAPTER

» Exploring the many types of decentralized assets

» Discerning truly decentralized assets from centrally managed assets

» Distinguishing native versus non-native tokens

Chapter 5 Decentralized Assets

As a decentralized yet secure method of recordkeeping, blockchain technology provides a vehicle by which to implement and deliver many different types of asset classes. Much like how a piece of paper can be used to print money, a stock certificate, or a car title, crypto can be used to represent a number of things. It all depends on the intent of the developers and what they are choosing to keep a record of.

The general groupings of asset types are not mutually exclusive, and tokens don't all fit neatly into a single category. Still, crypto assets all share one defining feature: the distributed ledger technology on which they are secured. From decentralized currencies to security tokens to memes, the range of what a crypto asset can represent is vast.

Moreover, not all crypto assets are truly decentralized; many are monitored and controlled by a central authority after issuance. For instance fiat-backed stablecoins, such as Tether (USDT) and USD Coin (USDC), are issued by an institution that is entrusted with keeping sufficient U.S. dollars or other reserves to back the supply of stablecoins that it issues. Similarly, security tokens are centrally issued by institutions that are responsible for providing the promised cash-flow claims, such as profits from the underlying business or investments made by the management team.

This chapter provides an overview of the broad range of crypto assets whose ownership and transaction records are secured in a decentralized fashion on a public blockchain. I've chosen to start the chapter with a description of native tokens. Although native tokens span numerous categories, they mostly function as decentralized currencies and utility tokens. I then proceed to describe many types of non-native tokens that are issued on existing blockchains.

Understanding Native Tokens

Native tokens share the common characteristic of serving as the base token or inherent currency of their own proprietary blockchains.

Some native tokens, such as bitcoin (BTC), were designed to serve as disintermediated currencies. The purpose of a *disintermediated* currency is to provide a global medium of exchange that is independent of a central authority, such as a bank or a government. Other examples in this category include Litecoin (LTC) and Bitcoin Cash (BCH).

Most other native tokens were designed to serve as utility tokens. A *utility token* provides access to a service or good within a given platform. For instance, ether (ETH) serves as the native token that fuels transactions on the Ethereum smart-contract platform. You need to pay ETH to transfer funds, deploy smart contracts, or access functions in an existing smart contract. Other examples in this category include ada (ADA) for Cardano and TRONIX (TRX), often simply called TRON, for the TRON Protocol.

Coins can shift categories and even straddle more than one category. For instance, ETH became so popular that it's also used as a disintermediated currency outside the Ethereum platform. Think of Walmart gift certificates, which are like utility tokens. The gift certificates are designed to be used to access goods and services within the Walmart platform. However, if Walmart becomes so popular that restaurants and movie theatres begin to accept Walmart gift certificates in place of cash, these gift certificates will have become a global medium of exchange that is now accepted outside the Walmart platform.

Figures 5-1 and 5-2 present examples of online vendors that accept BTC, LTC, and ETH, among other crypto, as forms of payment.

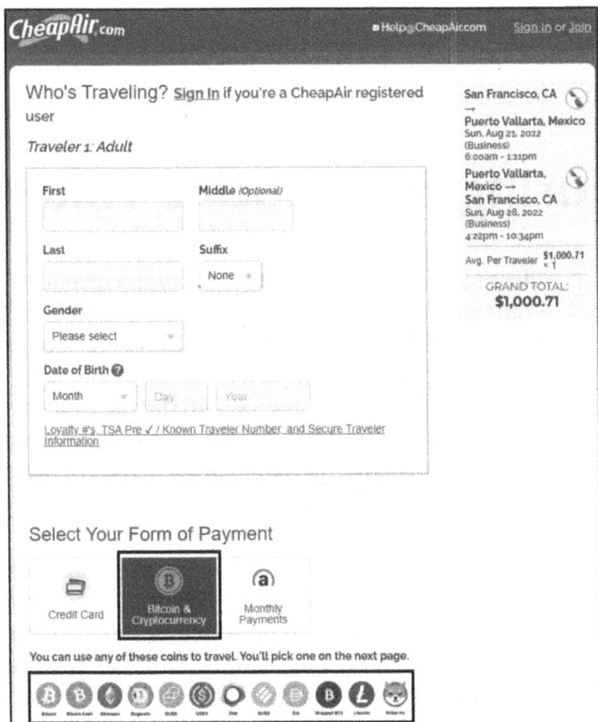

FIGURE 5-1: Using crypto to purchase a flight on CheapAir.com.

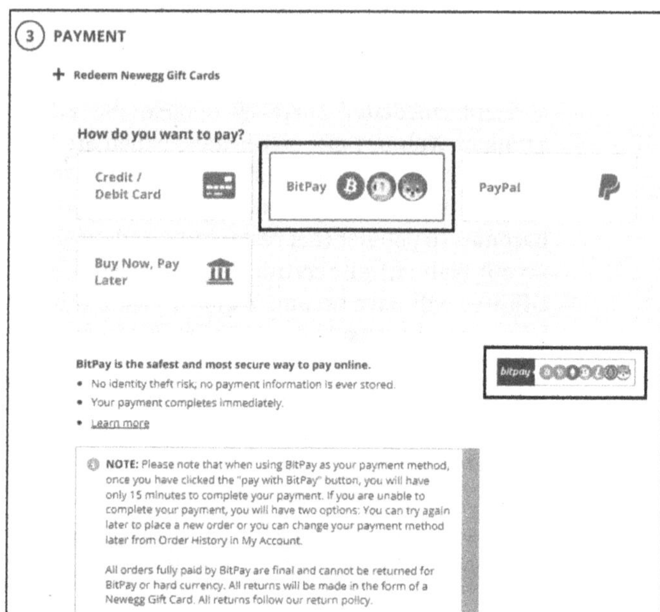

FIGURE 5-2: Using crypto to purchase hardware on Newegg.com.

Exploring Non-Native Tokens

Close to 21,000 exchange-traded cryptocurrencies were listed on CoinMarketCap as of the end of August 2022. Most crypto assets are not native tokens. Instead, they are built on and secured by an existing blockchain. After all, we really don't need 20,000 different blockchains that essentially provide the same record-keeping function. Also, having so many distinct blockchains would compromise the safety of each system, which depends on the size of the network.

Although there are now many serious contenders to be the number-one smart-contract platform, Ethereum remains the predominant blockchain on which to issue crypto assets, either as ERC-20 fungible tokens or as ERC-721 non-fungible tokens. Much like how you can have numerous tabs in an Excel spread-sheet to keep records of different things, Ethereum allows developers to carve out their own recordkeeping systems on a reliable and tamper-proof platform.

The following sections, from "Stablecoins" to "Meme coins," provide examples of non-native fungible tokens.

Stablecoins

So-called *stablecoins* derive their name from the soft one-to-one peg they seek to maintain with a chosen fiat currency, such as the U.S. dollar. (A soft peg allows some flexibility in the exchange rate, whereas a hard peg requires strict one-to-one adherence.)

Some stablecoins, such as Tether (USDT), are centrally controlled by a trusted party that controls the supply and is responsible for holding sufficient collateral — such as U.S. dollars or gold — to maintain the public's faith in its stablecoin. With a total market cap in excess of $180 billion, USDT is the largest stablecoin and the third largest cryptocurrency. It began as an ERC-20 token for use on Ethereum and later expanded to other blockchain platforms, such as TRON, Solana, and EOS.

Other stablecoins, such as Dai (DAI), are really decentralized loans backed by collateral (other crypto assets) that are locked in smart-contract accounts, known as vaults, to secure the DAI. These vaults are liquidated to burn some of the outstanding DAI if the collateral value sinks below a certain threshold. DAI is implemented as an ERC-20 token on the Ethereum blockchain. With a total market cap close to $7 billion, DAI is the largest decentralized (algorithmic) stablecoin and the twelfth largest cryptocurrency. (See Chapter 7 for more technical details on how DAI and other decentralized loans work.)

The stability of a stablecoin depends critically on the management (or mismanagement) of the stablecoin and ongoing public faith in the system. Whether the stablecoin is centrally managed and backed by traditional collateral or is algorithmically maintained by a nexus of smart contracts, stablecoins are not immune to a classic run on the bank.

Regulators are increasingly concerned about the seeming Wild West environment in which stablecoins have been operating. Their concerns were heightened by the recent catastrophic implosion of TerraUSD (UST), an algorithmic stablecoin that plummeted to just a few cents and has remained de-pegged from the U.S. dollar since May 2022. Overall, lawmakers are in favor of imposing capital requirements on stablecoin issuers like Tether Limited Inc. (for USDT) and Circle (for USDC). Perhaps the next move will be to require algorithmic stablecoins to undergo a formal credit rating process!

Wrapped tokens

Wrapped tokens allow for the synthetic use and trading of a native token from another blockchain. Much like how stablecoins are pegged to a fiat currency, wrapped tokens are pegged to a particular token.

For instance, you can't swap ETH for actual bitcoins (BTC) on the Ethereum blockchain, but you may have noticed that you can swap ETH for Wrapped Bitcoin (WBTC), which is issued as an ERC-20 token, via a DEX like Uniswap, as shown in Figure 5-3.

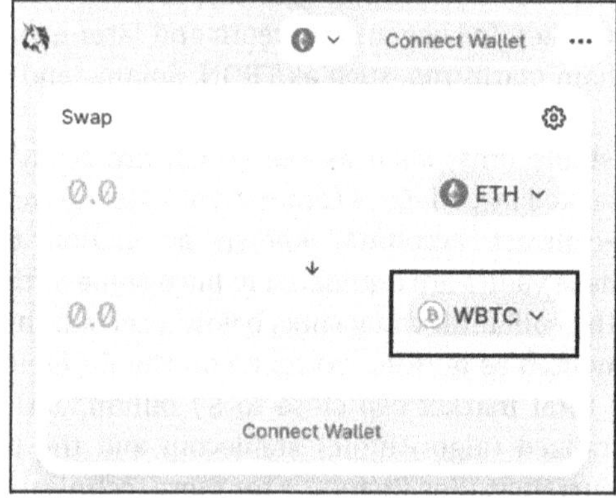

FIGURE 5-3: Trading Wrapped Bitcoin (WBTC) on Uniswap, a liquidity protocol on Ethereum.

Governance tokens

Governance tokens have become a popular way for development teams to elicit community participation in the ongoing management of a DeFi protocol after it has been deployed.

For instance, the Uniswap token (UNI) is an ERC-20 token that allows its holders to vote on various features of the Uniswap DEX protocols. Similarly, the SushiSwap token (SUSHI) is an ERC-20 token that allows its holders to vote on various features of the SushiSwap DEX protocols.

REMEMBER

Note that UNI and SUSHI are purely governance tokens and do not serve as utility tokens on the respective protocols.

- Specifically, you don't need UNI to execute a trade on a Uniswap liquidity pool, and you don't need SUSHI to execute a trade on a SushiSwap liquidity pool (unless, of course, you are planning to swap UNI or SUSHI).
- The Uniswap and SushiSwap protocols are built on the Ethereum blockchain, and thus, you need ETH, the native utility token of Ethereum, to transact on these DEXs.

In addition to voting rights, governance token holders also receive a portion of the fees earned on the protocol. SUSHI holders receive a portion of the 0.30 percent swap fee charged for trading in the SushiSwap liquidity pools, and UNI holders are expected to soon begin receiving a portion of the 0.30 percent swap fee charged for trading in the Uniswap liquidity pools.

Despite their uncanny resemblance to equity securities (which also provide voting and cash-flow rights), governance tokens have thus far managed to stay out of the SEC's crosshairs. The implications, though, would be huge — requiring their removal from any crypto exchange not registered as an Alternative Trading System (ATS).

Security tokens

Security tokens are tokenized securities, which represent equity ownership or other types of cash-flow claims in tokenized form. BCAP, an ERC-20 token issued by Blockchain Capital in 2017, is reportedly the first security token offering (STO) and was used to raise funds for its Blockchain Capital III Digital Liquid Venture Fund.

Other examples of security tokens include OSTKO, an ERC-20 token representing preferred equity shares in Overstock.com, and ArCoin, an ERC-20 token representing shares in the Arca U.S. Treasury Fund.

Meme coins

Some coins are simply meme coins that have no explicit monetary value or practical use associated with the coin at creation.

Dogecoin (DOGE), the most famous meme coin, is actually a native token with its own blockchain that was originally designed as a joke. DOGE is the largest meme coin and tenth largest cryptocurrency, with a total market cap close to $8.5 billion as of the end of August 2022.

Inspired by the success of DOGE, other meme coins followed in its wake. Shiba Inu (SHIB), launched as an ERC-20 token on Ethereum, is another runaway success with a total market cap in excess of $6.5 billion, making it the second largest meme coin and 14th largest cryptocurrency. Baby Doge Coin, launched as a BEP-20 token on the Binance Smart Chain, is far from its aspirational predecessors but has an impressive valuation nonetheless, with a total market cap in excess of $150 million!

Of course, meme coins can also shift or straddle other categories. Refer to Figures 5-1 and 5-2 (presented earlier) to see that both DOGE and SHIB are also accepted as forms of payment on CheapAir.com and Newegg.com.

Other intriguing (though far less successful) meme coins include FOMO Coin (accessed at `https://fomocoin.org/` and shown in Figure 5-4), and Jesus Coin (accessed at `https://www.jesuscoin.live/` and shown in Figure 5-5), both of which were also launched as ERC-20 tokens on the Ethereum blockchain.

FIGURE 5-4: FOMO Coin.

Much like the rise (and fall) of Beanie Babies in the 1990s, it's hard to predict whether a meme coin is destined for DOGE-like greatness (though, it certainly helps if vendors adopt the meme as a form of payment and Elon Musk tweets about it!).

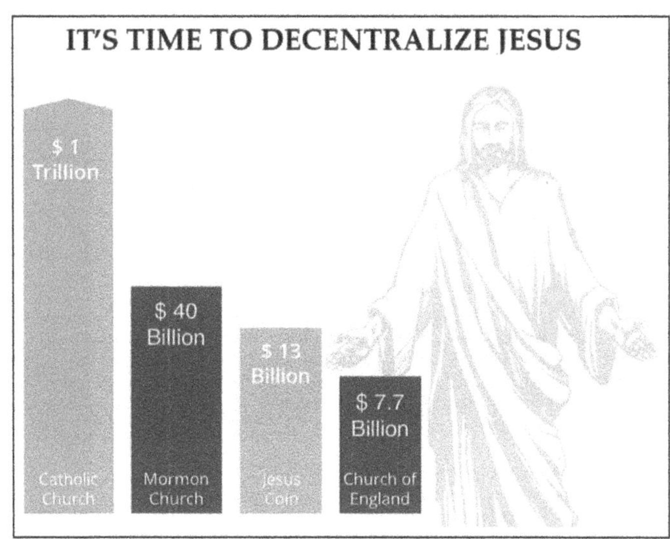

FIGURE 5-5: Jesus Coin.

Differentiating Non-Fungible Tokens (NFTs)

Finally, I would be remiss to ignore the category of non-fungible tokens (NFTs)!

Although NFTs also fall under the category of non-native tokens, I've assigned this group its own header to clearly demarcate it from the tokens covered previously, which are all fungible tokens.

NFTs are still relatively young, and thus far have mostly been designed to represent ownership of digital collectibles and gaming assets. However, many nascent projects are in various stages of planning and development. From NFT-izing the ownership records of luxury goods to event tickets to real estate, the possibilities are seemingly endless. Already, NFTs are being used to secure ownership and transaction records of digital property in decentralized metaverses, such as Decentraland and Sandbox, which are covered in Chapter 8. Perhaps more real-world analogues will soon follow!

IN THIS CHAPTER

» **Comparing DEXs and CEXs**

» **Explaining the role of liquidity providers and traditional order books**

» **Introducing automated market makers**

» **Exploring other types of decentralized exchanges**

Chapter 6

Decentralized Exchanges and Marketplaces

Whether you want to sell a car or a share of Microsoft stock, marketplaces exist to provide an organized way to gather and match those who want to sell with others who want to buy. *Liquidity* refers to the ability to quickly buy or sell at a fair price.

For instance, cars are relatively illiquid items. You would certainly find an immediate buyer for your car if you offered it at $1, but that's not a desirable sale price for you. On the other hand, Microsoft stock, which sees an average daily volume of 30 million shares (a measure of how many times the stock is bought and sold throughout the trading day), is highly liquid.

Liquidity in a marketplace is not just beneficial to those who want to immediately buy or sell a given asset. Active markets provide ongoing updates as to what an asset is worth. Although the value of your car fluctuates over time, you don't observe the price changes because, unlike Microsoft stock, your car is not being bought and sold 30 million times a day. Knowing what your assets are worth is important not only for retirement planning but also for accessing capital — for instance, if you want to pledge your assets as collateral to borrow money.

From ancient marketplaces to modern exchanges, technology has greatly improved liquidity across numerous asset classes by facilitating connections that were impossible even just decades ago. Much of the enhanced liquidity you now enjoy is owed to centralizing primitive peer-to-peer processes. But now, another disruptive technology has arrived to enable truly decentralized peer-to-peer exchanges in a way that is still disciplined and effective!

This chapter walks you through the basics of how modern exchanges function and explains the key differences between centralized exchanges (CEXs) and their decentralized counterparts (DEXs).

Understanding Liquidity Providers and Order Books

Before delving into DEXs, it's helpful to first consider how a centrally operated exchange works and how prices move throughout the day. If you've ever bought or sold stock, you're probably familiar with what's known as a *central limit order book* (CLOB).

Consider what happens when you place a market order through your brokerage firm to buy a share of Microsoft stock (MSFT). As the one initiating the trade, you are considered a liquidity taker. There are *liquidity providers* on the other end who collectively provide a valuable service — namely, they stand ready to buy MSFT from you when you want to sell and, conversely, to sell MSFT to you when you want to buy.

For instance, based on the quotes shown in Figure 6-1, you would be able to buy a share of MSFT for $287.60, and you would be able to sell a share of MSFT for $287.40. Thus, you sell low (at the *bid* price) and buy high (at the *ask* price), whereas liquidity providers buy low (at the bid) and sell high (at the ask). This bid-ask spread compensates them for their service; after all, they are the ones providing these quotes for the order book. In addition, many exchanges provide additional compensation to liquidity providers each time they provide the liquidity for a trade.

Microsoft Corporation (MSFT)
NasdaqGS - NasdaqGS Real Time Price. Currency in USD

287.02 -2.14 (-0.74%)
At close: 04:00PM EDT

Summary Company Outlook Chart Conversations Sta

Previous Close	289.16	Market Cap	2.141T
Open	290.85	Beta (5Y Monthly)	0.93
Bid	287.40 x 3100	PE Ratio (TTM)	29.74
Ask	287.60 x 900	EPS (TTM)	9.65
Day's Range	286.51 - 291.21	Earnings Date	Oct 24, 2022 - Oct 28, 2022
52 Week Range	241.51 - 349.67	Forward Dividend & Yield	2.48 (0.88%)
Volume	18,473,601	Ex-Dividend Date	Aug 17, 2022
Avg. Volume	28,335,859	1y Target Est	336.06

FIGURE 6-1: A snapshot of MSFT quotes from Yahoo! Finance on August 11, 2022.

But what if you want to place a very large order for MSFT? You don't get to buy an unlimited number of shares at the quoted ask of $287.60, nor do you get to sell an unlimited number of shares at the quoted bid of $287.40. You'll notice that there's a limited quantity, known as the *depth*, associated with each price in the order book.

If you want to sell a large quantity of MSFT, liquidity providers can't tell whether you are selling for liquidity reasons or because you know something negative about the firm. Thus, if your sell order exhausts the depth of 3,100 shares, the price moves down to the next bid in the order book. If you believe that MSFT is worth only $280, you'll keep selling MSFT, and as you exhaust the depth at each price point, the price will continue to move down until it hits $280, at which point you finally stop trading.

So you can see that there are really more than two prices. What you see in Figure 6-1 is really just the *innermost* bid and ask prices at the moment, known as the National Best Bid and Offer (NBBO). This basic information, which you get to see for free on `https://finance.yahoo.com`, is referred to as Level I quotes. The term "innermost" is meant to convey that all other bid prices are lower than the innermost bid and all other ask prices are higher than the innermost ask.

Beyond these innermost quotes, there's an entire order book of prices, which you don't see unless you pay for Level II quotes, and you don't get to add your own prices to the order book unless you purchase access to Level III quotes.

Centralized crypto exchanges follow a similar model. However, you get to see the entire order book, as shown in Figure 6-2, and even add your own quotes as a small player!

Suppose you want to buy 2 ETH on Coinbase. Based on the quotes shown in Figure 6-3, you would get

- 0.30000000 ETH at a price of $1,905.83 per ETH
- 1.31167412 ETH at a price of $1,905.97 per ETH
- The remaining 0.38832588 ETH at a price of $1,906.01 per ETH

Your order size would punch through three price levels in the Coinbase order book for ETH! In total, you would pay `(0.30000000 * $1,905.83) + (1.31167412 * $1,905.97) + (0.38832588 * $1,906.01) = $571.75 + $2,500.01 + $740.15 = $3,811.91` for your 2 ETH, at an average price of $1,905.96 (per ETH).

Overall, the price-discovery process moves prices up and down throughout the day based on the collective buyer-initiated versus seller-initiated activity.

FIGURE 6-2: Snapshot of Coinbase's ETH-USD order book on August 11, 2022.

Order Book 0.01

PRICE (USD)	AMOUNT (ETH)	AMOUNT (USD)
1906.06	0.25503022	486.10
1906.04	2.42512190	4622.38
1906.01	1.58700000	3024.84
1905.97	1.31167412	2500.01
1905.83	0.30000000	571.75

FIGURE 6-3: Zooming in on specific prices and depths from Figure 6-2.

Distinguishing between Custodial and Noncustodial Exchanges

When you buy Microsoft stock through a brokerage such as Fidelity or Charles Schwab, the stock you purchase is, by default, held in *street name.* That is, the stock is legally registered in the name of the brokerage firm rather than in your name (the brokerage takes *custody* of your stock).

Alternatively, you could contact your broker or the transfer agent for Microsoft and request the stock to be registered with a physical certificate issued in your name. This *noncustodial* approach entails a rather time-consuming process both at the front end, when you buy the stock, and again at the tail end, when you want to sell it. In fact, to later sell the stock, you need to transfer the physical certificate back to your broker or to the transfer agent. In the end, CeFi came about because the process was much simpler and faster to have trusted intermediaries serve as custodians of our financial claims and maintain their own private ledgers to keep track of who actually owns what.

In a similar fashion, if you buy or sell crypto on a centralized crypto exchange, the trades are executed very quickly, which is a benefit of centralized permissioned bookkeeping! Really, the crypto exchange is taking custody of your crypto assets, and the trades are recorded *off-chain* (on the exchange's internal, private ledger rather than on a public blockchain). For instance, suppose you want to exchange your ether (ETH) for some Dai (DAI) on a centralized exchange, such as Coinbase. (See Chapter 5 and Chapter 7 for more information on the DAI stablecoin.) Here's what this scenario entails:

- First, you need to transfer your ETH from your (noncustodial) wallet, such as MetaMask, to a (custodial) wallet on Coinbase.com. This transaction occurs *on-chain,* which means you need to wait for the transaction to be included in a block for execution. (Chapter 9 explains the process of validating and adding transactions to a public blockchain.)

  Because this transaction occurs on-chain, you'll later be able to see the transfer memorialized for all time on the public Ethereum blockchain.

» After the transaction is complete, your ETH is officially in Coinbase's accounts, to which Coinbase holds the private keys. Coinbase then keeps an internal record of who is the actual owner of the crypto in its custody.

  From here, all "trades" you make on Coinbase occur off-chain.

» Now that your ETH is in the Coinbase.com system, you can submit an order to sell ETH in exchange for DAI.

  This off-chain trade occurs very quickly and isn't recorded on the Ethereum blockchain. Instead, Coinbase simply updates its private ledger to note who now technically owns what (and Coinbase continues to maintain custody of the tokens).

» Finally, when you withdraw your newly acquired DAI from your custodial wallet on Coinbase.com to store it in a noncustodial wallet, this transaction occurs on-chain and you once again have total control (and responsibility!) of your crypto, and maybe even your destiny.

Exploring DEXs

Despite the safety and efficiencies provided by trusted intermediaries, some situations — even in developed economies — remain rife with inherent distrust of the central operator (just Google "dark pool" alongside "scandal" or "lawsuit"!). But if there is no central operator to distrust, the problem is solved.

In this section, I cover the two main types of DEXs: (1) decentralized order books and (2) automated market makers. In addition, some DEXs operate as hybrid liquidity models, which incorporate both the order-book and automated market-maker approach; and others operate as DEX aggregators, which are comparable to travel search engines, but for decentralized trading.

Irrespective of the specific DEX model, all DEXs share these key traits:

- **»** DEXs are noncustodial.

  Unlike CEXs, such as Coinbase or Gemini, a DEX does not take custody of your assets.

- **»** Transactions are executed via smart contracts on a public blockchain.

  Also unlike CEXs, DEXs don't rely on a trusted intermediary or central operator to route the orders or keep records. Instead, when you submit a transaction, you wait for your transaction to be included in the next block and executed according to the consensus protocol of the blockchain in question.

Decentralized order books

The first DEXs naturally implemented a fully on-chain, decentralized version of the central limit order book. However, this model quickly proved to be clunky and expensive. For one thing, imagine the frustration of paying transaction fees for each bid and offer price added to and removed from the order book. In addition, well-functioning order books need to update prices in a timely manner. In fact, liquidity providers on public equity exchanges are equipped to add and remove price quotes within less than one microsecond (that's one-millionth of a second!). In contrast, transactions on Ethereum are mined and executed in about 13 seconds during nonpeak times, and the process can take hours during times of extreme network volume.

The move to maintaining an off-chain order book with on-chain transactions produced problems of its own, where offers and bids that were no longer available were still displayed on the off-chain order book while the pending transactions were waiting to be mined and executed on-chain. (Imagine the disappointment of waiting in line for a sale, only to learn that the sale was over long before you arrived!)

Overall, decentralized order books highlight a key weakness in DeFi versus CeFi: the lack of liquidity in the absence of a central authority to efficiently aggregate orders and post prices, especially in a highly fragmented market.

Automated market makers

To address the weaknesses inherent in order-book DEXs, developers naturally sought other ways to implement permissionless liquidity pools governed by smart contracts known as *automated market makers* (AMMs).

An incredibly simple yet powerful way to implement an AMM is through a special class of *constant function market makers* (CFMMs) known as the *constant product market maker* (CPMM). First broached by Vitalik Buterin and popularized by the success of Uniswap, a multitude of tweaked implementations followed: SushiSwap! PancakeSwap! The list goes on.

In this type of DEX, liquidity pools are formed to allow trades between cryptocurrency pairs, which must both be supported by the underlying blockchain. For instance, you can't have an ETH/BTC liquidity pool, though, you may have noticed ETH/wBTC liquidity pools (wBTC, known as Wrapped Bitcoin, is an ERC-20-compliant token that is backed one-to-one with BTC). Blockchain compatibility isn't an issue with centralized exchanges, because the trades occur off-chain. In contrast, trades via a CPMM occur on-chain and are noncustodial (you maintain custody of your assets with your private keys).

Understanding the constant product market maker

This section illustrates how a CPMM works and demonstrates the significance of the famous constant product formula: `x * y = k`. For this example, I focus on trading pair ETH and USDT, which is an ERC-20-compliant token for the stablecoin Tether.

To begin an ETH/USDT liquidity pool, liquidity providers lock up an initial amount of ETH and USDT in a smart-contract account, where the initial ratio of ETH to USDT is determined by the prevailing exchange rate at the time. Thus, if ETH is currently worth 2,000 USDT, the liquidity pool can begin with, say, 100 ETH and 200,000 USDT (which maintains the `1:2,000` ETH-to-USDT ratio).

After the liquidity pool is formed, any trades that occur must maintain the original product, `k`, obtained by multiplying the initial quantity of ETH times the initial quantity of USDT: `100 * 200,000 = 20,000,000`. Thus, when traders access this liquidity pool to swap ETH for USDT, or vice versa, they must do so in a way that the resulting quantities (of ETH and USDT in the liquidity pool) maintain this constant product of `k = ` **`20,000,000`**.

For instance, suppose you want to exchange USDT for 1 ETH from this liquidity pool. Here's how you would go about doing so (the constant product appears in bold):

- To remove 1 ETH from the liquidity pool, you need to deposit enough USDT to maintain the `x * y =` **`20,000,000`** constant product.

  Specifically, you need to deposit 2,020.202 USDT to take 1 ETH, because `(100 - 1) * (200,000 + 2,020.202) =` **`20,000,000`**.
- Thus, if you think 1 ETH is worth at least 2,020.202 USDT, you'll make this trade. Then, the liquidity pool will hold 99 ETH and 202,020.202 USDT.
- Notice that if you want to take one more ETH from the pool, you now have to deposit 2,061.4307 USDT, because `(99 - 1) * (202,020.202 + 2,061.4307) =` **`20,000,000`**. (The price continually increases!)

On the other hand, suppose instead that you want to exchange your ETH for USDT. Here's what you need to do (again, the constant product appears in bold):

- In exchange for 1 ETH, you can pull out 1,980.198 USDT, because `(100 + 1) * (200,000 - 1980.198) =` **`20,000,000`**.
- Thus, if you think ETH is worth 1,980.198 USDT or less, you'll make the trade, and the liquidity pool will have 101 ETH and 198,019.802 USDT.
- Notice that if you want to exchange another ETH for more USDT from the pool, you can now pull out only 1,941.3706 USDT, because `(101 + 1) * (198,019.802 - 1,941.3706) =` **`20,000,000`**. (The price continually decreases!)

Ta da! In this CPMM model, your continued demand for ETH drives up its price, and your continued supply drives down its price, much like in an order-book model. Figure 6-4 demonstrates the quantities of ETH and USDT that satisfy the constant product `k = 20,000,000`.

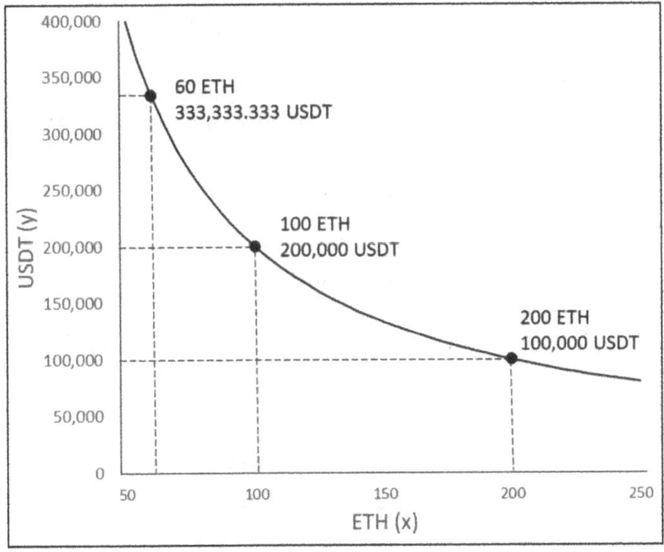

FIGURE 6-4: Plotting the constant product formula, `x * y = 20,000,000`.

Moreover, you'll notice that, just as in the order-book model, greater liquidity (or depth) in this CPMM model allows trades to have a lower price impact. For instance, suppose that you're dealing with a much larger pool that holds 100,000 ETH and 200,000,000 USDT, where the required constant product is `k = 100,000 * 200,000,000 =` **`20,000,000,000,000`**.

Here's how you would trade ETH for USDT and vice versa in this deeper and more liquid pool (the constant product appears in bold):

- To remove 1 ETH, you need to deposit only 2,000.02 USDT (rather than the 2,020.20 USDT required in the earlier example when the pool had less depth), and to remove another 1 ETH, you need to deposit only an additional 2,000.06 USDT (rather than 2,061.43 USDT, as in the earlier example). Specifically, notice that

- (100,000 – 1) * (200,000,000 + 2,000.02) = **20,000,000,000,000**.
- (99,999 – 1) * (200,002,000.02 + 2,000.06) = **20,000,000,000,000**.

» On the other hand, in exchange for 1 ETH, you can pull out 1,999.98 USDT (rather than just the 1,980.20 USDT you would get in the earlier example when the pool had less depth), and to exchange another 1 ETH, you can pull out an additional 1,999.94 USDT (rather than just 1,941.37 USDT, as in the earlier example). Specifically, notice that

- (100,000 + 1) * (200,000,000 – 1,999.98) = **20,000,000,000,000**.
- (100,001 + 1) * (199,998,000.02 – 1999.94) = **20,000,000,000,000**.

Take some time to behold the beauty of this very simple yet surprisingly powerful price discovery and trading mechanism!

Growing and shrinking an existing liquidity pool

After a liquidity pool has been formed, new liquidity providers can enter the pool at any time by providing quantities of ETH and USDT in a way that maintains whatever is the ETH-to-USDT ratio at the time. Then the constant product that must be maintained increases from there on out.

Here's how to provide liquidity to a pool that currently has 100 ETH and 200,000 USDT:

» To join this pool, you must lock up ETH and USDT in a `1:2,000` ETH-to-USDT ratio. For instance, you can contribute 10 ETH and 20,000 USDT.

» As a result, the pool now holds 110 ETH and 220,000 USDT. The new constant product to be maintained going forward is now `(100 + 10) * (200,000 + 20,000) = 24,200,000`, and you own `10 / (100 + 10) = 1/11` (approximately `9.091%`) of the pool.

You can reclaim your locked capital at any time, in a way that maintains the ETH-to-USDT ratio of the pool at the time you decide to remove your ownership stake. For example, suppose that a trader removes 10 ETH and deposits 22,000 USDT from the pool so that the pool now has `110 - 10 = 100 ETH` and `220,000 + 22,000 = 242,000 USDT` (notice the constant product of `100 * 242,000 = 24,200,000` is maintained). Here's how to reclaim your locked tokens from the pool after this trade:

- To exit this pool, you must withdraw ETH and USDT in quantities that maintain the `1:2,420` ETH-to-USDT ratio. You are still entitled to 1/11 of the pool, but you'll get back different amounts of ETH and USDT than you originally contributed (because the ETH-to-USDT ratio has shifted).
- Specifically, you can claim `100 * (1/11) = 9.09090909 ETH` and `242,000 * (1/11) = 22,000 USDT`, leaving behind 90.90909091 ETH and 220,000 USDT and shrinking the required constant product back down to `90.90909091 * 220,000 = 20,000,000` (what it was before you contributed to the liquidity pool!).

Thus, liquidity can be effectively crowdsourced and pooled across numerous participants in the network.

Paying up versus getting paid

The simplified examples in the preceding sections gloss over the fees incurred by traders to compensate the liquidity providers for locking up their ETH and USDT in the liquidity pool.

As a trader, you are a liquidity taker. Thus, you must pay a liquidity fee for accessing this service. For instance, Uniswap V2 imposes a 0.30 percent fee on trades, which is directly added to the liquidity pool. Specifically, in addition to the gas fees you must pay for the Ethereum transaction (explained in Chapter 9), you'll need to deposit additional funds in the amount of 0.30 percent of your trade to the liquidity pool. As a result, the constant product, `k`, increases with each trade to compensate liquidity providers for their valuable service.

Acknowledging limitations

Despite the powerful simplicity of CPMMs, this class of AMMs has obvious limitations.

From a trader's perspective, this model doesn't allow you to specify the price(s) at which you're willing to trade. For example, the difference between your expected price and execution price — referred to as *slippage* — can be quite high during times of high trading volume. Here's one possible scenario and its consequences:

- You submit a transaction to deposit 1 ETH to the liquidity pool when you observe that the pool consists of 100 ETH and 200,000 USDT (thus, expecting to get 1,980.198 USDT in exchange for your 1 ETH, because `(100 + 1) * (200,000 - 1,980.198) = 20,000,000 = k`).
- However, by the time your transaction is included in a block for execution, the pool may consist of 125 ETH and 160,000 USDT (note that `125 * 160,000 = 20,000,000 = k`).
- Thus, instead, you'd ultimately get 1,269.841 USDT in exchange for your 1 ETH (since `(125 + 1) * (160,000 - 1,269.841) = 20,000,000 = k`).

To address this issue, most CPMMs allow you to set your slippage tolerance as a percentage of the price ratio you observe at the time you submit your transaction. Of course, setting a generous tolerance level increases the likelihood that you'll trade, though possibly at an undesirable price point, whereas setting a strict tolerance level decreases the likelihood of a successful trade (somewhat akin to submitting a limit order rather than a market order when trading on an order-book CEX or DEX).

From a liquidity provider's perspective, this model doesn't allow you to specify the price(s) at which you're willing to provide liquidity. As a result, during times of high price volatility, the ratio of the tokens you deposited can change drastically — a situation referred to as *impermanent loss*. Consider this scenario:

- You join an ETH/USDT liquidity pool that has 100 ETH and 200,000 USDT, to which you contribute 10 ETH and 20,000 USDT (which maintains the `1:2,000` ETH-to-USDT ratio).

» With this contribution, you own 1/11 of the pool, which now has a required constant product of `k = (100 + 10) * (200,000 + 20,000) = 24,200,000`.

» Subsequently, traders may repeatedly exchange ETH for USDT, leaving the pool with 125 ETH and 193,600 USDT (note that `125 * 193,600 = 24,200,000 = k`).

» You still own 1/11 of the pool (which amounts to 11.3636 ETH and 17,600 USDT), but ETH has now declined in value from 2,000 USDT (at the time you entered the pool) to 1,548.80 USDT (now).

» Although you're now entitled to more ETH than you contributed to compensate for getting back less USDT than you contributed, you may not have wanted to provide liquidity across all these price points.

To address this issue, newer CFMMs (such as Uniswap V3) are deviating from the CPMM model to allow liquidity providers a lower and upper bound on ratios at which their locked tokens can be accessed for trades. Of course, tight bounds naturally reduce liquidity and reintroduce the inefficiencies inherent in order-book DEXs.

Hybrid liquidity and aggregators

With the success and increasing popularity of DEXs, hybrid protocols and DEX aggregators naturally followed. For instance, IDEX v3 reportedly saw more than $100 million in exchange volume within the first two weeks of launching its hybrid protocol, which combines the order-book model with the AMM model, in December 2021. Moreover, much like how travelers often check Orbitz before booking a flight, DeFi traders are now accustomed to checking 1inch, a DEX aggregator.

Navigating Marketplaces for Non-Fungible Goods

Much of this chapter was devoted to the exchange of fungible assets, given the interesting challenges that arise in attempting to price and provide liquidity for a quantity of items that are essentially identical (meaning that, for the most part, you don't care which specific ETH or dollar bill or share of Microsoft stock you receive as long as you receive the correct quantity).

Naturally, the exchange of non-fungible assets is inherently more complex than that of fungible assets. There's really no way to implement an AMM because, by definition, there is only one of each unique item. Perhaps you have an antique vase — or an NFT of an antique vase! — that you'd like to sell (see Chapter 5 for more on NFTs). You can

- » Call up everyone you know to see whether your friends or your friends' friends would like to buy the NFT.
- » List the NFT on a marketplace for $1 million and wait for a buyer.
- » List the NFT with an auction house and accept the highest bid.

The first option falls under primitive DeFi, whereas the second and third options can be facilitated by a modern CeFi or DeFi marketplace. However, no true DeFi marketplaces for NFTs exist yet.

For instance, consider OpenSea, accessed at `https://opensea.io/`, which allows users to buy and sell NFTs on its platform. Although OpenSea is noncustodial (you maintain custody of your crypto and NFTs) and transactions are executed on-chain (you don't rely on a private ledger maintained by OpenSea), it's still a centrally hosted marketplace that has the authority to deny particular listings or to deny access to particular users. Thus, this platform is very much like eBay, which is also noncustodial but is not permissionless. To be clear, the beauty and DeFi-ness of a DEX like Uniswap doesn't just lie in its quality as a noncustodial exchange. *Anyone* can essentially "list" a token on Uniswap without permission by creating a liquidity pool for it. Then, in a permissionless fashion, anyone can take liquidity (trade against) or provide additional liquidity to the pool.

None of this is to say that something is inherently wrong with OpenSea — simply that it isn't permissionless or truly decentralized. The upside is that the UI/UX is much friendlier and more beautiful than any DeFi platform to date!

IN THIS CHAPTER

» Explaining collateralized lending protocols

» Introducing flash loans

Chapter 7
Decentralized Lending and Borrowing

Much like how technology has facilitated liquid exchanges of assets, it has also greatly facilitated borrowing and lending activity. After all, matching borrowers to lenders is just another type of marketplace.

There are many similarities between DeFi loans and CeFi loans. The key difference is that DeFi loans are implemented through a nexus of smart contracts that are settled and executed in a decentralized manner rather than by trusting a central bookkeeper to maintain a proper account of who owes what. This chapter explains how decentralized lending protocols are designed to make longer-term collateralized loans as well as extremely short-term uncollateralized loans.

For simplicity's sake, in this chapter I focus on decentralized borrowing and lending protocols built on the Ethereum blockchain, which remains the predominant smart-contract platform for DeFi activity. Keep in mind, though, that these concepts apply to decentralized lending protocols built on other blockchains.

Making a Collateralized Loan

Suppose you decide to lend money to someone whom you don't fully trust to repay you. What do you do? Require collateral!

For instance, suppose the borrower pledges a risky asset currently worth $100 as collateral, and further suppose that this risky asset could suddenly drop in value to $80. If you want to issue a riskless loan (and are okay charging a low interest rate), you should lend, at most, $80 against this collateral. Then, in the worst case, if the borrower disappears, you can sell the collateral and still make yourself whole.

If you feel comfortable issuing a risky loan (and want to charge a greater interest rate), you can lend more than $80 against this collateral. Of course, you accept the possibility that you may not be made whole in the end.

This simple example describes a practice known as *overcollateralization*, which means that the borrower pledges more collateral than the actual loan amount. As a lender, the ongoing loan-to-value (LTV) ratio you should require depends on

- How risky the collateral is
- How difficult the collateral is to liquidate
- How much risk you're ultimately willing to assume

With CeFi loans, the collateral is held by the designated lender or trusted third party, and the lender monitors conditions to determine whether and when to call the loan. With DeFi lending protocols, the collateral is locked in a smart-contract account, and smart-contract functions monitor price feeds to determine whether and when to liquidate the collateral and close out the loan.

Understanding the Compound lending protocol

Compound, a decentralized lending protocol demonstrated in Chapter 4, assigns a *collateral factor* to each token ranging from 0 to 90 percent. A collateral factor of 0 percent means that you can't use that particular token as collateral in a loan, whereas a collateral factor of 90 percent means that you can maintain a loan balance up to 90 percent of the value of that token.

Keep in mind that your loan balance accrues interest and grows over time in accordance with an *annual percentage yield* (APY) based on the specific token(s) you borrow. Any pledged collateral also grows at a specified APY, where the *supply APY* (the annualized rate at which your pledged collateral grows) is less than the *borrow APY* (the annualized rate at which your loan balance grows) for any given token.

As a borrower, it's your responsibility to continually monitor market conditions to ensure that your loan balance doesn't exceed your maximum allowance, which triggers liquidation to protect lenders. Liquidation can be triggered if your collateral declines in value, the tokens you borrowed increase in value, or the collateral factor decreases. You should be prepared to post additional collateral or repay part of your loan long before your loan balance reaches your maximum allowance.

Forced liquidation is costly and unpleasant for the borrower. On Compound, anyone can opt to participate as a liquidator, scouring the Compound-verse for unhealthy accounts where a borrower's loan balance exceeds the maximum allowance. These liquidators repay part of the loan in exchange for a portion of the loan collateral. For their trouble, they receive additional loan collateral determined by the *liquidation incentive,* which, on Compound, is currently set to 8 percent.

For instance, suppose you lock up $1,000 worth of Uniswap tokens (UNI) as collateral. Specifically, you'll send your UNI to a Compound smart-contract account and receive tokens in return, known as *cTokens,* that represent claims to your locked collateral. Because UNI currently has a collateral factor of 75 percent, you can borrow up to $750 worth of tokens against the $1,000 worth of UNI collateral you've pledged.

Say you decide to borrow $600 worth of Tether (USDT), a stablecoin. If your UNI collateral declines in value to $800 (and the USDT you borrowed is still valued at $600), then your loan balance sits right at your new maximum allowance of `0.75 * $800 = $600`. If you sit back and do nothing, a liquidator will notice your underwater account as soon as the value of your collateral dips a fraction below $800, and can liquidate up to 50 percent of your position. Specifically, the following can happen:

- The liquidator can repay half of your $600 loan — $300 worth of USDT — on your behalf.
- In return, the liquidator takes `$300 * 1.08 = $324` worth of UNI from your pledged collateral (based on the current 8 percent liquidation incentive).
- In the end, you are left with a loan balance of `$600 - $300 = $300` worth of USDT and `$800 - $324 = $476` worth of UNI collateral, bringing your account back to a healthy status because `300 / 476 = 63%`, which is less than the 75 percent collateral factor.

In contrast, suppose you proactively liquidate some of your collateral to repay $300 worth of your USDT loan before the liquidator sweeps in. Here's what would happen in this alternative scenario:

- You could sell $300 worth of your UNI collateral to repay $300 worth of your USDT loan. (Of course, there are gas fees and other market frictions here, but nowhere near to the 8 percent liquidation incentive!)
- In the end, you are (again) left with a loan balance of `$600 - $300 = $300` worth of USDT, but this time you now have `$800 - $300 = $500` worth of UNI collateral remaining, leaving you better off than in the earlier forced liquidation scenario that left you with just $476 worth of UNI collateral.

Moreover, if you are proactive in monitoring your LTV ratio, you could choose to liquidate far less while keeping your account above water. For instance, you could sell just $100 worth of your UNI collateral to repay $100 worth of your USDT loan before the forced liquidation is triggered. In this case, you are now left with `$800 - $100 = $700` worth of UNI collateral and a loan balance of `$600 - $100 = $500` worth of USDT, bringing your account back to a healthy status since `500 / 700 = 71.4%`.

Overall, you're simply better off proactively managing your LTV ratio to avoid the penalties that come with forced liquidation!

Follow these steps to view the collateral factor, borrow APY, and supply APY on Compound for a given token:

1. **Go to** `https://compound.finance/`.
2. **Click the Markets link at the top of the Compound main page, as shown in Figure 7-1.**

   You arrive at the Market Overview page, as shown in Figure 7-2.
3. **Click any of the tokens in the All Markets box to see further details for that particular token.**

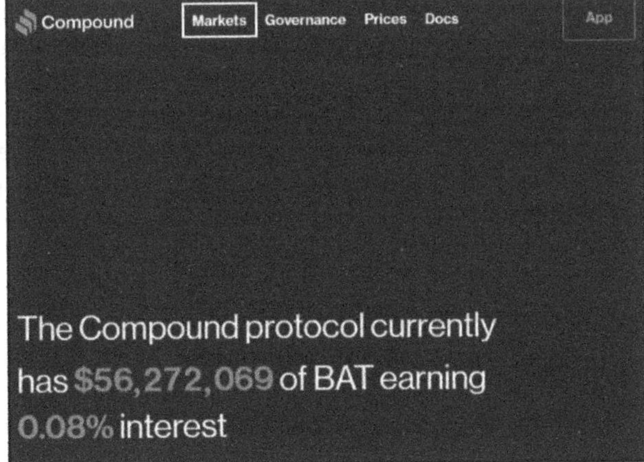

FIGURE 7-1: The Compound main page.

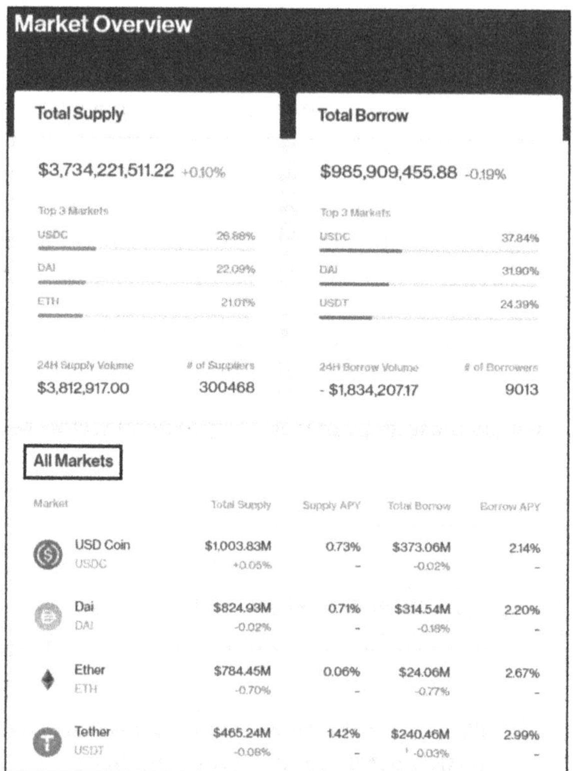

FIGURE 7-2: The Compound Market Overview page.

Compound market details for ETH, presented in Figure 7-3, show a supply APY of 0.06 percent versus a borrow APY of 2.67 percent. Thus, any ETH supply locked on Compound effectively grows by 0.06 percent annually, whereas if you choose to borrow ETH, your ETH loan balance effectively grows by 2.67 percent annually. At the time of the snapshot, the total supply of locked ETH available to potential borrowers was 481,276 ETH.

Figure 7-3 also shows a current collateral factor of 82 percent for ETH. Thus, at a valuation of $1,582.33, you could borrow up to `0.82 * $1,582.33 = $1,297.51` worth of other tokens on the Compound protocol for each ETH you lock up as collateral.

TIP

Of course, you don't want to borrow the maximum possible amount at the outset to avoid the possibility of immediately triggering liquidation. Common practice is to borrow up to 80 percent of your maximum allowance to provide yourself a healthy buffer as prices fluctuate over time.

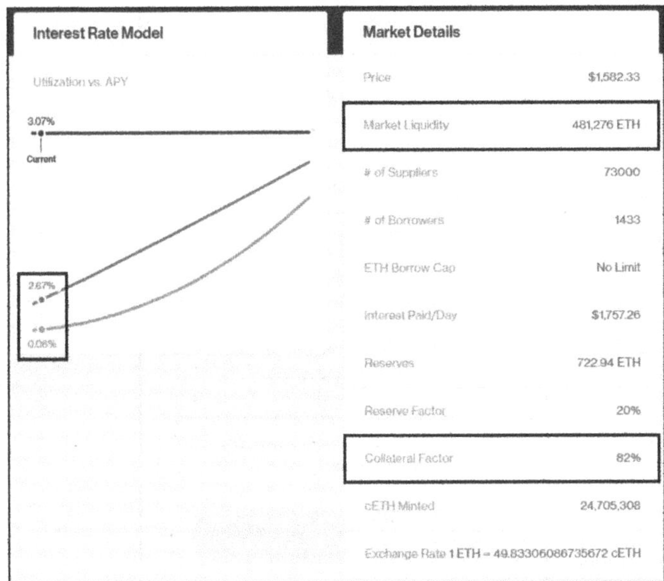

FIGURE 7-3: Market details for ETH on Compound.

Other collateralized lending protocols, such as Aave, follow similar procedures, though the exact terminology and percentages differ from protocol to protocol.

Revisiting DAI: A collateralized loan turned stablecoin

Now that you've seen how collateralized DeFi loans work, this section walks you through the basic steps as to how DAI, an *algorithmic stablecoin* (introduced in Chapter 5), is generated. You'll quickly see the defining characteristics that essentially make this stablecoin a special type of overcollateralized loan. Figure 7-4 shows key loan metrics under the Maker (ETH-C) protocol, accessed at `https://oasis.app/borrow/`.

Suppose you lock up $1,000 worth of ETH as collateral in a Maker vault contract account — specifically, under the Maker (ETH-C) protocol. Based on a 170 percent liquidation ratio (also known as a *minimum collateral ratio*), as shown in Figure 7-4, you can mint up to `1,000 / 1.7 = 588.24` DAI against your locked ETH.

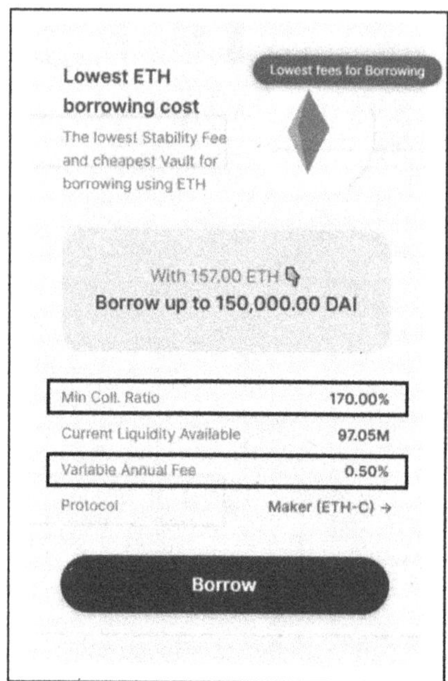

FIGURE 7-4: Key metrics for the Maker (ETH-C) lending protocol.

Say you decide to mint 500 DAI, which puts your collateral-to-debt ratio at a healthy 200 percent. With this 500 DAI, you can turn around and purchase additional ETH (which, in turn, can be locked up in the Maker vault contract account to mint even more DAI!).

Later, to reclaim your locked collateral, you'll have to return the 500 DAI plus a stability fee, which is currently 0.50 percent APY. Thus, you'd have to repay `500 * 1.0050 = 502.50` DAI to unlock your ETH in one year.

However, along the way, your ETH collateral may decline in value, from $1,000 to $850, triggering the 170 percent liquidation ratio. To avoid forced liquidation, you'll need to either repay some of the DAI (along with the commensurate stability fee) sooner or deposit more ETH as collateral to ensure that your collateral-to-debt ratio remains above the 170 percent minimum requirement.

Otherwise, your vault will be automatically liquidated to ensure the safety and stability of DAI, and the liquidator will collect a 13 percent liquidation penalty for their service.

Specifically, under the forced liquidation scenario:

- $500 + ($500 * 0.13) = $565 worth of your collateral (plus the stability fee incurred on the 500 DAI loan to date) will be liquidated to repay your total outstanding debt, with the additional $65 being kept by the liquidator.
- You keep the remaining $850 - $565 = $285 worth of ETH.

Yes! DAI is indeed a collateralized loan!

Using price feeds: What is the collateral worth?

As you can see from the examples in the previous sections, continuous updates on the value of the loan collateral are critical to assessing the health of the loan. To determine whether a borrower's account is underwater, participants of a decentralized lending protocol need access to reliable pricing information. This information can be obtained through the following:

- **On-chain sources, such as pricing data obtained from DEXs like Uniswap and SushiSwap.** Because MakerDAO and Uniswap both operate as smart contracts on the Ethereum blockchain, MakerDAO can submit a transaction to access data stored in any Uniswap smart contract.

  For instance, for an ETH-backed loan on MakerDAO, the protocol can continuously check the DAI-to-ETH ratio in the DAI/ETH Uniswap liquidity pools to assess whether the liquidation ratio has been breached. (See Chapter 6 for more information on how price discovery occurs in DEXs based on automated market makers.)
- **Off-chain sources, such as pricing data obtained from CEXs like Coinbase and Gemini.** Because blockchains are closed systems, MakerDAO can't directly access ETH prices posted on, say, Coinbase. Thankfully, oracle services like Chainlink have established reliable data feeds that continuously aggregate off-chain information (such as ETH prices from Coinbase) and submit the data to an on-chain smart-contract account for use by other protocols on the same network. (See Chapter 9 for more information on oracles.)

Compound's Open Price Feed uses a combination of the Chainlink Data Feed for a given token along with the time-weighted average price based on the ratio of the token pair on Uniswap V2 liquidity pools. Similarly, MakerDAO's Medianizer maintains a list of trusted price feeds, known as a *whitelist*, to use in arriving at a continuously updated reference price.

Implementing a Flash Loan

A *flash loan* is a special type of loan that allows users to borrow funds without posting collateral. However, the funds must be repaid quickly (within the same block!) for successful execution. Flash loans were first implemented and popularized by Aave (which, separately, also offers collateralized lending protocols).

Why might this be a valuable service? The next two sections compare how you would attempt to capture an arbitrage profit from price differences you observe on two different CEXs (without using flash loans) versus on two different DEXs (using flash loans). (In finance, an *arbitrage* opportunity refers to an opportunity to purchase an asset in one venue and then immediately sell it to another to capture a profit from the price discrepancy.)

A tale of two CEXs: Arbitraging without flash loans

Suppose you notice that you can buy 1 ETH for 1,500 USDT on Coinbase and sell 1 ETH for 2,000 USDT on Kraken — an incredible opportunity!

However, neither Coinbase nor Kraken will allow you to execute these trades under the promise that you'll ultimately deliver 1,500 USDT to Coinbase and 1 ETH to Kraken. Coinbase requires that you already have the USDT settled and ready in your Coinbase account if you want to place an order to buy another crypto with USDT on Coinbase. Likewise, Kraken requires that you already have the ETH settled and ready in your Kraken account if you want to place an order to sell ETH on Kraken. The following two scenarios look at how this market feature impacts your ability to profit from temporary price discrepancies across CEXs.

Scenario 1

You have 1,500 USDT in your Coinbase account, and no funds in your Kraken account.

Suppose you notice that you can buy 1 ETH for 1,500 USDT on Coinbase and sell 1 ETH for 2,000 USDT on Kraken. You can use the 1,500 USDT in your Coinbase account to buy 1 ETH. Next, you'll have to submit a transaction to send this 1 ETH from your Coinbase account to your Kraken account. Then you'll have to wait for this on-chain transaction to be mined with 20 confirmations, which can take five minutes (or longer), before your ETH deposit on Kraken is considered settled and confirmed.

By the time your ETH is confirmed and settled in your Kraken account, the prices will surely have evolved, and you will no longer have the same profit opportunity you originally observed (to sell ETH for 2,000 USDT).

Thus, you'll need to have a stockpile of funds ready in your respective accounts on both exchanges to take advantage of any price discrepancies you observe.

Scenario 2

You have 200 ETH and 400,000 USDT, with 100 ETH and 200,000 USDT in your Coinbase account and the other 100 ETH and 200,000 USDT in your Kraken account.

Again, suppose you notice that you can buy 1 ETH for 1,500 USDT on Coinbase and sell 1 ETH for 2,000 USDT on Kraken. You can place an order to buy 1 ETH for 1,500 USDT on Coinbase, leaving you with `100 + 1 = 101` ETH and `200,000 - 1,500 = 198,500` USDT in your Coinbase account.

At the same time, you can sell 1 ETH for 2,000 USDT on Kraken, leaving you with `100 - 1 = 99` ETH and `200,000 + 2,000 = 202,000` USDT in your Kraken account.

Now your combined wealth across your Coinbase and Kraken accounts is `101 + 99 = 200` ETH and `198,500 + 202,000 = 400,500` USDT. Overall, your total wealth has gone up by 500 USDT (minus the trading fees charged by Coinbase and Kraken) and you've successfully captured the profit from this price discrepancy!

Overall, you can see that trying to profit from price discrepancies across CEXs is very capital intensive. You'd have to keep lots of ETH and USDT on each exchange, ready to be immediately deployed as soon as you see amazing profit opportunities.

This example also highlights the costs and inefficiencies inherent in immediate settlement. It's nice to have the time to gather the funds or the assets you've agreed to exchange before the actual trade needs to be settled. In U.S. securities markets, institutions are afforded two business days, commonly referred as T+2.

The next section looks at how flash loans have democratized delayed settlements and reduced the capital intensity required to trade.

A tale of two DEXs: Arbitraging with flash loans

Suppose you observe a Uniswap ETH/USDT liquidity pool that has 1,000 ETH and 1,500,000 USDT, with constant product `k = 1,000 * 1,500,000 = 1,500,000,000`. At the same time, you observe a SushiSwap ETH/USDT liquidity pool that has 1,000 ETH and 2,000,000 USDT, with constant product `k = 1,000 * 2,000,000 = 2,000,000,000`. (See Chapter 6 for more information on how CPMMs and the constant product formula work.)

Because the ETH-to-USDT ratio in the Uniswap pool is `1:1,500` and the ETH-to-USDT ratio in the SushiSwap pool is `1:2,000`, you can see that ETH is underpriced in the Uniswap pool relative to the SushiSwap pool. So how can you take advantage of this opportunity? You'd code up a smart contract to execute the following sequence of steps:

1. **Submit a transaction to the Aave flash loan protocol to borrow 1,500 USDT.**
2. **Take your borrowed USDT and submit a transaction to deposit 1,500 USDT in exchange for 0.999 ETH from the Uniswap ETH/USDT pool.**

   This swap maintains the original constant product `(1,000 - 0.999) * (1,500,000 + 1,500) = 1,500,000,000` for this liquidity pool.

3. **Take this ETH you just got from the Uniswap pool and submit a transaction to deposit 0.999 ETH in exchange for 1,996.008 USDT from the SushiSwap ETH/USDT pool.**

   This swap maintains the original constant product `(1,000 + 0.999) * (2,000,000 - 1,996.008) = 2,000,000,000` for this liquidity pool.

4. **Submit a transaction to repay the 1,500 USDT you borrowed from the flash-loan protocol plus a 0.09 percent fee (totaling `1,500 * 1.0009 = 1,501.35` USDT).**

5. **Cross your fingers and toes and hope that all transactions are included in the next block.**

If all goes well, then ta-da! You are left with a handsome profit of `1,996.008 - 1,501.35` = **494.658 USDT** (minus swap fees charged by Uniswap and SushiSwap and transaction fees incurred on Ethereum) — all without having to keep a large amount of up-front capital on hand!

Noting the caveats: The steep price of failure

The previous section's example has conveniently ignored the role of transaction fees in the likelihood of success. When you take these transaction fees into account, quite a lot of risk is involved in attempting to take advantage of this profit opportunity.

Specifically, you incur fees on Ethereum for each of the transactions you submit in your attempt to execute this flash-loan-financed arbitrage. If the final transaction to repay the flash loan isn't included in the same block, the initial transaction to borrow 1,500 USDT fails, and all subsequent transactions fail. Although you don't pay swap fees on Uniswap or SushiSwap if an exchange isn't made, you're still charged transaction fees on Ethereum for failed transactions! (See Chapter 9 for details as to how gas prices impact likelihood and speed of execution and how total transaction fees are determined.)

Overall, as part of your strategy, you'd need to specify relatively high gas prices to increase the likelihood that all your transactions are successfully included in the next block. At the same time, you don't want to rack up so much in total transaction fees that you're left without a profit at the end. So if you stand to net $495 from this sequence of transactions, you might specify a high enough gas price to bring your total transaction fees to, say, $400. But what if someone else, who sees the same opportunity, is willing to pay $450 in transaction fees?

In the end, you may lose out on the profit opportunity while racking up eye-watering fees on your failed transactions. Yes, the price of failure can be quite steep!

Caveats aside, you can still behold the amazingness of flash loans, which provide small players the opportunity to be day traders without requiring immense amounts of capital up front. (All you need is sufficient ETH in your account to pay for the transaction fees.)

Manipulating markets (the dark side of flash loans)

Flash loans can also be exploited for more manipulative use cases, such as to generate false volume or inflated prices.

How might such endeavors work? Suppose you have an NFT, around which you want to create some hype. To do so, you plan to list the NFT for sale and buy it from yourself at a buzzworthy sum — say, for 1,000 ETH. If you already have a lot of crypto wealth, you can easily execute this wash trade by simply purchasing the NFT from yourself using a second account. However, if you don't have that amount of crypto wealth on hand, you can still execute this plan using borrowed funds from a flash loan.

For simplicity's sake, suppose that Account 1 is the account holding the NFT, and Account 2 is the account you'll use to purchase the NFT from Account 1. Here is the sequence of transactions required to make this wash trade:

1. **Submit a transaction from Account 2 to the Aave flash loan protocol to borrow 1,000 ETH.**

2. **From Account 2, submit a transaction to purchase the NFT for 1,000 ETH from Account 1.**
3. **From Account 1, submit a transaction to transfer the 1,000 ETH back to Account 2, the account you used to take on the flash loan.**
4. **From Account 2, submit a transaction to repay the 1,000 ETH you borrowed from the flash-loan protocol plus the required 0.09 percent fee (totaling `1,000 * 1.0009 = 1,000.90` ETH).**

If all goes as planned, you'll have generated a 1,000 ETH transaction price for your NFT — all for the price of 0.90 ETH paid to the Aave flash-loan protocol plus the transaction fees for each of the transactions in the above sequence. Not so pricey considering that marketing campaigns cost money!

WARNING

Of course, wash trades are, at best, unethical when it comes to manipulating prices or volume in crypto markets (and are totally illegal when it comes to manipulating securities markets)! Also, you risk the public shame and humiliation if someone traces your tracks and exposes your attention-thirsty scheme.

IN THIS CHAPTER

» **Discovering decentralized metaverses**

» **Getting started on Decentraland**

» **Exploring things to do in the metaverse**

Chapter 8 Decentralized Metaverses

Sci-fi enthusiasts have long been fascinated by the prospect of virtual open worlds. The earliest iterations of such worlds allowed nonlinear gameplay, though the interactions were limited to simulated characters within the game.

By the late 1990s, the 56K dial-up modem enabled households to access the internet at speeds that allowed for more meaningful virtual experiences. *Massively multiplayer online role-playing games* (MMORPGs) soon followed, and games like Ultimate Online (1997) and Everquest (1999) allowed thousands of actual players to interact through avatars in the online realm.

Soon after these developments, broadband cable internet allowed for truly immersive virtual experiences, and Second Life (2003) emerged as the first credited implementation of a *metaverse* — a meta universe facilitating social connections by way of a three-dimensional online world that mimics the physical world. Second Life players, known as residents or inhabitants, are part of an internal economy. Within this virtual world, players can buy, sell, or rent property (including land) and create virtual items of their own. In fact, some Second Life inhabitants have maintained lucrative businesses selling Second Life virtual items on eBay which are then transferred (from the seller to the buyer) within the online Second Life world.

And now, armed with the technology to implement modern DeFi, decentralized metaverses are the natural next step to democratizing metaverses and virtual economies! This chapter takes you on a brief tour of the latest developments and gets you started on Decentraland, a popular decentralized metaverse.

Introducing Decentralized Virtual Economies

A decentralized metaverse is collectively owned and managed by its citizens. These virtual worlds are implemented as browser-based, open-source protocols, where you can make friends, buy land, host events, attend concerts, create assets, and launch businesses. The currency and assets of the metaverse are issued and secured on a public blockchain, and the metaverse follows a DAO-style method of governance, where votes are typically apportioned based on land ownership within the metaverse.

Sadly, decentralized metaverses are also (currently) characterized by rather primitive graphics that may disappoint you if you were expecting Halo-level production quality. Also, these metaverses still have quite a lot of undeveloped terrain, which can make random exploration feel unfulfilling and even frustrating. Nonetheless, keep in mind that the interfaces are rapidly developing, much like how many of the DeFi applications covered in this book have vastly improved in just the last several years.

Paving the way for real-world possibilities

Virtual real estate and other gaming assets in a decentralized metaverse are implemented as NFTs, which may very well serve as a pilot for real-world analogues. After all, if million-dollar plots of virtual land can be secured as ERC-721 non-fungible tokens on Ethereum, perhaps the recordkeeping system for real estate in the physical realm will be ready to follow suit (especially in developing economies with less reliable recordkeeping systems). Much like how cute digital cats paved the way for a game-changing technology, lighthearted virtual worlds may provide the inspiration to push further exploration and development of more value-adding and elegant real-world uses of blockchain technology.

TECHNICAL STUFF

NON-FUNGIBLE KITTIES: PAVING THE WAY FOR EIP-721

CryptoKitties, the first commercially successful NFT, debuted in 2017 at a time when ERC-20 fungible tokens were all the rage. These adorable digital cats were so overwhelmingly popular that news headlines emphasized not only their eye-popping prices but also the substantial congestion their breeding and trading activity added to the Ethereum network. The first figure in this sidebar shows sample *cattributes* from the CryptoKitties Catalogue.

In the wake of CryptoKitties's success, the ERC-721 Non-Fungible Token Standard soon followed, and an entire movement was born! Sometimes it takes cute kitties and strange mutant apes, shown in this sidebar's second figure, to further DeFi development!

(continued)

(continued)

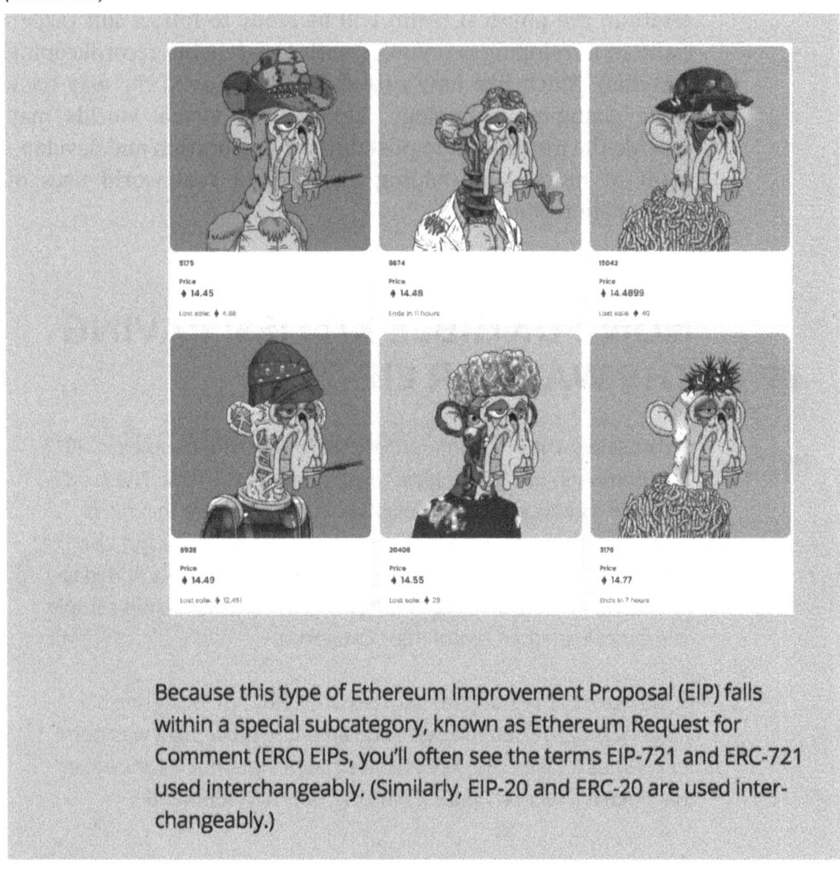

Because this type of Ethereum Improvement Proposal (EIP) falls within a special subcategory, known as Ethereum Request for Comment (ERC) EIPs, you'll often see the terms EIP-721 and ERC-721 used interchangeably. (Similarly, EIP-20 and ERC-20 are used interchangeably.)

Discovering decentralized metaverses

Quite a few decentralized metaverses are now in various stages of development. It's difficult to assess the total dollar value of a metaverse economy, which includes not only its fungible currency (which is easier to value) but also its non-fungible assets such as real estate and other unique items (which are much harder to value). That said, as of the end of August 2022, the two largest decentralized metaverses by total market cap of their fungible currencies are Decentraland and The Sandbox, each with a total market cap close to $1.5 billion for their MANA and SAND currencies, respectively.

Of the two, Decentraland is more mature and further along in development. Also, Decentraland is closer to the feeling of a virtual open-world experience reminiscent of The Sims or Second Life, which has no explicit game rules for progression (arguably like real life). Instead, citizens wander freely, socialize, and find their own purpose in Decentraland. Although The Sandbox also incorporates these features, it distinctly provides more structured purpose through play-to-earn games where users are presented with quests. Other so-called metaverses, such as Axie Infinity, are even further from the Second Life model, with a clearly defined mission to collect, breed, and battle digital pets in Pokémonesque fashion

Other interesting metaverses, such as the Otherside, have a role-playing flair with a centrally developed narrative and universe. Although the format doesn't yet fit the decentralized-metaverse mold, developers are working on a decentralized metaverse for players to explore after they complete an 11-part journey to "the other side."

Experiencing Decentraland

Getting started on Decentraland is quick and easy after you've set up a compatible Web3-enabled wallet, such as MetaMask. (Refer to Chapter 3 on how to download, install, and set up your MetaMask wallet.) Follow these steps to enter this popular, decentralized metaverse:

1. **Click the fox icon in your browser's toolbar, log in to your MetaMask account, and make sure you're connected to the Ethereum Mainnet.**

   TIP

   Review the subsection in Chapter 3 on "Getting test ETH" for a refresher on how to change networks on MetaMask.

2. **Point your browser to** `https://play.decentraland.org/`.
3. **Click the Continue with Wallet button located in the Play Using Your Wallet box.**

   A window pops up, allowing you to select your wallet type.

4. **Select the MetaMask option.**
5. **Follow the series of pop-up prompts to connect your account.**

   A page appears on which you can customize your avatar.

6. **When you're satisfied with your avatar, click the Done button located at the bottom-right corner of the page.**

   A screen appears, asking you to name your avatar.

7. **Enter your desired onscreen name and then click the Next button.**

   A page outlining the Terms of Service and Privacy Policy appears.

8. **When you're ready, click the I Agree button. (You need to scroll to the bottom of the agreement language before the I Agree button is activated.)**

   Ta-da! You arrive at Genesis Plaza, where Alice, a cute floating mentor, greets you and provides a tutorial on the basic navigation tools and features.

After completing the tutorial, you can wander around to explore the Decentraland metaverse. You can even pop into various events, such as block parties and art exhibits. Figure 8-1 shows my avatar attending an art exhibit, where the various pieces on display are linked to NFTs for purchase on OpenSea (a marketplace for NFTs).

FIGURE 8-1: My avatar at an art exhibit on Decentraland.

TIP

If you experience issues accessing Decentraland via your browser, you can download and install the Decentraland desktop client from `https://decentraland.org/download/`. The desktop client is far less memory intensive but is currently available only for Windows PCs.

Exploring the Metaverse

Here are some examples of what you can do so far on the popular metaverse platform, Decentraland.

- **Make friends.** With themed districts and established hangouts, Decentraland is designed for you to find like-minded others.
- **Attend events.** In addition to art galleries, Decentraland has a continuous lineup of block parties, game nights, concerts, and even multiday music festivals. Its first music festival, the Metaverse Festival held in October 2021, featured headliners like Deadmau5 and Paris Hilton.
- **Visit your favorite stores.** Large brands have begun establishing a presence in decentralized metaverses. For instance, Samsung, a multisegment manufacturing conglomerate, has a virtual store in Decentraland, as shown in Figure 8-2, that is modeled after its flagship Samsung 837 physical store in New York City (837 is its street number). Sotheby's, a high-end auction house, has established a virtual gallery in Decentraland's art district, as shown in Figure 8-3.
- **Start a business.** With an increasingly robust and diverse economy, you can set up a shop to sell products or services on Decentraland.
- **Get a job.** Yes, businesses in the metaverse are hiring! For instance, the Tominoya Casino in Decentraland hired live hosts to welcome guests into the virtual casino, as shown in Figure 8-4. Hosts are paid every month in DAI or Decentral Games (DG) tokens.

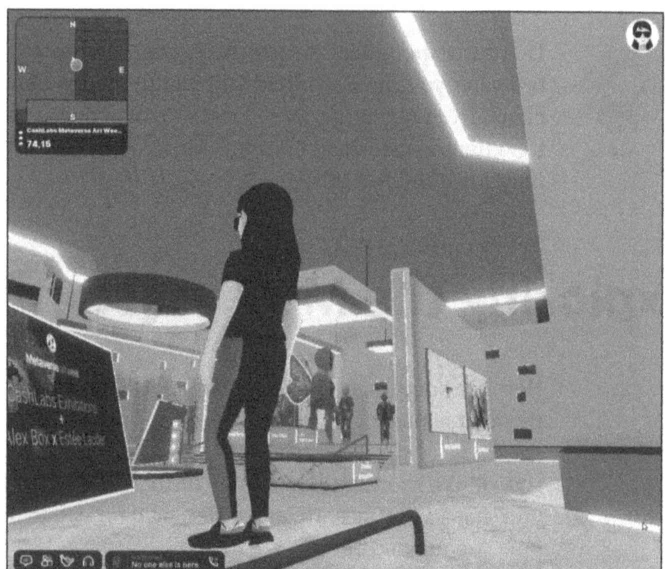

FIGURE 8-2: Entering Samsung 837x in Decentraland.

FIGURE 8-3: Sotheby's gallery in Decentraland.

This Casino in Decentraland Is Hiring (for Real)

Decentraland's Tominoya Casino is paying real people to staff the virtual pit in a job that game developers usually reserve for bots.

By Danny Nelson Mar 18, 2021 at 1:50 p.m. PDT Updated Sep 14, 2021 at 5:29 a.m. PDT

A peek inside the casino

FIGURE 8-4: Paid jobs in Decentraland in the news.

- **Become a real estate mogul.** If you managed to get in on Decentraland early on, you're probably holding quite a bit of virtual land that has appreciated in value. You can follow the likes of the Metaverse Group, a digital real estate company (very cutely and aptly headquartered in Decentraland) that rents out land and provides custom development services.

Decentralized metaverses are still in their infancy, but you can see that the community is already teeming with activity and excitement. In less than five years, the blockchain world has progressed from non-fungible kittens to multibillion-dollar virtual worlds. Overall, the possibilities are vast and continually developing!

3

Developing Your Own DApp: A Step-by-Step Guide

IN THIS PART . . .

Discover how transactions are validated and added to the blockchain.

Compare different smart-contract platforms.

Learn how to write, compile, and deploy a smart contract on Ethereum and other EVM-compatible blockchains.

Follow a step-by-step guide to integrate your back-end smart contract with your front-end web application.

IN THIS CHAPTER

» Getting to know blockchain-based distributed ledgers

» Explaining consensus mechanisms that secure public blockchains

» Understanding how transactions are validated and added to the blockchain

» Accessing off-chain information

Chapter 9
DeFi Building Blocks

Before you dive into the practical details and instructions for deploying a smart contract, it's helpful to gain a high-level understanding of distributed ledger technology and how public, permissionless systems operate in a way that is reliable and safe. My goal in this chapter is to present concepts that broadly pertain across smart-contract platforms, using the specifics of Ethereum to illustrate those concepts.

Absorbing the information in this chapter is not a necessary prerequisite to implementing the step-by-step guides provided in later chapters, but it will help you understand the ecosystem on which you'll build your DeFi protocols.

That said, if you're feeling restless for some hands-on action, you can skip straight to Chapter 11, "Launching a Smart Contract on Ethereum."

Introducing Public Blockchains

At the heart of modern markets is the recordkeeping system that secures and validates transactions. Well-established institutions, such as Fidelity or Bank of America, have long been accepted as trusted intermediaries to keep a proper account of ownership and transfers.

However, instead of relying on trusted intermediaries, imagine a recordkeeping system (a *distributed ledger*) that is

- **Permissionless (or public):** Anyone can participate in both reading and writing to the recordkeeping system.
- **Distributed:** Replicated copies of the records are distributed and maintained across all participants.
- **Trustless:** The records are reliable and tamper proof, despite being permissionless and distributed (safety of the system doesn't hinge on the trustworthiness of participants).
- **Autonomous:** The system runs without centralized leadership (that is, it's a decentralized autonomous organization, or DAO, introduced in Chapter 2).

Most distributed ledgers are currently implemented as blockchain-based ledgers, which are often simply referred to as a public *blockchain*. In a blockchain-based ledger, transaction records are grouped into blocks that are cryptographically linked in a linear fashion, as shown in Figure 9-1. Closing out a block to begin a new one requires agreement across participants, referred to as *nodes*, through a process known as the *consensus mechanism*. The consensus mechanism differs from blockchain to blockchain. In a well-designed blockchain, participants should not be able to alter the records in a given block after that block is closed. Thus, blockchains are designed to be *append-only* and otherwise *immutable* (new blocks of information can be added but prior blocks cannot be altered).

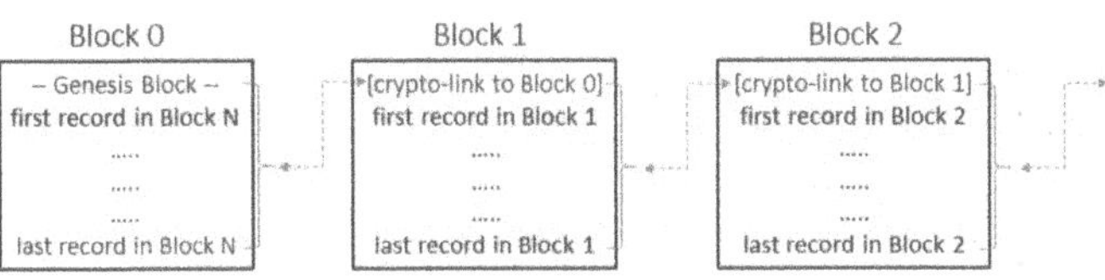

FIGURE 9-1: A simplified representation of a blockchain-based ledger.

BITCOIN: THE WORLD'S MOST FAMOUS BLOCKCHAIN

The concept of a cryptocurrency built on a permissionless and trustless electronic payment system dates back to the 1990s (see the b-money whitepaper, accessed at `www.weidai.com/bmoney.txt`).

However, it wasn't until January 3, 2009 — the date of Bitcoin's genesis block (also referred to as Block 0, as shown in this sidebar's first figure) — that the first widespread and successful execution of this idea took root. Although Bitcoin's founder (or founders) never explicitly reference the term "blockchain" in their seminal whitepaper (accessed at `www.bitcoin.org/en/bitcoin-paper`), the distributed timestamp server they describe indeed depicts the implementation of what we now widely refer to as a public blockchain. Overall, their goal was to provide an "electronic payment system based on cryptographic proof instead of trust, allowing any two willing parties to transact without the need for a trusted third party."

Block Hash

000000000019d6689c085ae165831e934ff763ae46a2a6c172b3f1b60a8ce26f

Summary

Height	0	Relayed By	unknown
Confirmations	740,844	Difficulty	2.54 K / 1.00
Block Size	285 Bytes	Block Reward	50.00000000 BTC
Stripped Size	285 Bytes	Fee Reward	0 BTC
Weight	1,140	Tx Count	1
Time	2009-01-03 10:15:05	Tx Volume	0 BTC

(continued)

(continued)

Since its inception, Bitcoin's price, popularity, and infamy have exploded, now with a current market capitalization close to $600 billion USD (see the second figure in this sidebar). With estimated holdings in excess of 1,000,000 BTC, Bitcoin's creator (or creators) — known only by the pseudonym "Satoshi Nakamoto" — would easily make the top 100 in Forbes's annually published list titled "The Richest People In the World."

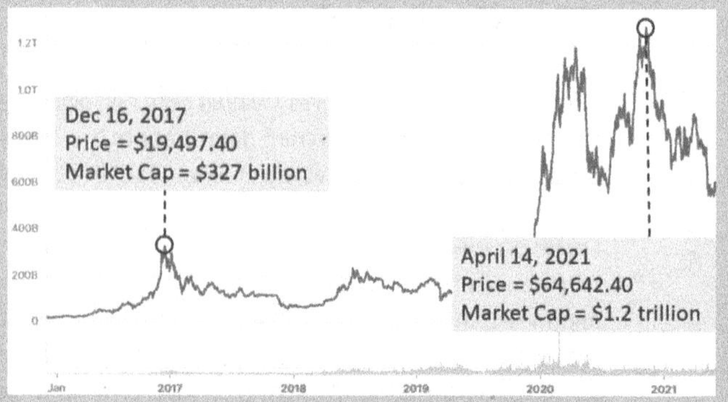

Throughout the years, crypto-enthusiasts and curious dabblers alike have continued the debate as to the true identity of Bitcoin's founder (or founders), sometimes with strange and interesting speculations, some of which have even (mostly jokingly) pointed to Kim Jong Un (see the final figure in this sidebar).

But the potential revelations weren't all fun and games. In 2014, *Newsweek* published an article claiming to have discovered the identity of Satoshi Nakamoto: a man named Dorian Prentice Satoshi Nakamoto. In response, Mr. Nakamoto attempted to crowdfund capital to sue *Newsweek*, saying that the article had harmed him and his family.

In stark contrast, some have actively clamored to be recognized as Satoshi Nakamoto. In 2016, Craig Steven Wright published a blog post providing a digital signature that he claimed was cryptographic proof that he was Bitcoin's founder. Within 90 minutes, astute Redditors pointed out that Mr. Wright's so-called proof was actually a simple reencoding of a signature in one of Satoshi Nakamoto's earlier transactions on the Bitcoin blockchain.

And so, the legendary and elusive Satoshi Nakamoto remains at large.

Grasping the importance of a native token

In contrast to a typical firm like Microsoft or Amazon, public blockchains like Bitcoin and Ethereum are not run by an executive team that determines who will participate and what tasks they will be assigned. So it's natural to wonder how a disparate group of participants, operating independently and without centralized leadership, can autonomously yet collectively manage to keep the platform up to date and running smoothly.

The native token to a public blockchain serves this critical governance function that allows a decentralized and autonomous network to collectively operate without a leader. For one thing, the native token incentivizes community members to provide the computing power that ensures the trustless safety of the permissionless system. Native tokens are used to pay for transactions on the platform, which are used to compensate validators. For instance, validators on Bitcoin earn a mining reward along with transaction fees paid in bitcoins (BTC).

In addition, the external market value of the native token incentivizes community members to contribute to the ongoing development of the platform. Consider an autonomous collective of homeowners. Even in the absence of centralized leadership, the homeowners are nonetheless incentivized to collectively keep their neighborhood safe and clean to ensure the value of their native tokens — in this case, their respective homes.

Much like how home values incentivize homeowners to maintain their neighborhoods, the external market value of a public blockchain's native token incentivizes ongoing maintenance and improvements to the platform to ensure that the platform remains a viable and desirable place to transact. After all, the safety and value of these platforms depend on maintaining a critical mass of network participants. There's no value to being the only participant on Tinder, and there's no value to being the only participant on Bitcoin.

As newer and faster blockchains have popped up, the Ethereum community has been furiously working to implement a major update to their platform (known colloquially as Ethereum 2.0, or *The Merge*) to ensure that they don't lose substantial market share to other platforms over time.

Understanding key pairs and digital signatures

When you create an account, your wallet service generates a private and public key pair that, in essence, represents your "account." This key pair enables you to digitally sign transactions to prove that you are the rightful account owner.

TECHNICAL STUFF

For instance, to create an Ethereum account, your wallet service randomly generates a 64-digit hexadecimal number between `0` and `FFFFFFFFFFFFFFFFFFFFFFFFFFFFFFFEBAAEDCE6AF48A03BBFD25E8CD0364141`. Then, a compatible public key must be derived via the `secp256k1` Elliptic Curve Digital Signature Algorithm. The corresponding public address is derived by applying the `keccak256` hash function to the public key, keeping only the last 40 hexadecimal digits (of the 64-digit hexadecimal code produced by the `keccak256` hash function), and prepending the final result with `0x`. A given private key has more than one compatible public key.

FROM DECIMALS TO HEXADECIMALS AND BACK

Unlike the decimal numbers that you're more familiar with, hexadecimal numbers follow a base-16 notational system. Each digit in a base-16 number is represented by one of the following 16 characters: 0, 1, 2, 3, 4, 5, 6, 7, 8, 9, A, B, C, D, E, or F, where A is the hexadecimal representation of the decimal value 10; B is the hexadecimal representation of the decimal value 11; and so on.

In a base-10 (decimal) notational system, after a unit reaches 9, the tens place is increased by one, and the ones place is reset to zero. Similarly, in a base-16 (hexadecimal) notational system, after a unit reaches F, the tens place (or perhaps here, it's more appropriately referred to as the "sixteens place") is increased by one, and the ones place is reset to zero. Thus, the decimal number `15` translates to F in hexadecimal notation, and the decimal number `16` translates to `10` in hexadecimal notation.

To convert a hexadecimal number to its decimal equivalent, take the decimal value of each digit and multiply by 16 to the power of *X*, where *X* represents the placement number of the digit. Placement numbers increase from right to left, with zero being the placement number for the rightmost digit in the ones place.

For instance, the hexadecimal number `138` translates to $(1 * 16^2) + (3 * 16^1) + (8 * 16^0) = 312$ in decimal notation. Similarly, the hexadecimal number 5F2B translates to $(5 * 16^3) + (15 * 16^2) + (2 * 16^1) + (11 * 16^0) = 24{,}363$ in decimal notation.

REMEMBER

If you created an Ethereum account using the MetaMask wallet service (as shown in Chapter 3), you can access your public address and private key as follows:

1. **Click the MetaMask fox icon in your browser's toolbar, and sign in to your MetaMask account.**

   Your public address is centered prominently toward the top of the main drop-down menu, as shown in Figure 9-2. To copy this value, you can simply click your public address.

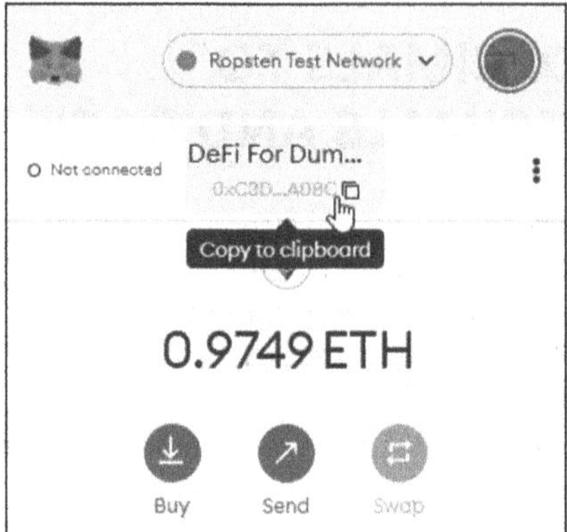

FIGURE 9-2: Accessing your account's public address on MetaMask.

2. **Click the vertical ellipsis located to the right of your public address.**

   A drop-down menu appears, as shown in Figure 9-3.

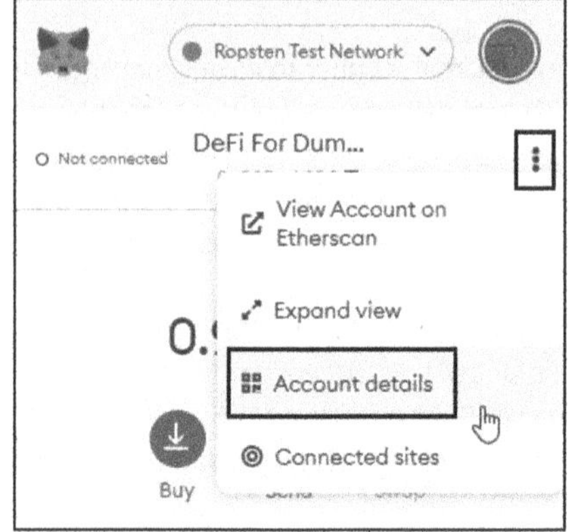

FIGURE 9-3: Accessing the Account Details option from the MetaMask drop-down menu.

3. **Select the Account Details option.**

   A screen appears, displaying your full public address and corresponding QR code, as shown in Figure 9-4.

4. **Click the Export Private Key button.**

   A screen appears, prompting you for your MetaMask password to unlock your account's private key, as shown in Figure 9-5.

FIGURE 9-4: The Account Details screen on MetaMask.

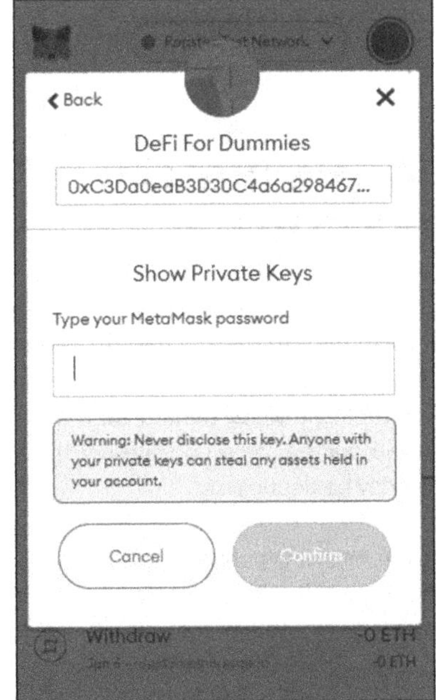

FIGURE 9-5: Unlocking your account's private key on MetaMask.

5. **Type in your MetaMask password, and click the Confirm button.**

   Ta da! Your account's private key is revealed. Now that you have the private key to your account, you can use this key to access your Ethereum account from any other wallet service you want to try out.

WARNING

   The private key is the literal key to accessing the funds in your account. Do *not* share your private key!

Your public/private key pair has the following properties:

- Using your public/private key pair, you can digitally sign transaction requests, ensuring that only you can spend the funds in your account.
- Validators on the network can apply your public key to your digital signature to verify the legitimacy of the transaction request.
- Sharing your public key does not reveal your private key (much like how sharing your email address does not reveal the password to your email account).

CRACKING THE DIGITAL SIGNATURE CODE

You may wonder how key pairs work to credibly demonstrate account ownership without actually providing the private key itself. The following simplified example demonstrates how key pairs can be used to generate verifiable digital signatures. The example also demonstrates that without the correct private key, the resulting digital signature can quickly be debunked.

Suppose you have the following public/private key pair generated for your account: Key_{pub} = `{3, 33}` and Key_{priv} = `{7}`. To submit a transaction to send 5 ETH to another account, you would take the following steps:

1. Take the transaction amount, 5, to the power of 7 (from Key_{priv}) and divide by 33 (from Key_{pub}).

The remainder from this division, 14, is your digital signature for this transaction.

2. Submit your transaction to the network, including this digital signature alongside your request to transfer 5 ETH.

3. Validators on the network will apply your publicly known Key_{pub} = {3, 33} to decode your digital signature for this transaction by taking 14 (your digital signature) to the power of 3 (from Key_{pub}) and then dividing by 33 (also from Key_{pub}).

   The remainder from this division, 5, comes out to the exact transaction amount you requested! Thus, your digital signature proves that you are the rightful owner of this account. Notice that validators used only your public key and digital signature to verify your status as the rightful account holder. (You didn't have to divulge your private key.)

4. After the legitimacy of your transaction request is verified, the transaction will sit in a pool of pending transactions that will eventually be added to the blockchain.

Now suppose that an unauthorized user wants to submit a fraudulent transaction request to send 5 ETH from your account to their own. This unauthorized user can see your public key but doesn't have access to your private key.

1. First, this bad actor must guess your private key. Suppose they (incorrectly) guess that it is equal to 12.

2. The bad actor will now take the transaction amount, 5, to the power of 12 (rather than the correct Key_{priv} = {7}) and divide by 33 (from the publicly known Key_{pub} = {3, 33}).

   The remainder from this division, 25, is the bad actor's digital signature for this transaction.

3. The bad actor will submit this transaction to the network, including this (invalid) digital signature alongside their request to transfer 5 ETH from your account to theirs.

4. Validators on the network will, again, apply your publicly known Key_{pub} = {3, 33} to decode the digital signature for this transaction by taking 25 (the invalid digital signature) to the power of 3 (from Key_{pub}) and then dividing by 33 (also from Key_{pub}).

(continued)

(continued)

This time, the remainder from this division, 16, does not equal 5 (the transaction amount that was requested).

Thus, the transaction request will be rejected, and the unauthorized user will fail in their attempt to pilfer ETH from your account. Yay!

Touching on other types of distributed ledgers

More recent developments to improve throughput and scalability have led to other types of distributed ledgers that do not use a linear blockchain-based design. These newer designs focus on an asynchronous validation process using a *directed acyclic graph* (DAG) that does not group transactions into blocks.

For instance, IOTA has implemented a DAG-based architecture, which they call the Tangle. In this system, participants who want to submit a transaction must first validate at least two other transactions on the Tangle. As shown in Figure 9-6, the node submitting the latest transaction *X* has validated two other transactions on the Tangle. As additional transactions continually arrive, transaction *X* will be validated in time also.

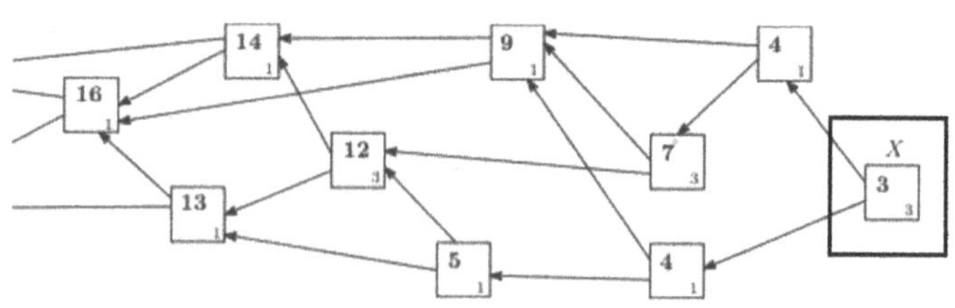

FIGURE 9-6: Simplified representation of IOTA's DAG-based Tangle (from the Tangle whitepaper).

Similarly, Hedera has implemented a DAG-based ledger, which they call the Hashgraph. In this system, the participant submitting a transaction selects any other participating node in the network. The selected node must validate the transaction and begin to propagate the information to other nodes, who, in turn, confirm (or deny) the transaction and repeatedly propagate the information across the network.

It's important to note that these DAG-based ledgers are susceptible to tampering if a malicious user controls just one-third of the network. In contrast, under the blockchain-based designs implemented by Bitcoin and Ethereum, a malicious user must gain control of at least 51 percent of the network to be reasonably likely to successfully tamper with confirmed records. Overall, these DAG-based systems aren't yet tried and true like the more established blockchain-based designs.

Accordingly, current DAG implementations aren't yet fully open source or decentralized. For example, in IOTA, validations must reference a milestone that is issued only by a permissioned node known as the Coordinator.

Throughout the rest of this chapter (and this book), I focus solely on blockchain-based protocols.

Explaining Consensus Mechanisms

In stark contrast to private records, public blockchains are replicated and maintained across all participants in the system who have read/write access without needing permission from a central authority. So what is guaranteeing the permissionless yet trustless security of these public recordkeeping systems? After all, neither you nor I can simply decide to gain read/write access to Bank of America's records without official authorization and clearance.

A blockchain's *consensus mechanism* dictates the system of rules that determines how nodes across the network reach consensus as to what constitutes a valid block of information that can be added to the ledger. The consensus mechanism must be designed such that

- The system is *fault tolerant* (it continues to operate even in the face of a few malicious or faulty nodes)

» The system is *safe* (its records are reliable and tamper proof)

The consensus mechanism must strike a balance between *liveness* and *safety*. On one end of the spectrum, a system can be 100 percent live by approving all transactions irrespective of whether they are valid. On the other end, a system can be 100 percent safe by not allowing any transactions to execute.

Proof of Work (PoW)

The idea behind proof-of-work (PoW) is to require a computationally difficult puzzle that is extremely time consuming to solve but easy to verify after a solution is provided. In these systems, closed blocks of information are incredibly difficult to manipulate because of the onerous process required to validate and execute transactions.

Try out the following exercise to gain a better understanding of what a proof-of-work problem entails:

1. **Go to** `https://xorbin.com/tools/sha256-hash-calculator`.
2. **In the large Data text box, type in** Seoyoung Kim **and then click the Calculate SHA256 Hash button.**

   The 64-digit hexadecimal code, `854f4c75f7845a5997 4714c3baf4bdd9dac34dbafb0722c4c568ecf41051a839`, appears in the SHA-256 Hash text box, as shown in Figure 9-7. This process is known as *hashing*.
3. **Repeatedly hash different inputs to see if you can find one that generates the following SHA-256 hash code: `496aca80e4d8f29fb8e8cd816c3afb48d3f103970b3 a2ee1600c08ca67326dee`. (Hint: There is more than one answer!)**

   After some trial and error, you can get a sense of the onerous process involved in trying to find an input that produces the required hash code. However, if you're provided with a solution (the word *block*), you can quickly and easily verify that it produces the required hash code.

4. **Type** block **in the Data text box and then click the Calculate SHA256 Hash button.**

   Ta da! The required code, `496aca80e4d8f29fb8e8cd-816c3afb48d3f103970b3a2ee1600c08ca67326dee`, appears in the SHA-256 Hash text box.

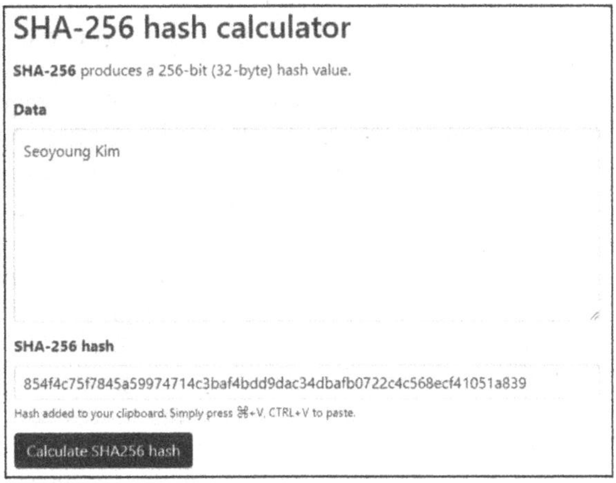

FIGURE 9-7: The Xorbin SHA-256 calculator.

PoW-based systems, such as Bitcoin, require validators on the network, known as *miners*, to solve a computationally taxing problem to earn the right to add a new block of transactions to the blockchain. Specifically, miners repeatedly hash a block of pending transactions, racing to be first to find an arbitrary value, known as a *nonce*. This nonce, when combined and then hashed with the contents of the block in progress, must produce a hash code that satisfies the consensus protocol's mathematical standards (typically to produce a hash code with a minimum number of leading zeros).

After a nonce is found, the winning miner broadcasts this nonce alongside the block of transactions. Then the next speed race begins. Because the nonce is easy to verify but incredibly difficult to produce, dishonest nodes would require an inordinate amount of computing power to alter closed blocks of transaction records.

Proof of Stake (PoS)

Because PoW-based systems are computationally cumbersome and energy intensive by design, newer blockchains are increasingly opting for proof-of-stake (PoS) protocols. In fact, Ethereum is also expected to move to a PoS-based consensus mechanism; however, this shift to "Ethereum 2.0" has been in the works for years, and at the time of this writing, the Ethereum Mainnet still relies on a PoW protocol.

In contrast to PoW-based systems, which require sufficient computational effort to be the next validator, PoS-based systems require sufficient stake in the system. Under a PoS protocol, potential validators must *stake* their native tokens, effectively locking their staked tokens in a designated smart contract. Validators are selected from this pool to propose new blocks and to approve proposed blocks. Greater stake proportionately increases the likelihood of being selected as a validator. Some PoS-based systems allow smaller participants to pool their staked wealth (known as *leased proof-of-stake*), and others have a fixed set of delegates who are elected by participants whose voting power increases with their staked wealth (known as *delegated proof-of-stake*).

To prevent dishonest behavior, developers have proposed a punitive component to PoS protocols, whereby validators are penalized for proposing or approving invalid blocks in a process referred to as *slashing*. Under these *punitive proof-of-stake* protocols, a validator may even lose their entire staked wealth depending on the severity of their mistake(s). Systems currently implementing punitive PoS include Polkadot (accessed at `https://polkadot.network/`) and Celo (accessed at `https://celo.org/`).

Proof of XYZ

With ongoing testing and development, newer PoS-based systems are providing scalable solutions that enhance liveness without sacrificing safety. For instance, Solana's scalability is achieved by a combination of a PoS-based consensus protocol and a *proof of history*, a variation of a *verifiable delay function*

(VDF) that provides proof of sequential validation. In this system, a set of transactions is validated and digitally signed in sequence by each validator. Thus, transactions are swiftly and optimistically confirmed with minimal delay and prior to reaching system-wide consensus.

Overall, compared to battle-tested PoW-based implementations, PoS-based architectures are far less computationally intensive to operate but are more mathematically complex to design in a way that is fault tolerant and safe. As PoS-based implementations mature, developers have continued to address practical and theoretical weaknesses in their PoS protocols while dramatically improving transaction times and network scalability.

Following a Day (or a Second) in the Life of a Transaction

Effectively transacting with the DeFi protocols described in Part 2 of this book depends critically on the timing and speed of the sequence of transactions you submit. Thus, a greater understanding of how transactions are processed is a critical part of any serious DeFi player's arsenal.

You've now seen the various mechanisms that allow public blockchains to function in a way that provides trustless security and reliability while being permissionless. So to put it all together, this section takes a more detailed look at the factors impacting the speed and successful execution of a transaction after it's submitted.

REMEMBER

Because Ethereum remains the predominant smart-contract platform, I focus my explanations and examples on how transactions are processed on the Ethereum network. Keep in mind that the exact details differ from platform to platform, but the general concepts presented here hold true across different platforms.

Determining transaction fees

Transaction fees play a pivotal role in the speed and successful execution of your transaction. When submitting a transaction to the Ethereum network, you must specify your desired *gas limit*, *max priority fee*, and *max fee* for the transaction:

- **Gas limit:** The transaction's gas limit specifies the maximum units of gas you're willing to expend to execute the transaction. (In the parlance of Ethereum, *gas* refers to the computing power spent on executing transactions.) Here are two things to keep in mind when setting the gas limit:
  - For simple tasks, such as sending ETH from one account to another, the required gas usage is known in advance to be 21,000 units.
  - The computational complexity of many other, not-so-simple transactions — which entail interacting with smart contracts and which, in turn, may trigger additional calls to other smart contracts — are difficult to assess prior to execution. In these cases, the gas limit protects you from paying for unexpectedly complicated tasks, particularly ones that may have faulty loops.
- **Max priority fee:** The max priority fee specifies the additional price you're willing to pay, per unit of gas, above and beyond the prevailing *base fee,* which is dynamically adjusted based on network congestion.
- **Max fee:** The max fee specifies the maximum price you're willing to pay per unit of gas, ensuring that you're not unpleasantly surprised by the final bill if there's an unanticipated surge in the base fee.

You can think of the gas limit as the maximum gallons of gas you're willing to burn to get from Point A to Point B, whereas the max fee is the maximum price you're willing to pay per gallon of gas. In general, the max priority fee and max fee you specify should increase with the extent of your desperation to be included in the next block added to the blockchain.

The gas limit times the max fee you specify provides an upper bound on the total *transaction fee* you'll be charged for your transaction. You can think of this upper bound as the money you would need to have on hand before embarking on a road trip. If your road trip requires less gas than expected, you'll pocket the remaining funds. Similarly, you'll be charged only for the units of gas actually used to ultimately complete your requested transaction. However, you'll still need sufficient funds at the onset of your request to cover the entire gas limit times the max fee.

To make life easier, wallet services such as MetaMask provide dynamically adjusted default recommendations for your transaction's gas limit, max priority fee, and max fee. If you want to override MetaMask's default recommendation, you can do so by following these steps:

1. **From the main MetaMask menu, click the Send button, specify a recipient, specify the amount of ETH to send, and click the Next button.**

   The next screen displays the estimated gas fee, as shown in Figure 9-8.

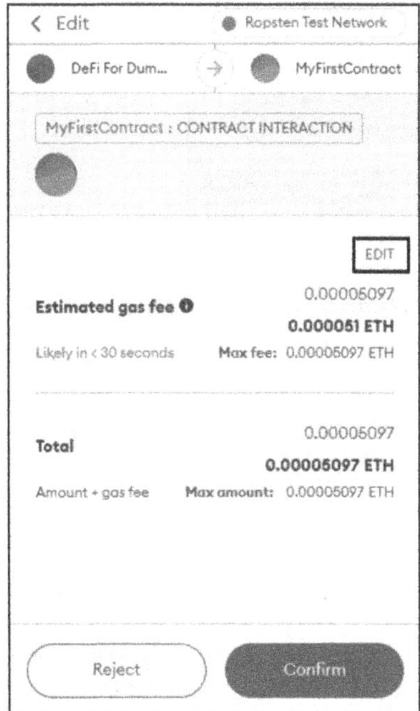

FIGURE 9-8: Estimated gas fee for a transaction submitted through MetaMask.

2. **Click the Edit link.**

   The next screen displays blunt radio-button options to edit the priority of your transaction (from Low to Medium to High), as shown in Figure 9-9.

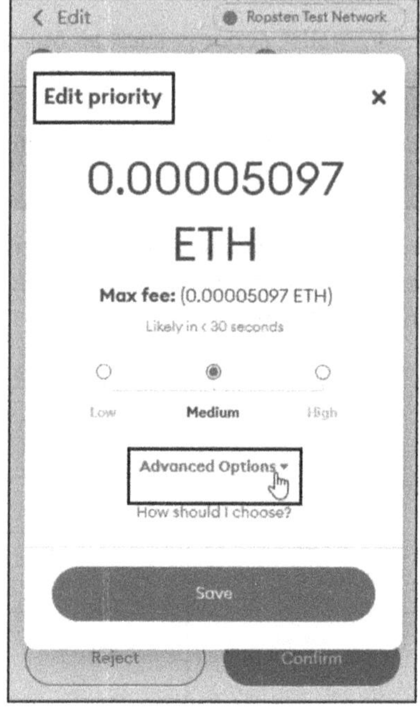

FIGURE 9-9: Edit Priority options on MetaMask allow users to toggle from Low to High priority pricing for the transaction.

3. **On the Edit Priority screen, click the Advanced Options link.**

   The next screen displays the Gas Limit, Max Priority Fee (GWEI), and Max Fee (GWEI) text boxes, as shown in Figure 9-10.

   These text boxes allow you to specify your exact desired amount for each metric, where the max priority fee and the max fee must be specified in *gwei.* One ETH is equal to 1 billion gwei, and 1 gwei is equal to 1 billion wei, where 1 wei is the smallest denomination of ETH (much like how 1 cent is the smallest denomination of the USD).

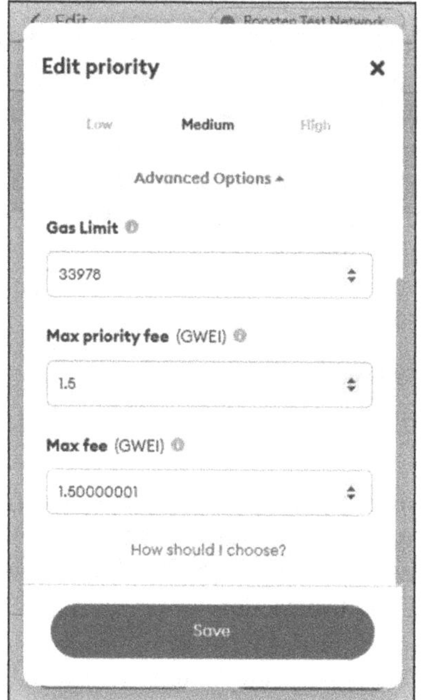

FIGURE 9-10: The advanced Edit Priority page on MetaMask allows you to specify your exact limit and fees for the transaction.

The final bill you incur, known as the transaction fee, is determined after your transaction is mined and added to the blockchain. Specifically, the transaction fee is calculated by taking the actual gas usage required to execute the transaction times the actual *gas price* you incur per unit of gas used.

This gas price you're ultimately charged is determined by the sum of your specified max priority fee and the prevailing base fee at the time of execution, subject to the upper limit imposed by the max fee you specified.

For instance, suppose you specify a max priority fee of 3 gwei and a max fee of 22 gwei. Here are two possible scenarios:

- If the base fee turns out to be 17 gwei, you'll be charged `17 + 3 = 20 gwei` per unit of gas used.
- On the other hand, if the base fee turns out to be 20 gwei, you'll be charged `min{(20+3), 22} = 22 gwei` per unit of gas used.

You pay only for the units of gas used to execute your transaction. So if your specified gas limit exceeds your actual gas usage, you'll be refunded the difference: `(max fee * gas limit) - transaction fee`. For instance, consider the transaction with a TxHash of `0x537bca12942244896df41c898f93d433f7bafa7a76f8617d80d21888fb056214` (shown in Figure 9-11). Initial transaction details are as follows:

- **Gas limit:** 50,733 units
- **Max priority fee:** 1.5 gwei
- **Max fee:** 20.744684053 gwei

At the outset, when this transaction was submitted to the network, 50,733 (gas limit) * 20.744684053 gwei (max fee) = 1,052,440.056 gwei (0.0010524401 ETH) is set aside to pay for the execution of this transaction.

After being included in a block and executed, the actual gas usage of this transaction comes out to 41,321 units, which is less than the specified gas limit of 50,733 units.

In addition, the prevailing base fee for transactions in this block is 17.283388757 gwei. Thus, the gas price charged per unit of gas usage is set to 18.783388757 gwei for this transaction. Here's how the gas price and transaction fee were determined:

- Specifically, 17.283388757 gwei (base fee) + 1.5 gwei (max priority fee) = 18.783388757 gwei, which is less than the specified max fee of 20.744684053 gwei.
- Thus, the transaction successfully completes execution, with a transaction fee of 18.783388757 gwei (gas price) * 41,321 units (gas usage) = 776,147.4068 gwei (0.0007761484068 ETH).
- In addition, the unused funds are returned to the originating account: 1,052,440.056 gwei (funds set aside) – 776,147.4068 gwei (actual transaction fee) = 276,292.6492 gwei (0.0002762926492 ETH).

Transaction Fee:	0.000776148406827997 Ether ($0.87)
Gas Price:	0.000000018783388757 Ether (18.783388757 Gwei)
Gas Limit & Usage by Txn:	50,733 | 41,321 (81.45%)
Gas Fees:	Base: 17.283388757 Gwei | Max: 20.744684053 Gwei | Max Priority: 1.5 Gwei
Burnt & Txn Savings Fees:	Burnt: 0.000714166906827997 Ether ($0.80) Txn Savings: 0.000081042682926016 Ether ($0.09)

FIGURE 9-11: Sample fee breakdown of a successful transaction in Block 14988638.

WARNING

Keep in mind, though, that if the total gas required to successfully complete your transaction exceeds your specified gas limit, you'll be still be charged the gas price times the gas used up until the transaction failed. After all, miners still contributed computing power to mine your transaction. For instance, consider the transaction with a TxHash of `0x62b554e84de6dfc7354e6ed269d6260f3c1cfb1a7d23bb97465f28f226c2a758` (shown in Figure 9-12). Initial transaction details are as follows:

- **Gas limit:** 448,046 units
- **Max priority fee:** 2 gwei
- **Max fee:** 37.532123074 gwei

At the outset, when this transaction was submitted to the network, 448,046 (gas limit) * 37.532123074 gwei (max fee) = 16,816,117.61 gwei (0.01681611761 ETH) is set aside to pay for the execution of this transaction.

After being mined and included in a block, the computational complexity of this transaction is discovered to be greater than the gas limit during execution. Thus, further processing is terminated after expending 446,734 units of gas.

Because the prevailing base fee for transactions in this block is 18.976246082 gwei, the gas price charged per unit of gas usage is set to 20.976246082 gwei for this transaction. Here's how the gas price and transaction fee were determined:

- Specifically, 18.976246082 gwei (base fee) + 2 gwei (max priority fee) = 20.976246082 gwei, which is less than the specified max fee of 37.532123074 gwei.

» Thus, this (unsuccessful) transaction incurs a transaction fee of 20.976246082 gwei (gas price) * 446,734 units (gas usage) = 9,370,802.317 gwei (0.009370802317 ETH).

» The originating account is refunded the unused funds: 16,816,117.61 gwei (funds set aside) – 9,370,802.317 gwei (actual transaction fee) = 7,445,315.293 gwei (0.007445315293 ETH).

» This transaction will need to resubmitted with a higher gas limit to prevent another failed submission.

FIGURE 9-12: Sample fee breakdown of an unsuccessful transaction in Block 14988632.

Finally, if you're looking at transactions included in blocks that were mined prior to August 5, 2020, you'll notice a single gas price specified rather than a max priority fee and max fee. The current system in place, as I've outlined in this section, took effect upon the implementation of EIP-1559, which partitioned the gas price into separate base-fee and priority-fee components and introduced dynamic adjustments to block-level gas limits from one block to the next.

Understanding transaction times

Block times on Ethereum typically range from 12 to 15 seconds. However, if you've submitted transactions to the Ethereum network, you've likely noticed that you're not always included in the next block. So what is causing these delays?

Each block is constrained by a dynamically adjusted block-level gas limit, which limits the number of transactions (by aggregate complexity) that can be included in a given block. Specifically, the aggregated gas limits of the selected pending transactions cannot exceed the prevailing block-level gas limit. If the pool of pending transactions, known as the *memory pool* (or *mempool*), contains more pending transactions than can fit in the current block, miners must prioritize which pending transactions to select.

Enter the priority fee! In each speed race, the successful miner who is first to find the winning nonce receives a *block reward* that is composed of a fixed portion along with a variable portion:

- The fixed portion of the block reward is currently 2 ETH.
- The variable portion of the block reward is determined by the sum of each transaction's priority fee times the units of gas used to complete the transaction. The de facto *priority fee* portion of each transaction's final gas price can be derived by this formula: `min{(base fee + max priority fee), (max fee)} - (base fee)`.

For instance, for Block 14978386, the miner's 2.178583456187095628 ETH (`2 + 0.956594429822178759 - 0.778010973635083131`) block reward, as shown in Figure 9-13, can be decomposed as follows:

- The first term, 2 ETH, is the fixed portion of the block reward.
- The second term, 0.956594429822178759 ETH, is the sum of transaction fees across the 403 transactions selected for this block.
- The third term, 0.778010973635083131 ETH, is the base-fee portion of the total transaction fees. Specifically, 25.963636059 gwei (base fee) * 29,965,409 units (total gas used) = 778,010,973.6 gwei (0.7780109736).
- The block's total transaction fees (0.956594429822178759 ETH) minus the portion attributed to base fees (0.778010973635083131 ETH) provides the portion attributed to priority fees (0.178583456187095628 ETH), which serves as the variable portion of the block reward.

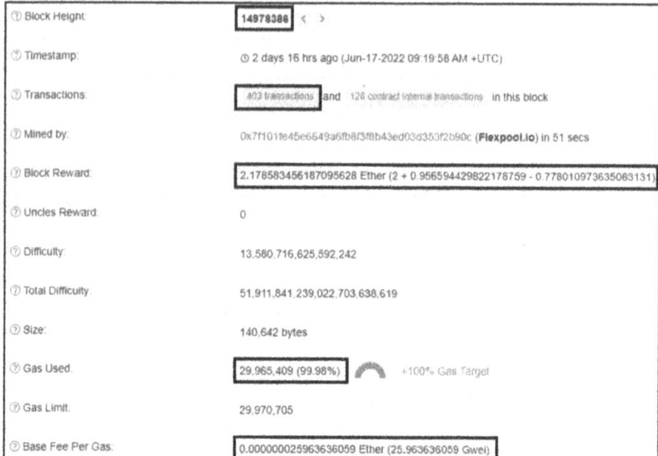

FIGURE 9-13: Details of Block 14978386.

When the contents of the mempool exceed the allowable block-level gas limit, miners are generally incentivized to select as many transactions as possible with the highest priority fees. Miners also watch out for unrealistically high gas limits attached to a transaction, because they are compensated only for the actual gas used in execution. As a result, a pending transaction may be included in the next block or may be forced to wait a few (or many!) rounds before finally being mined.

In addition, you may have noticed that many applications don't immediately consider your transaction to be "confirmed" after it has been mined and added to the blockchain. Because the newest blocks are the most vulnerable to attack, applications often require your transaction to be numerous blocks deep, based on the perceived safety of the blockchain.

Suppose, to the contrary, that clients and applications consider transactions to be fully settled once they are included in the latest block. A group of malicious nodes could then collude to launch a double-spend attack as follows:

1. The malicious group submits a transaction to send ETH to a shared custodial account on Kraken, a popular crypto exchange in the United States.

2. After their pending transaction is mined and executed:

   a. This malicious group moves to immediately convert the ETH to USD and withdraw the money from Kraken to another account.

   b. At the same time, this group secretly and furiously works to resolve a series of nonces until their alternative chain, which does not include this transaction to transfer ETH to Kraken, exceeds the length of the main chain.

3. The malicious group can now broadcast their (longer) alternative chain, which overwrites the main chain as the majority consensus.

4. All transactions from the honest chain that are not part of the malicious chain are reversed, so the malicious group can re-spend their ETH.

5. Because Kraken has already allowed the group to withdraw USD, Kraken is left paying the cost of this double-spend attack.

To prevent these attacks, for ETH transfers, Kraken requires your transaction to be 20 blocks deep before considering the funds to be settled. On the other hand, for ETC (Ethereum Classic), which has suffered numerous double-spend attacks, Kraken requires the transaction to be 40,000 blocks deep. (International checks clear faster than an ETC transfer!) Figure 9-14 provides additional examples of confirmation requirements and corresponding estimates of total wait times until external fund transfers are made available.

Cryptocurrency	Confirmations required	Estimated Time* If included in the next block
Bitcoin (BTC)	4 confirmations	EST 40 minutes Dependent on Fee
Ethereum (ETH)	20 confirmations	5 minutes
Ethereum Classic (ETC)	40,000 confirmations	6.5 days
Flow (FLOW)	30 confirmations	1 minute
Polkadot (DOT)	25 confirmations	2 minutes
Solana (SOL)	N/A	Near-instant

FIGURE 9-14: Sample confirmation requirements on Kraken.

Tracing the journey of a transaction

The following steps walk you through the journey of a transaction from inception to execution:

1. You submit your (digitally signed) transaction to the Ethereum network, specifying your gas limit, max priority fee, and max fee.

2. Assuming your digital signature is valid and you have sufficient funds in your account, your transaction will be assigned a unique code, known as the transaction hash (*TxHash*), and placed in the memory pool of pending transactions (also known as *mempool*), waiting to be mined and added to the blockchain.

   For example, you can follow the journey of a specific transaction, `0x29019f7d22d7e5c0e5abdc008dbc18a15f8856bc172766ccc32f842587d33786`, on the `etherscan.io` block explorer. Figure 9-15 shows this transaction sitting in the mempool, and Figure 9-16 shows the specific details of this pending transaction:

   - The gas limit was set to 99,244 units.
   - The max priority fee was set to 1.5 gwei, and the max fee was set to 33.250323159 gwei.

3. Miners take pending transactions from the mempool and race to find the corresponding proof-of-work nonce to win the right to add the latest block of transactions to the blockchain.

   Whether your pending transaction is immediately included in the next block or is relegated to wait a few cycles depends on the extent of network congestion and the max priority fee you specified when submitting the transaction.

4. After a miner, who has selected your transaction, finds the winning nonce, your transaction will be included in the latest block and added to the blockchain.

Notice that the transaction you're following, `0x29019f7d22d7e5c0e5abdc008dbc18a15f8856bc172766ccc32f842587d33786`, has now been included in Block 14978386 of the Ethereum blockchain, as shown in Figure 9-17.

FIGURE 9-15: A snapshot of the mempool of pending transactions.

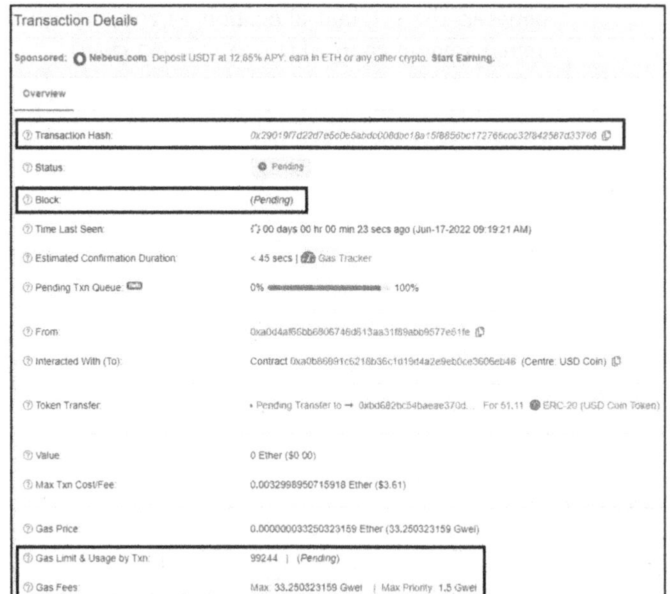

FIGURE 9-16: A pending transaction waiting in the mempool.

The gas price paid, per unit of gas used to complete this transaction, is equal to 27.463636059 gwei, which is the sum of the 25.963636059 gwei base fee and the 1.5 gwei max priority fee. (This sum is less than the specified max fee of 33.250323159 gwei.) The total actual gas usage here is 60,825 units, which is less than the specified gas limit of 99,244. Thus, the actual transaction fee incurred for this transaction is equal to 60,825 units * 27.463636059 gwei = 1,670,475.663 gwei (0.0016704757 ETH). Of this actual transaction fee, 60,825 units * 1.5 gwei = 91,237.5 gwei (0.0000912375 ETH) goes toward the miner's block reward.

The total amount originally allocated for this transaction is 3,299,895.072 gwei (determined by the max price, 33.250323159 gwei, times the gas limit, 99,244). Because this total amount is less than the actual transaction fee incurred, the unused portion is returned to the originating account. That unused portion is 1,629,419.409 gwei, which was determined by the difference between the original allocation (3,299,895.072 gwei) and the actual amount charged (1,670,475.663 gwei).

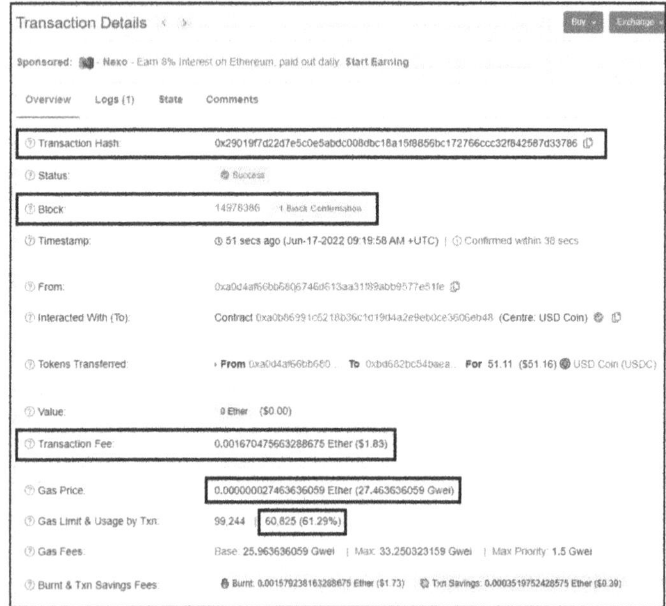

FIGURE 9-17: A confirmed transaction is now part of Block 14978386 on the Ethereum blockchain.

Streamlining the Development Process

Consider your various credit cards. Because they come in a standard size and shape, you can easily hold different cards from various issuers without requiring a different wallet when you switch cards. The standardization across cards also allows vendors to use the same physical credit-card processor irrespective of the card being used. Thus, standardization ensures *interoperability,* meaning that your product will be compatible with existing clients and services.

Standardization also allows you to combine and recombine various components to suit your specific needs. For instance, consider the sizing of studs and anti-studs used on children's building bricks. The standardized shapes and sizes allow for a myriad of effortless stacking solutions. Thus, standardization promotes *composability,* meaning that you can effortlessly combine and augment existing products to arrive at custom solutions that fit the needs of a particular client.

Similarly, the DeFi community has established development standards to ensure that a diverse set of independent players can seamlessly and effectively interact. You don't have to adhere to these standards when implementing your own smart contracts, but following commonly accepted guidelines will save you a lot of frustration and make your protocol more attractive to other participants in the system.

Leveraging smart-contract libraries

Depending on your chosen platform, many open-source libraries exist to provide developers with pre-vetted base contracts that follow the established development standards of the platform in question. For instance, OpenZeppelin (accessed at `https//www.openzeppelin.com`) provides ready-made ERC-20 and ERC-721 compliant implementations that allow you to quickly create a fungible or non-fungible token on Ethereum.

Oracles: A Blockchain's Divine Access to the Outside World

Public blockchains like Ethereum operate as closed systems, much like a computer that is disconnected from the internet, where functions on the network can access only *on-chain* data and code that is stored on the blockchain in question. Thus, although external applications and players can access the functions and data housed on a public blockchain, transactions within the network cannot issue an HTTP request to access *off-chain* information.

The self-contained nature isn't restrictive if you simply plan to use the blockchain as a payments system, because all the information required to transfer funds from one account to the other (transaction history and account balances) is recorded and kept on the blockchain. But what if you want to implement a decentralized betting application that is designed to accept funds and pay participants based on, say, whether a particular team wins the Super Bowl? Or perhaps you'd like to implement a decentralized derivative product that pays participants based on whether the S&P 500 Index exceeds a predefined benchmark. You need a way to get this off-chain data onto the blockchain so that your on-chain smart contract can use this information to compensate the winning accounts.

Thankfully, this problem has a straightforward solution! You can develop a separate off-chain application, alongside your on-chain smart contract, to gather the desired information. Then this application, called an *oracle,* can submit a transaction that provides the off-chain data to your smart contract.

Your oracle can be centrally operated, or, as a dedicated DeFi purist, you can opt for a decentralized implementation. With the explosion of dApps in recent years, the demand for reliable oracle services has risen commensurately. Several well-known oracle services include:

- **Chainlink:** `https://chain.link/`
- **Provable:** `https://provable.xyz/`
- **Witnet:** `https://witnet.io/`

IN THIS CHAPTER

» Explaining layer 1 (L1) and layer 2 (L2)

» Comparing (L1) base protocols

» Exploring off-chain (L2) scaling solutions

Chapter 10 Smart-Contract Platforms

Following the widespread adoption and soaring market values of Bitcoin and Ethereum, many new blockchains have spawned to address the inefficiencies that come with these old-school protocols. With promises to achieve greater throughput and faster transaction times, a common theme across these scaling solutions is the collective shift from proof-of-work (PoW) to proof-of-stake (PoS). Another trend is the rise of so-called *layer 2* off-chain (or, more accurately, off-layer-1) scaling solutions.

» Layer 1 (L1) refers to the base blockchain. Bitcoin and Ethereum are examples of L1 blockchains.

» Layer 2 (L2) refers to an off-chain scaling solution whose transactions are ultimately reconciled and secured on the L1 protocol it was designed to scale. These L2 scaling solutions come in many different shapes and sizes, each with their own advantages and disadvantages.

No solution has yet disproven the famous *blockchain trilemma*, which holds that in trying to achieve scalability, security, and decentralization, one feature must always be sacrificed. But in such an exciting and rapidly developing space, who knows what is around the corner!

I highly recommend reading the full chapter to gain a better understanding and appreciation of the existing solutions and ongoing challenges in achieving truly secure and decentralized scalability. That said, this chapter is not a necessary building block to successfully implement the instructional guides provided in Chapters 11, 12, and 13.

TIP

Thus, if you're feeling impatient, you can easily skip this conceptual chapter and jump straight to the next chapter (Chapter 11, "Launching a Smart Contract on Ethereum").

Diving into Layer 1: Comparing Base Protocols

This section describes several well-known blockchain-based layer 1 (L1) protocols for smart-contract development. For each platform covered in this section, I provide the following information:

- **Year:** The year the main network went live
- **Native Token:** The ticker symbol for the network's native token
- **Consensus Protocol:** The process used by the network to reach agreement when adding transactions to the blockchain
- **Epoch Length:** The turnaround cycle to determine adjustments to the difficulty level (for proof-of-work protocols) or the next set of validators (for proof-of-stake protocols)

- **Network Permissions:** What permissions (if any) are required to participate as a validator or miner on the network
- **Primary Language:** The most commonly used programming language for smart-contract development on the platform
- **Average Block Time:** The average time between block formations
- **Block Limit:** The upper-bound on the total transactions, either by message size or computational complexity, that can be included in a single block
- **Confirmations Required:** How many blocks deep a transaction must be before Kraken and Coinbase, respectively, consider the deposit to be fully settled
- **L2 Platform(s):** Examples of off-chain scaling solutions alongside the ticker of the token used to transact on the L2 protocol
- **Proposal Process:** The process used by the network participants to propose network updates and standards to be approved for adoption by the community

REMEMBER

Keep in mind that protocols are updated over time, some more frequently than others. For reference, the information provided here represents the prevailing network standards as of July 2022.

Bitcoin

Despite its continued reign as the largest native token by market cap, Bitcoin hasn't gained much traction for DeFi activity beyond its role as a decentralized payment system. Nonetheless, as the OG of public blockchains, I would be remiss to forgo Bitcoin in my review of well-known L1 protocols.

Here is Bitcoin in a nutshell:

- **Year:** 2009
- **Native Token:** BTC
- **Consensus Protocol:** Proof of Work (PoW)

- **Epoch Length:** 2,016 blocks (2 weeks)
- **Network Permissions:** Anyone can obtain the necessary hardware and download the appropriate software to join the network as a miner (validator)
- **Primary Language:** Bitcoin Script
- **Average Block Time:** 10 minutes
- **Block Limit:** 1MB
- **Confirmations Required:** 4 (Kraken), 2 (Coinbase)
- **L2 Platform(s):** Lightning Network (BTC), Liquid Network (L-BTC)
- **Proposal Process:** Bitcoin Improvement Proposals (BIPs), accessed at `https://github.com/bitcoin/bips`

Throughout the years, Bitcoin has remained relatively simple in the computational functions it supports. However, with some creative maneuvering, more expressive smart contracts are possible to implement on the Bitcoin blockchain. For instance, so-called *colored coins*, introduced in 2012, were designed to represent ownership records of off-chain assets by piggybacking on the trustless security of the Bitcoin blockchain. This secondary layer of recordkeeping was implemented as a Bitcoin transaction submitted with additional metadata to reference the desired asset. With the advent of newer, more flexible platforms, colored coins have naturally lost their appeal.

Ethereum

Given the clear demand for a more flexible protocol, Ethereum was created to provide a platform expressly designed to implement more customized applications while maintaining the decentralized, yet tamper-proof, recordkeeping system established by Bitcoin. Now, seven years after its Mainnet went live, Ethereum remains the predominant platform for DeFi developers.

Here is Ethereum in a nutshell:

- **Year:** 2015
- **Native Token:** ETH

TAPPING AROUND TAPROOT

Despite the seeming lack of curb appeal, many developers view Bitcoin's simplicity as a feature rather than a drawback to the platform. Given the Bitcoin community's relatively strict adherence to the protocol's original underpinnings, the base protocol is unlikely to ever support fully expressive smart contracts.

However, a recent and exciting exception is the proposed Taproot upgrade, which is designed to aggregate signatures of a multisignature (multisig) transaction for validation rather than to validate each signature separately. This upgrade, if accepted by the community of Bitcoin miners, would enhance both the efficiency and privacy of transactions processed on the network, which, in turn, could very well accelerate the development of more expressive smart contracts on L2 protocols.

With the proposal of BIP-0343, Bitcoin miners began the voting process, known as *activation signaling,* where miners must include the specified signal in the blocks they mine to convey support for Taproot. The signaling period began at block `681,408` on May 1, 2021 and will end at block `760,032`, which is expected to close sometime in August 2022. If 90 percent of blocks mined during this period signal support for Taproot, all miners will be required to incorporate this upgrade by block `762,048` (approximately two weeks after the end of the signaling period).

Thus, the jury's still out on Taproot, but the verdict will likely be in by the time this book hits shelves!

- **Consensus Protocol:** Proof of Work (PoW)
- **Epoch Length:** 30,000 blocks (5 days)
- **Network Permissions:** Anyone can obtain the necessary hardware and download the appropriate software to join the network as a miner (validator)
- **Primary Language:** Solidity
- **Average Block Time:** 13 seconds
- **Block Limit:** Dynamically adjusted gas limit, with a target of 15 million units and an upper bound of 30 million units

» **Confirmations required:** 20 (Kraken), 14 (Coinbase)

» **L2 Platform(s):** Arbitrum One (ETH), Optimism (OP)

» **Proposal Process:** Ethereum Improvement Proposals (EIPs), accessed at `https://eips.ethereum.org/`

For years, the Ethereum community has been anticipating a shift from PoW to PoS. In fact, a *difficulty bomb* was embedded into the protocol early on, with the view to spur the development of on-chain scaling solutions for the network. The difficulty bomb was designed to progressively, but dramatically, increase block times by triggering stepwise increases in the computational difficulty of the proof-of-work puzzle that miners must solve. This difficulty bomb has been delayed (by way of EIPs, of course!) numerous times, with the latest delay (EIP-5133) pushing the difficulty bomb from exploding in June 2022 to approximately September or October 2022.

This historic shift to PoS may (also!) have occurred by the time you read this. Following the migration from PoW to PoS, Ethereum plans to achieve further on-chain scaling through the use of *shard chains*, which effectively split the network data to lighten each node's load without sacrificing general network consensus.

Ethereum Classic

Although the Ethereum blockchain itself has never been hacked, externally owned accounts (EOAs) and smart-contract accounts on Ethereum have been breached. Most notably, in mid-2016, a critical vulnerability in smart-contract design culminated in a major hack on a smart-contract account known as The DAO. This security breach resulted in the theft of roughly 3.6 million ETH. In a controversial sequence of events, the Ethereum community, under the guidance of the Ethereum Foundation, voted to alter the blockchain records to restore the stolen funds.

The vast majority of the Ethereum community migrated to this forked blockchain path with the rewritten history. However, a sizable minority, who were adamantly opposed to violating the immutability of the blockchain, remained and continued to support the original legacy chain. Thus, the rebranded Ethereum Classic was born, and major crypto exchanges swiftly moved to support and list the nonforked native token, ETC.

With a substantially smaller network of miners, the Ethereum Classic blockchain has suffered a series of double-spend attacks. In response, Coinbase even required an ETC transaction to be 20,000 blocks deep before considering the deposit to be fully settled! More recently, in April 2022, Coinbase relaxed this confirmation requirement to 3,000, though Kraken still requires 40,000 confirmations and Gemini simply doesn't support ETC.

Here is Ethereum Classic in a nutshell:

- **Year:** 2016
- **Native Token:** ETC
- **Consensus Protocol:** Proof of Work (PoW)
- **Epoch Length:** 60,000 blocks (10 days)
- **Network Permissions:** Anyone can obtain the necessary hardware and download the appropriate software to join the network as a miner (validator)
- **Primary Language:** Solidity
- **Average Block Time:** 13 seconds
- **Block Limit:** 8 million units of gas
- **Confirmations required:** 40,000 (Kraken), 3,000 (Coinbase)
- **L2 Platform(s):** N/A (none yet)
- **Proposal Process:** Ethereum Classic Improvement Proposals (ECIPs), accessed at `https://ecips.ethereumclassic.org/`

Like the Bitcoin community, Ethereum Classic remains more conservative in its adherence to core principles, with the mantra to "move slowly and don't break things" and to "keep Ethereum Classic *classic*." Interestingly, Ethereum Classic intends to remain a PoW-based protocol. Accordingly, the difficulty bomb on Ethereum Classic was first delayed (ECIP-1010) and then removed altogether (ECIP-1041). Perhaps after Ethereum (finally!) executes its transition to PoS, an influx of miners may migrate to Ethereum Classic.

Binance Smart Chain

Also referred to as BNB Smart Chain, or simply BSC, the Binance Smart Chain is EVM-compatible, which dramatically lowers the switching cost for developers (as you'll directly experience if you follow the hands-on portion of both Chapters 11 and 12). To achieve faster transaction times, the Binance Smart Chain employs a delegated proof-of-stake consensus protocol, where the top 21 candidates, ranked by total staked BNB, are selected every 24 hours to serve as validators.

Validator candidates must self-stake a minimum of 10,000 BNB to be included in the candidate pool. At the current price of approximately $235 per BNB, this minimum threshold translates to $2.35 million! (Figure 10-1 shows the BNB price path from August 2021 to July 2022, accessed at `https://coincap.io/assets/binance-coin`.) Smaller players can participate by delegating their BNB to any of the candidates in the pool of prospective validators, thereby essentially casting their votes for who serves as the 21 delegates in the next 24-hour cycle. Malicious or otherwise faulty validators are subject to slashing, where the validator's own stake (but not the delegated stake) is seized and redistributed.

FIGURE 10-1: A recent BNB price path.

In addition to shorter block times relative to Ethereum, the Binance Smart Chain also allows a much higher gas limit per block. The current limit is at 100 million units of gas, with the view to incrementally increase the gas limit by 25 million until reaching the targeted upper bound of 200 million by the end of 2022.

Here is the Binance Smart Chain in a nutshell:

- **Year:** 2020
- **Native Token:** BNB
- **Consensus Protocol:** Delegated Proof of Stake (DPoS)
- **Epoch Length:** 24 hours
- **Network Permissions:** Anyone can join the validator candidate pool by staking at least 10,000 BNB (and, of course, obtaining the necessary hardware and software)
- **Primary Language:** Solidity
- **Average Block Time:** 3 seconds
- **Block Limit:** Gas limit of 100 million units
- **Confirmations Required:** N/A (not supported by Kraken or Coinbase)
- **L2 Platform(s):** Autobahn (TXL)
- **Proposal Process:** BNB Evolution Proposals (BEPs), accessed at `https://github.com/bnb-chain/BEPs`

Although BNB trading is not currently supported by Kraken (or Coinbase or Gemini), international exchanges that accept BNB vary quite a bit in their confirmations required, ranging from 1 confirmation (crypto.com) to 25 confirmations (CEX.IO).

Other EVM-Compatible Networks

In addition to Binance Smart Chain, other PoS-based EVM-compatible L1 protocols include:

- **Fantom,** which launched in 2019, with average block times of 1 second and native token FTM

- **Celo,** which launched in 2020, with average block times of 5 seconds and native token CGLD
- **Avalanche,** which launched in 2020, with average block times of 2 seconds and native token AVAX
- **Cronos,** which launched in 2021, with average block times of 6 seconds and native token CRO

Like Binance Smart Chain, these L1 protocols also employ Solidity as their primary smart-contract language and are supported by MetaMask.

TRON

TRON's dedication to building a truly decentralized internet was solidified early on with its acquisition and integration of BitTorrent, an established behemoth in the peer-to-peer decentralized file-sharing space.

TRON employs a delegated proof-of-stake consensus protocol, where the top 27 candidates, referred to as *super representatives*, are elected every 6 hours to serve as validators. Any TRX holder can participate in the voting process by staking their TRX to receive one vote, referred to as TRON Power (TP), per TRX staked.

TRON doesn't impose an explicit minimum stake requirement to be included in the candidate pool. Candidates simply pay a 9,999 TRX fee to be included in the super-representative election. At the current price of approximately $0.07 per TRX (`https://coincap.io/assets/tron`; see Figure 10-2), this initiation fee is roughly $7,000.

- **Year:** 2018
- **Native Token:** TRX
- **Consensus Protocol:** Delegated Proof of Stake (DPoS)
- **Epoch Length:** 6 hours
- **Network Permissions:** Anyone can join the validator candidate pool by paying a 9,999 TRX fee (and, of course, obtaining the necessary hardware and software)

- **Primary Language:** Solidity
- **Average Block Time:** 3 seconds
- **Block Limit:** 2,000,000 bytes
- **Confirmations Required:** 20 (Kraken), N/A (not supported by Coinbase)
- **L2 Platform(s):** BitTorrent Chain (BTTC)
- **Proposal Process:** TRON Improvement Proposals (TIPs), accessed at `https://github.com/tronprotocol/TIPs`

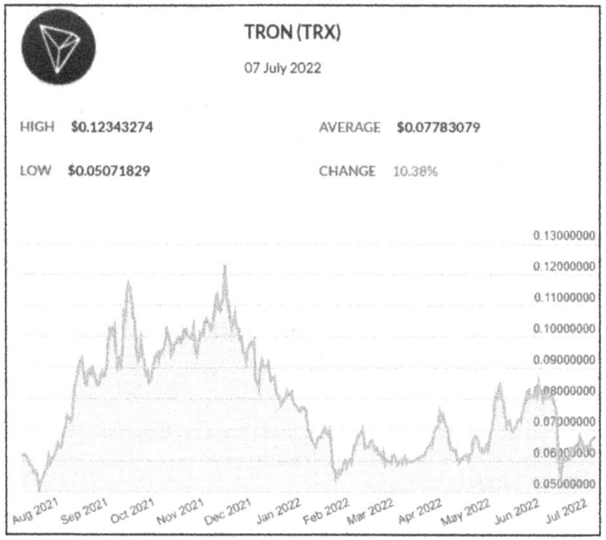

FIGURE 10-2: The TRX price path from August 2021 to July 2022.

TRON is mostly EVM-compatible with some key differences, for instance, in some of the built-in functions and operation codes (opcodes), contract-address generation, and transaction-fee structure. Accordingly, MetaMask doesn't support network connections to the TRON Mainnet.

Flow

Brought to you by Dapper Labs (home of CryptoKitties and NBA Top Shots!), Flow is secured by a leased proof-of-stake consensus protocol that employs an assembly-line process with separate but overlapping functions for each node type. This multinode architecture consists of the following nodes:

- *Collection nodes,* which manage the memory pool of pending transactions.
- *Consensus nodes,* which form and validate transactions into blocks.
- *Execution nodes,* which execute the transactions.
- *Verification nodes,* which verify the Execution nodes' work product.

Potential validators must apply to operate a node, and punitive slashing is currently decided on a case-by-case basis.

The minimum stake required to be a node operator can be quite steep, with Execution nodes requiring a minimum stake of 1.25 million FLOW. At the current price of approximately $1.30 per FLOW (`https://coincap.io/assets/flow`; see Figure 10-3), this minimum threshold translates to $1.63 million. The minimum required stake to operate a Collector, Consensus, or Verification node is 250,000, 500,000, and 135,000 FLOW, respectively. Smaller players can participate by staking their FLOW with a confirmed node operator.

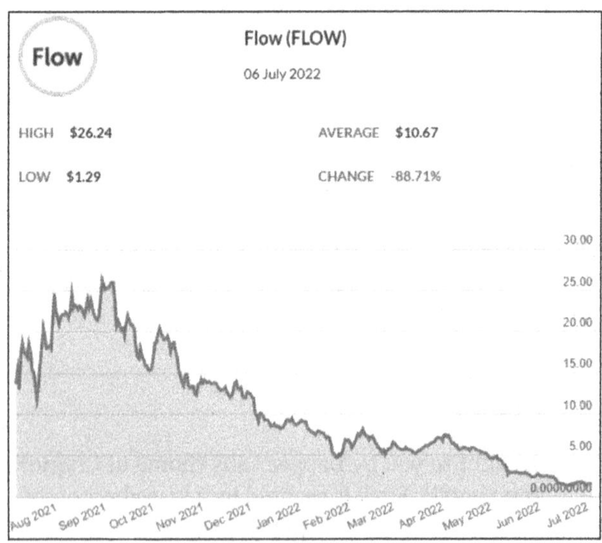

FIGURE 10-3: FLOW price path from August 2021 to July 2022.

Flow measures epochs by the number of *consensus views*, which is dynamically adjusted to ensure that each epoch lasts approximately one week. Prior to the start of each epoch, Flow's protocol reviews each node to confirm sufficient stake and computing power. Nodes meeting the minimum requirements are included in an *identity table*, which signifies the nodes authorized to participate in the next epoch.

Here is Flow in a nutshell:

- **Year:** 2020
- **Native Token:** FLOW
- **Consensus Protocol:** Leased Proof of Stake (LPoS)
- **Epoch Length:** 1 week
- **Network Permissions:** Validator candidates who want to operate a Collection, Consensus, or Verification node must fill out an application for review by the Flow Foundation (applications to operate an Execution node are not currently being accepted)
- **Primary Language:** Cadence
- **Average Block Time:** 2 seconds
- **Block Limit:** 100 results
- **Confirmations Required:** 30 (Kraken), 0 (Coinbase)
- **L2 Platform(s):** N/A (none yet)
- **Proposal Process:** Flow Improvement Proposals (FLIPs), accessed at `https://github.com/onflow/flow/tree/master/flips`

Although the Flow documents refer to staking as "delegating," I classify the Flow consensus protocol as *leased* PoS to differentiate PoS protocols that have elected delegates for each epoch from those that allow simple pooling.

Cardano

Despite its highly anticipated yet disappointing rollout of fully expressive smart-contract functionality in late 2021, Cardano continues to command the respect of developers and the overall market. Cardano is unique in its commitment to a truly decentralized yet safe reliance on proof of stake based on vetted, peer-reviewed research that has been accepted and presented at academic conferences.

Validators in this system are referred to as *stake pool operators.* Anyone can start a stake pool, and there isn't a minimum self-staking requirement. However, other (nonoperator) participants in the network are unlikely to stake their ADA with a stake pool operator who pledges little to no ADA of their own. The likelihood of being randomly selected to form a block increases proportionately with total staked ADA (but only to a certain limit to encourage decentralization).

Under Cardano's current protocol, known as *Ouroboros Praos,* each epoch consists of 432,000 one-second slots. Prior to the start of each epoch, a *leader log* is generated to dictate which stake pool operator(s) will serve as slot leaders who are responsible for forming blocks. A given slot may randomly be assigned more than one leader or no leader at all. Overall, the algorithm is designed, on average, to draw a slot leader every 20 slots. Thus, on average, each epoch consists of 21,600 blocks formed approximately every 20 seconds. Notably, Cardano's protocol doesn't implement punitive slashing and has no designs to do so.

Here is Cardano in a nutshell:

- **Year:** 2017
- **Native Token:** ADA
- **Consensus Protocol:** Leased Proof of Stake (LPoS)
- **Epoch Length:** 432,000 one-second slots (5 days)
- **Network Permissions:** Anyone can obtain the necessary hardware and download the appropriate software to start a stake pool
- **Primary Language:** Plutus
- **Average Block Time:** 20 seconds
- **Block Limit:** 88KB
- **Confirmations Required:** 15 (Kraken), 10 (Coinbase)

- **L2 Platform(s):** N/A (none yet)
- **Proposal Process:** Cardano Improvement Proposals (CIPs), accessed at `https://cips.cardano.org/`

Although there aren't yet any L2 solutions for Cardano's mainnet, the highly anticipated Hydra test protocol was recently launched in March 2022 as a public L2 state channel to test the promise of its off-chain scalability on the Cardano Testnet.

Solana

Solana's claim to fame lies in its impressive progress toward achieving its theoretically derived limit of 710,000 transactions per second. Solana's protocol accomplishes greater speed through (1) parallel validation and optimistic processing, coupled with (2) a variation of a *verifiable delay function* (VDF) to confirm the sequence of validated and processed entries that comprise the finalized "block."

In this process, transactions are grouped into *entries*, which are broken down into smaller *shreds*, which are then propagated across nodes for validation. Each node optimistically processes each transaction as it's received so that the execution delay is minimal after the block is finalized and confirmed. Solana's VDF, referred to as the *proof of history*, allows nodes to swiftly confirm the correct order of entries, thus enabling this piecemeal processing of entries (without having to wait for an entire block to be formed before beginning the propagation and validation across nodes).

Anyone can start a validator node with as little as 1 SOL to be entered in the candidate pool to be the next leader, and nonvalidators can participate by staking their SOL with their chosen validator(s). Solana hasn't yet implemented punitive slashing, though developers plan to update the protocol to not only slash the stake of a faulty validator but also slash the stake of those who backed the faulty validator.

Each epoch under this system consists of 432,000 slots. Prior to the start of each epoch, a *leader schedule* is generated to randomly assign a leader to each slot. Slot leaders are responsible for forming blocks, and a validator node's likelihood of being selected increases proportionately with its total stake.

Here is Solana in a nutshell:

- **Year:** 2020
- **Native Token:** SOL
- **Consensus Protocol:** Leased Proof of Stake (LPoS)
- **Epoch Length:** 432,000 slots (2–4 days)
- **Network Permissions:** Anyone can obtain the necessary hardware and download the appropriate software to start a validator node
- **Primary Language:** Rust, C++
- **Average Block Time:** < 1 second
- **Block Limit:** 32,000 shreds (up to 128,000 transactions)
- **Confirmations Required:** 30 (Kraken), 35 (Coinbase)
- **L2 Platform(s):** N/A
- **Proposal Process:** Feature Proposal Program, accessed at `https://spl.solana.com/feature-proposal`

There aren't any L2 solutions built for Solana, and developers aim to continually ensure on-chain scaling solutions as the network grows.

Floating Up to Layer 2: Off-Chain Scaling Solutions

Now that you've seen the basics of some well-known L1 protocols, this section provides an overview of the various types of L2 scaling solutions. L2 implementations come in many different flavors, but the main distinctions lie in the following:

- Whether the off-chain scaling is implemented via the use of (1) *state channels*, (2) *plasma chains*, or (3) *rollups*.
- Whether transactions are (1) executed *optimistically* and later challenged via *fraud proofs*, or (2) verified prior to execution and settlement via *validity proofs*.

Current L2 solutions are not immune to the widely held blockchain trilemma, where scalability is achieved by sacrificing either safety or decentralization.

A common theme across different L2 implementations is that transactions are processed outside of layer 1, which eases network burden and allows for faster execution. These off-chain (or, more accurately, off-L1) computations are ultimately settled and secured on the L1 base network through an on-chain smart contract. Thus, L2 solutions achieve speed while also enjoying greater security than if they operated as completely independent, standalone chains.

REMEMBER

Keep in mind that, like many developments in the blockchain world, L2 scaling solutions are still in their infancy. As with any new protocols, you should proceed with a healthy amount of caution and skepticism.

State channels

In case you were wondering what enabled Twitter to allow users to swiftly and seamlessly tip with Bitcoin, the answer is through state channels (and, of course, Strike — a Bitcoin wallet and payment services provider).

State channels achieve scalability by settling only the opening and closing transactions of each channel on the L1 base protocol. Wallet services designed for a given state-channel protocol typically operate numerous nodes to continuously open two-way channels with each of its clients.

Opening a channel requires each party to deposit and lock native tokens in a multisig smart contract on the L1 protocol. Then, the parties transact indefinitely (as long as the net activity doesn't exceed the contract account's balance), and all these interim records between parties are maintained off-chain. When the channel is ultimately closed, the contract account on the L1 protocol disburses the appropriate funds to each party based on the net activity that occurred while the channel was open.

Because all other interim records and computations are kept off-chain, users experience faster confirmations and lower overall transaction costs. However, because state channels depend on network connectivity through open channels, users cannot transfer funds to participants on the L1 network who are not active on the L2 state-channel network.

The simplest type of state channel is a *payment channel*, such as the Lightening Network, which provides an off-chain scaling solution for Bitcoin. With payment channels, the only state changes recorded are for beginning and final account balances when the channel is opened and when it is closed.

Plasma chains and sidechains

Similar to state channels, plasma chains also keep much of the transaction data and computations off-chain. However, for enhanced security, plasma chains submit cryptographic proof of the current state at regular intervals to the L1 chain. In contrast, state channels reconcile with the L1 chain only when the channel is opened and when it is closed.

Plasma chains are implemented as a separate blockchain with its own consensus protocol. A smart contract on the L1 chain serves as a bridge, allowing users to lock up native tokens in the bridge contract in a one-to-one exchange for tokens on the plasma chain, where the representative transactions are executed and periodically published to layer 1.

In this sense, plasma chains are very similar to *sidechains*, with the important distinction that sidechains do not submit cryptographic proof of state back to layer 1.

Rollups

A *rollup* is also implemented as a separate blockchain with its own consensus protocol. However, in contrast to state channels and plasma chains, rollups record information about every transaction performed back on layer 1. Transactions are still executed off layer 1, but rollups piggyback off the security of the L1 base protocol by submitting bundles of transactions, as data, to be recorded to a specially created rollup contract on L1.

Because hundreds of transactions performed on layer 2 can be *rolled up* and submitted as a single transaction on layer 1, the underlying L1 network's transaction fee is distributed across hundreds of transactions executed on L2, thereby dramatically reducing transaction fees while also increasing speed.

Fraud proofs versus validity proofs

Whether implementing a state channel, plasma chain, or rollup, developers must also decide how their L2 protocol will ultimately validate and settle transaction outcomes on the L1 chain.

Optimistic protocols execute transactions under the optimistic assumption that they are valid. *Fraud proofs* are used to challenge validity if a transaction is suspect. Thus, transactions are executed swiftly and cheaply on layer 2, but, given the necessary challenge period, participants must wait out this time frame before they can withdraw funds locked in the smart contract on layer 1.

Specifically, to deter potential fraud, operators on this type of L2 protocol must post collateral, typically referred to as a *bond*, for each bundle of L2 transactions they execute, roll up, and post on layer 1. Then the entire layer 2 network has a fixed amount of time, typically called the *challenge period*, to check the operator's work and to challenge fraudulent state changes. The challenger must also post a bond with their challenge. If proven wrong, the challenger's bond is slashed, and if proven correct, the faulty operator's bond is slashed. After the challenge period has passed, the bond is released and the transactions in question are considered permanently settled.

In contrast, "pessimistic" protocols rely on cryptographic *validity proofs*, known as *zero-knowledge* (ZK) proofs, to demonstrate validity prior to execution and settlement. To economize on computation and storage, these validity proofs must be designed to prove the validity of the off-chain computations without having to actually show and re-execute these computations.

Thus, unlike fraud proofs, which entail a mechanically cumbersome process of replaying prior transactions, ZK proofs provide quick and easy verification. As a result, participants can enjoy faster withdrawals of funds locked up in smart contracts on layer 1, because there is no challenge period to wait out. However, ZK proofs are far more mathematically complex to design in a way that ensures safety.

Arbitrum One and Optimism are examples of optimistic rollups for Ethereum that are EVM-compatible. There aren't (yet!) any ZK validity-proof–based rollups that are EVM-compatible, though several projects are under development. dYdX and zkSync are examples of ZK rollups designed for L2 asset transfers.

Crossing Cross-Chain Bridges

With the explosion in blockchain platforms, cross-chain bridges are popping up to enable participants from one network to cross over to another. Bridges are implemented as smart contracts, with a bridge contract account holding native tokens on one blockchain and the corresponding bridge contract on another blockchain issuing tokens compatible with that network.

However, the seeming convenience comes with many risks. For one thing, bridges are susceptible to double-spend attacks, much like Coinbase and Kraken. Thus, bridges are balancing speed and convenience against safety. After all, the value proposition of the bridge declines with the lockup period required for withdrawals.

Moreover, smart-contract vulnerabilities compound on these innate problems. Earlier in July 2021, THORChain was exploited by a relatively friendly hacker, who left notes explaining other vulnerabilities and famously added "[d]o not rush code that controls 9 figures" before absconding with approximately $8 million worth of tokens. At the time, roughly $100 million worth of tokens, collectively, were locked in THORChain bridge contracts.

More recently, cross-chain bridges have suffered far more public and catastrophic hacks. Solana's Wormhole lost more than $300 million worth of tokens to hackers in February 2022, and just one month later, Axie Infinity's Ronin Bridge lost more than $600 million to hackers. The most recent heist suffered by the Horizon Bridge in June 2022 totaled close to $100 million.

Overall, cross-chain bridges are not off to a great start, and seemingly less convenient methods are at least far less risky.

IN THIS CHAPTER

» Explaining account types (externally owned versus contract accounts)

» Introducing the key elements of a smart contract

» Writing, compiling, and deploying your smart contract

» Following and interacting with your smart contract after deployment

Chapter 11
Launching a Smart Contract on Ethereum

A *smart contract* is a software program, defined by a set of code and data, that lies dormant until triggered by an external transaction. When called, smart contracts automatically enforce and execute a series of deterministic rules. Overall, they provide the logical foundation on which decentralized applications (dApps) are built. Indeed, the myriad of DeFi implementations presented in Part 2, "Diving into the Burgeoning DeFi Space," rely on smart contracts for back-end processes. This chapter walks you through how to deploy and subsequently interact with your first smart contract on Ethereum!

REMEMBER

To follow the hands-on portion of this chapter, you will need to have completed some key steps in advance. I assume that you have already installed the MetaMask browser extension and set up your wallet with a funded account (see Chapter 3).

TIP

I highly recommend reading the full chapter to gain a better understanding of smart-contract design. However, if you're feeling antsy, you can skip the section on "Understanding Smart Contracts" and head straight down to "Launching Your Smart Contract."

Understanding Smart Contracts

It's easy to grasp at a high level what smart contracts are and what they're intended for, but the actual logistics remain murky even for many DeFi enthusiasts. My goal here is to shed some light inside this black box, beginning with an overview of what the nascent life of a smart contract looks like.

The birth of a smart contract

Suppose you want to crowdfund the development of a new project. Well-established options, such as Kickstarter and Indiegogo, provide (CeFi) platforms for you to raise funds in this manner. However, these firms charge a premium for the service they provide. For instance, Kickstarter currently charges 5 percent of the total funds raised in addition to payment processing fees equal to $0.20 plus 3 percent of each contributor's amount pledged. Indiegogo levies a similar fee on funds raised through its platform.

Another option is to deploy a smart contract on Ethereum for this same purpose. Here's how this process works:

1. First, you write and compile your code.
2. Next, you submit your compiled bytecode as a transaction to the Ethereum network without specifying a recipient.

   Note that this is different from the typical transactions you may be more familiar with — namely, transactions to send funds (ETH) from one account to another.

3. After your transaction has been mined and included on the Ethereum blockchain, a special contract account is created and assigned an address as part of this process.

   Contract accounts can hold a balance (hence, the obvious fundraising use case!) and can be designed to, say, record the balance and addresses of all accounts contributing to the contract account.

Now, before delving into the key features of a smart contract, it will be helpful to gain some more clarity as to what a *contract account* is and how it differs from a so-called "regular" account.

Contract accounts versus "regular" (externally owned) accounts

The account you create using MetaMask (in Chapter 3) is what's formally known as an *externally owned account* (EOA). EOAs are most commonly referred to simply as "accounts" (so they are far more common than their name suggests).

Here are a few things to keep in mind when it comes to accounts (a.k.a. EOAs):

- **You need an EOA to submit transactions to the Ethereum network.** For instance, EOAs can initiate transactions to: (1) transfer funds to another EOA (or to a contract account); (2) call functions housed in a contract account; or (3) deploy bytecode to create a new contract account. Transactions between two EOAs can only be requests to transfer funds.
- **Creating an EOA is quick and simple (when using wallet services such as MetaMask), and, importantly, is free (it doesn't cost any ETH to create an EOA)!** When you create a new EOA, your wallet service takes care of the fancy mathematical footwork to generate a key pair for you: a private key, which should never be shared; and a corresponding public address, which you can share with anyone to receive funds.

You can think of your account's public address as you would your email address. Anyone can send you emails if they know your email address. However, they can't access your emails without the password. Likewise, you need the EOA's private key to access and spend funds.

» **An EOA is not a wallet, and a wallet is not an EOA.** Wallet services, such as MetaMask, provide a friendlier user interface to help you manage your Ethereum accounts in the way that Microsoft Outlook provides a (questionably) friendlier user interface to help you manage your email accounts. Much like how you can access your emails without the use of Microsoft Outlook, you can access your accounts without the use of MetaMask.

On the other hand, *contract accounts*, which are often referred to simply as "smart contracts" or "contracts," are not free to create. You incur a transaction fee to create a new contract account, as you'll experience hands-on later in this chapter when you go through the motions to deploy your code onto the Ethereum Mainnet (or a testnet, such as Ropsten).

A few things to keep in mind when it comes to contract accounts:

» **You first need an EOA (with sufficient funds).** You need this account to submit the transaction to create a new contract account on the Ethereum network. Thus, contract accounts are not free to create. (It will cost some ETH.)

» **Contract accounts cannot be used to initiate transactions.** After being deployed, your smart-contract code lies dormant until called by a transaction. A contract account can be called by another contract account, but the sequence of calls must originate from an EOA.

  Thus, although you pay a transaction fee to create a contract account, you do not pay any ongoing maintenance fees. When your contract account is later accessed, the fees are paid by the EOA that initiates the transaction to call your contract account. In fact, the EOA that makes this initial transaction must pay the fees for any and all subsequent calls to other contract accounts that occur as a result of the original transaction.

» **After your contract account is created, it will be assigned a public address.** This public address allows you and others to track and interact with your new smart contract. Anyone with the address to your contract account is free to call any of the public or external functions in your contract, view any of the information in contract storage, and view all transactions and event logs associated with your contract account.

  In contrast to EOAs, contract accounts do not have private keys. After all, contract accounts cannot initiate transactions, so private keys are unnecessary for contract accounts.

Going forward, I typically refer to EOAs simply as accounts. Contract accounts are always specified as such. I never simply say "account" when referring to a contract account (and neither should you!).

Smart-contract languages

The Remix IDE, which you'll soon use in the hands-on instructional portion of this chapter, provides compilers for source code written in either the Solidity or Yul programming language. (See the nearby "Solidity: History in the Making" sidebar for more about the Solidity language.) I've chosen to proceed with Solidity, which is not only simpler than Yul (for humans) to understand but is also the most commonly used language across smart-contract developers on Ethereum.

In the classification of programming languages from high to low, Solidity is considered a high-level language, and Yul is considered an intermediate language. At one end of the spectrum, high-level languages are much easier for humans to read and debug but cannot be directly interpreted by the machine. At the other end of the spectrum, low-level languages come closest to providing instructions that can ultimately be understood and executed at the machine level. Sitting at the lowest level is machine code itself, which consists of a sequence of machine-level instructions expressed entirely in binary or hexadecimal format.

SOLIDITY: HISTORY IN THE MAKING

Solidity is an open-source programming language developed and maintained under the direction of a core team, often referred to as the Solidity Team, which is sponsored by the Ethereum Foundation. The language was first proposed in 2014 by a founding member of Ethereum with the view to specifically support smart-contract development on the Ethereum platform.

Before Solidity's widespread adoption, smart contracts on Ethereum were more commonly written in Serpent, and, to a lesser extent, in Mutan and Lisp-Like Language (LLL). In fact, the original Ethereum whitepaper, accessed at `https://www.ethereum.org/en/whitepaper`, references only Serpent (and not Solidity) as "one of our high-level languages," because Solidity had not yet been developed when the original whitepaper was released.

Within just a few years of its initial release, Solidity quickly became the most active language used to write smart contracts on Ethereum and was also the most actively maintained. Solidity's popularity has even spread beyond the Ethereum development community and has since been adopted by other smart-contract platforms such as Celo, TRON, and BNB Smart Chain, to name a few.

Still, Solidity is in its infancy and is rapidly developing. Accordingly, the core team continues to precede version numbering with a 0, following the Semantic Versioning Specification (accessed at `www.semver.org`), where major version 0 denotes software still in initial development. The most recent Solidity release is numbered 0.8.14.

Thus, once you've written your source code in Solidity, you need to compile your code to produce the following:

- » The *bytecode*, which is the machine-level translation of the more readable source code. Your compiler will also produce the corresponding *opcodes* (short for operation codes) which closely map to the machine-level instructions while using more readable language to specify what the processor should do. For instance, the machine-level hexadecimal code `0x52` is represented by `MSTORE` in opcode, and `0xF0` is represented by `CREATE`.

» The *application binary interface* (ABI), which provides a blueprint for navigating and interacting with the contract's data and functions.

Anatomy of a smart contract

A smart contract is defined by its *functions* and *variables* that will be housed at the contract account address on the Ethereum (or other public) blockchain. In addition to what's housed in contract *storage*, you can define *events* to log specific information associated with your contract over time.

Variables

In writing your contract code, you can access pre-defined *global variables* as well as define custom variables of your own.

Global variables (also known as *environment* variables) provide useful information about the current transaction or overall state of the blockchain. For instance, `msg.sender` contains the address of the account from which the current transaction was initiated, and `block.number` contains the current block number.

As a statically-typed language, Solidity requires custom variables to be declared prior to execution. In addition to specifying the variable type (for instance, whether the variable will store a string, address, or number), you'll also need to decide whether the variable should be retained in contract storage and whether it can be accessed by other external contracts:

» **Permanence/Storage:** *Memory variables* (also known as *local variables*) are designed to store temporary values that are not retained from one iteration to another. In contrast, *state variables* are retained in contract storage between calls.

» **Accessibility:** State variables can be *public* (contents accessible to any and all smart contracts) or *private* (strictly accessible only to the contract in which it's declared). State variables can also be designated as *internal,* which allows them to be accessed by derived contracts (contracts inheriting code from the contract in question). You don't incur any transaction fees to simply view a contract's state variable without changing its contents (known as a "read-only" call).

Keep in mind that public-versus-private accessibility of a state variable pertains only to whether external contracts can access the information stored in that variable. External contracts cannot directly alter the contents of a public variable ("public" visibility does not give permission to external contracts to alter data). Although external contracts cannot access private or internal variables, these state variables are still part of their contract's storage on the public blockchain, which can be viewed by anyone ("private" visibility does not keep the information hidden from more curious and ambitious users).

Nonetheless, public variables are much simpler to view. The act of declaring a public variable also generates a read-only `getter()` function associated with the public variable. A private variable is not accompanied by a corresponding `getter()` function to view its contents, and thus must be viewed within a core dump of the entire contract storage (making it a task only for more curious and ambitious readers!).

Functions

In building out the functionality of your contract, you can access *built-in* functions as well as implement custom functions of your own.

The built-in functions provided by Solidity are predefined to perform common tasks. For instance, `address.send()` is programmed to send the specified quantity of ETH to the specified `address`, and `selfdestruct(address)` is programmed to clear the contract's storage and send the remaining ETH balance to the specified `address`.

When implementing your own custom functions, you need to specify the function's accessibility to other external contracts. Functions can be designated as *public* (accessible to any and all smart contracts); *internal* (not accessible to external contracts but accessible to derived contracts); or *private* (strictly accessible only to the contract in which it's declared).

Functions can also be designated as *external.* As with public functions, external functions are accessible to any and all smart contracts, but they are always treated like the public functions of an external contract (even when called from within the same contract, in which case the command to call this function must be preceded by `this`).

In addition, you have the option to implement a special `constructor()` function to be executed only once. You can include (at most) one `constructor()` function in your contract, using this function to specify the set of code to be executed only when the smart contract is first created. Hereafter, this function cannot be called again.

Events

Event logs provide a cost-effective way for you to store historical state changes on the Ethereum blockchain without requiring additional storage space within your contract account.

For instance, suppose you'd like to maintain a record of prior information stored in a state variable. You can define an event in your contract to specify what information should be added to the event log associated with your contract account on the Ethereum blockchain. Then you can call this event, using the `emit` command in your code, to pass along the contents of the state variable before you alter it.

Multiple inheritance: Can you have three or more parents?

Composability is a critical part of the Ethereum ecosystem (see Chapter 9 for details about composability). Accordingly, Solidity and Yul both support multiple inheritance, which allows a smart contract (known as the *derived* or *child* contract) to inherit the features (code) of other smart contracts (known as the *base* or *parent* contracts). Thus, you can quickly and easily create a custom solution by building from a combination of predeveloped contracts from well-vetted libraries, such as OpenZeppelin (accessed at `www.openzeppelin.com`).

There is no explicit cap on the number of parents from which a derived contract can inherit (hence the term *multiple inheritance*). However, this practice can lead to a rather complicated inheritance family tree, and the added complexities inherent in multiple inheritance can lead to serious vulnerabilities. After all, as the number of parents (and grandparents, and great grandparents!) in your family tree grows, developers and auditors must comb through ever more source files of code. They must be well versed in the rules of inheritance to keep track of what's ultimately inherited and what's not. They must also keep track of conflicting declarations across files and how these conflicts are handled at compilation.

For now, you can get started with implementing and deploying a simple parentless contract. Later, in Chapter 13, "Launching Your First DeFi Product," you can see an example of how to leverage prebuilt contracts in developing your own protocols.

Launching Your Smart Contract

This section provides a step-by-step guide to deploying your first smart contract onto the Ropsten Testnet. The same steps apply when deploying to the Ethereum Mainnet when you're ready and willing to spend some real ETH.

REMEMBER

Keep in mind that Ropsten may be deprecated by the time you read this book. All the provided instructions remain the same, but you may prefer to use a different test network. Refer to the Introduction for more details.

Using the Remix IDE

In preparing to launch a smart contract, you first need to set up an integrated development environment (IDE) to edit, compile, and ultimately deploy your code. For this example, I use the Remix IDE as a one-stop shop that quickly and easily provides everything you need to deploy and subsequently interact with your smart contract. To get started, follow these steps to create a new file on Remix:

1. **Go to** `remix.ethereum.org`**.**

TECHNICAL STUFF

In the past, the secure version of Remix (accessed via `https://` as opposed to `http://`) was unable to connect to MetaMask. This issue has since been addressed, and you can now enjoy an HTTPS connection to Remix without losing functionality.

2. **From the main page, click the New File link, as shown in Figure 11-1.**

Alternatively, you can click the Create New File icon (symbolized as a blank page) in the File Explorer browser pane on the left, as shown in Figure 11-2.

You see a new, unnamed file populate in the File Explorer browser pane, as shown in Figure 11-2.

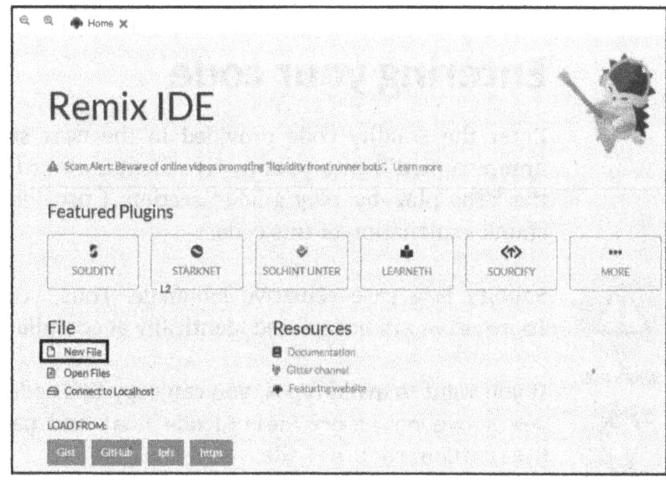

FIGURE 11-1: The Remix IDE main page.

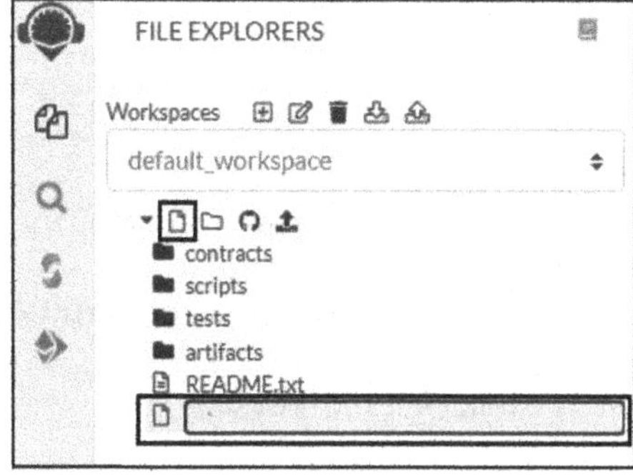

FIGURE 11-2: The Remix File Explorer browser pane.

3. **Type** MyFirstContract.sol **and press Enter to name your new file.**

   A new tab, with the name of the file, appears in the main browser pane, as shown in Figure 11-3.

Great work! You're now ready to enter your code.

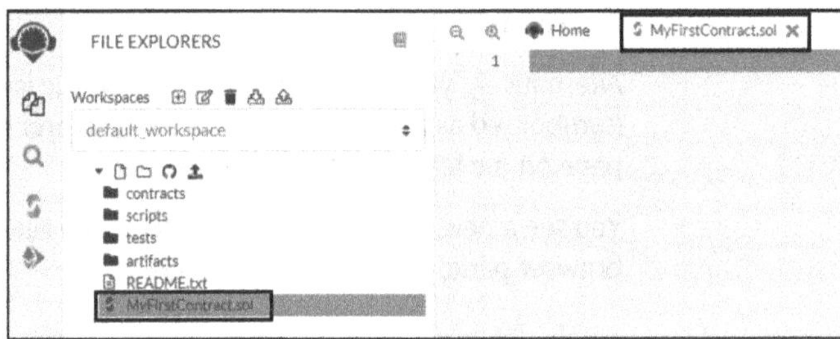

FIGURE 11-3: The MyFirst-Contract.sol open tab on Remix.

Entering your code

Enter the Solidity code provided in the next section ("Code, uninterrupted") into your `MyFirstContract.sol` file. Later, in the "The play-by-play guide" section, I provide a chunk-by-chunk explanation of this code.

WARNING

Solidity is a case-sensitive language. Thus, `LogReceive` and `logreceive` are not treated identically at compilation.

TIP

If you want to avoid typos, you can copy this code directly from `www.seoyoungkim.com/defifdcode.html` and paste it in your `MyFirstContract.sol` file.

Code, uninterrupted

```
pragma solidity 0.8.14;

contract MyFirstContract {
    event LogReceive(address _from, uint256
  amount);
    event LogWithdraw(address _to, uint256
  amount);
    event LogMsg(string message);
```

```
    string public storedMsg;
    address public owner;

    constructor() {
        storedMsg = "DeFi For Dummies";
        owner = msg.sender;
        emit LogMsg(storedMsg);
    }

    receive() external payable {
        emit LogReceive(msg.sender, msg.value);
    }

    function withdraw(
        address payable _to,
        uint256 amount
    )
        public
    {
        require(
            msg.sender == owner,
            "not the owner"
        );
        require(
            address(this).balance >= amount,
            "insufficient funds"
        );
        _to.transfer(amount);
        emit LogWithdraw(_to, amount);
    }

    function updateMsg(
        string memory newMsg
    )
        public
    {
        storedMsg = newMsg;
        emit LogMsg(storedMsg);
    }

}
```

The play-by-play guide

TIP

Before proceeding to compile, I recommend that you take a look at the following chunk-by-chunk explanation of the source code. However, if you prefer to maintain your hands-on momentum, you can skip straight ahead to "Compiling your code."

```
pragma solidity 0.8.14;
```

This first line of code is the Solidity version pragma, which ensures that your code is not compiled under incompatible compiler versions. Here, the version pragma specifies that this source code should be compiled only under version 0.8.14.

```
contract MyFirstContract {
```

The next line begins defining the contract, `MyFirstContract`. Notice that, as a curly-bracket language, Solidity uses curly brackets to begin and end blocks of code. Notice also that statements are delimited by semicolons.

```
  event LogReceive(address _from, uint256
amount);
  event LogWithdraw(address _to, uint256
amount);
    event LogMsg(string message);
```

These lines define three separate events: `LogReceive`, `LogWithdraw`, and `LogMsg`. When emitted, these events are designed to log the values of the specified arguments passed to the event. For instance, when the `LogWithdraw` event is emitted, the recipient account's address and the amount withdrawn will be recorded to the blockchain's ledger as an event log associated with this smart-contract account.

```
  string public storedMsg;
    address public owner;
```

These lines declare two public state variables: `storedMsg`, which is a string, and `owner`, which is an account address. The latest values of these public state variables will be retained in contract storage and accessible to other smart contracts.

```
    constructor() {
        storedMsg = "DeFi For Dummies";
        owner = msg.sender;
        emit LogMsg(storedMsg);
    }
```

This block of code defines the special `constructor()` function, which is executed only once — when the smart contract is first deployed.

The first line within this function initializes the text being stored in the `storedMsg` state variable, and the second line initializes the account address being stored in the `owner` state variable. Specifically, `msg` is a global structure variable (also known as a struct) containing key information about the current transaction, and `sender` is a member of this struct containing the address of the account initiating the transaction.

The third line within this function emits the `LogMsg` event, passing the contents of `storedMsg` to be recorded to the contract's event log.

```
    receive() external payable {
        emit LogReceive(msg.sender, msg.value);
    }
```

This block of code enables the contract account to receive funds. Here, the `receive()` function has been defined to emit the `LogReceive` event, passing the address of the account sending funds to the contract account (`msg.sender`) along with the amount of funds sent (`msg.value`) to be recorded to the contract's event log.

```
    function withdraw(
        address payable _to,
        uint256 amount
    )
        public
```

This block of code declares a public function, `withdraw()`, that accepts two arguments: the address of the account to receive withdrawn funds (`_to`) and the amount, specified in wei, to be withdrawn from the smart-contract account (`amount`). `_to` and amount are memory variables whose values are not retained in contract storage between calls.

REMEMBER

In Etherum, wei denotes the smallest denomination of ETH, with 1 ETH being equal to 1,000,000,000,000,000,000 = 10^{18} wei.

```
    {
        require(
            msg.sender == owner,
            "not the owner"
        );
        require(
            address(this).balance >= amount,
            "insufficient funds"
        );
        _to.transfer(amount);
        emit LogWithdraw(_to, amount);
    }
```

This next block of code defines the withdraw() function.

The first two statements in this function are calls to a built-in Solidity function, require(), which is designed to terminate the current function call if the specified condition is violated. For instance, the first require statement checks whether the account calling the withdraw() function is the authorized owner of this smart-contract account. If this condition is not met, the unauthorized function caller will receive the message not the owner, and the withdraw() function call will terminate without executing. The second require statement checks whether the smart-contract account contains sufficient funds to meet the withdrawal request.

Assuming that the required conditions are met, the third statement transfers funds from the smart-contract account to the specified recipient (_to). The final statement emits the LogWithdraw event, passing the address of the account receiving funds from the contract account (_to) along with the amount of funds withdrawn (amount) to be logged.

```
    function updateMsg(
        string memory newMsg
    )
```

```
        public
    {
        storedMsg = newMsg;
        emit LogMsg(storedMsg);
    }
```

This block of code defines a public function, `updateMsg()`, that accepts one argument: the `newMsg` specified to replace the contents of the `storedMsg` state variable. The final statement emits the `LogMsg` event, passing the new contents of `storedMsg` to be logged.

```
}
```

Finally, a closing curly bracket marks the end of the entire block of contract code.

Compiling your code

Now that you've created your `MyFirstContract.sol` file and pasted in the source code from the previous section, you're ready for compilation. Follow these steps to compile your source code.

1. **Click the Solidity Compiler icon in the navigation toolbar located on the far left, as shown in Figure 11-4.**

   The Solidity Compiler page appears in the left browser pane, as shown in Figure 11-5.

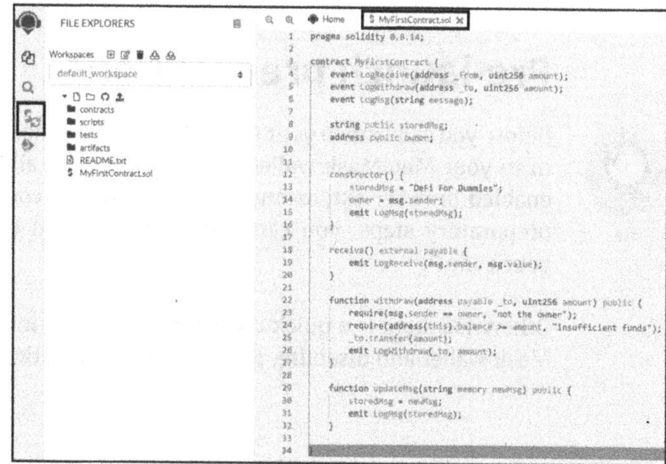

FIGURE 11-4: The `MyFirst-Contract` source code ready for compilation on Remix.

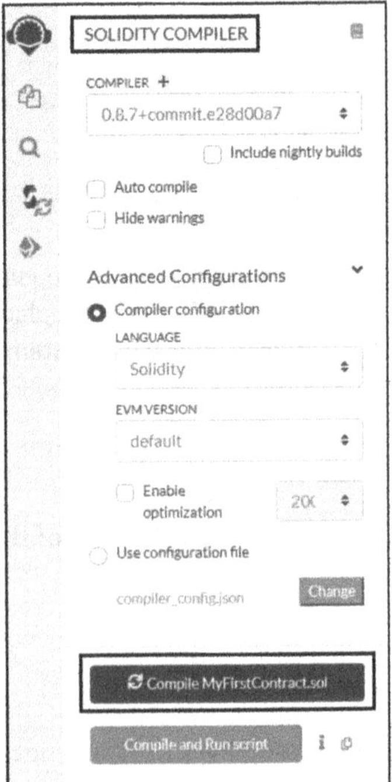

FIGURE 11-5: The Solidity compiler browser pane on Remix.

2. **From the Solidity Compiler browser pane, click the Compile MyFirstContract.sol button.**

   Compilation details appear at the bottom of the Solidity Compiler browser pane, as shown in Figure 11-6. This pane also contains two additional icons that allow you to copy the corresponding ABI and bytecode.

Pre-launch preparations

TIP

Before you can launch your smart contract, you need to be logged in to your MetaMask wallet and have disabled all other Web3-enabled browser extensions. If you've already completed these preparatory steps, you can skip straight down to "Deploying your code."

Otherwise, here is a quick refresher on logging into your MetaMask wallet and disabling potentially problematic extensions:

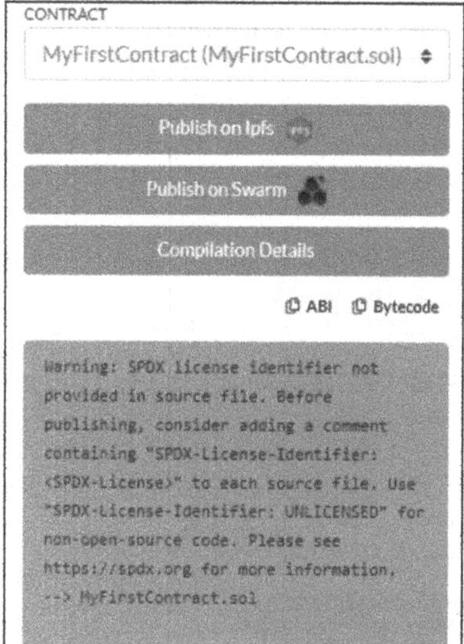

FIGURE 11-6: Accessing compilation details on the Solidity compiler browser pane on Remix.

1. **Click the MetaMask fox icon in your browser's toolbar.**

   The MetaMask drop-down menu appears, as shown in Figure 11-7.

   REMEMBER

   Refer to Chapter 3 if you need a refresher on navigating MetaMask.

2. **From the MetaMask drop-down menu, select your desired network and sign in to your account.**

   In Figure 11-7, I've selected the Ropsten Testnet. When you're ready to spend (and possibly lose!) real ETH, you can switch to the Ethereum Mainnet instead.

   REMEMBER

   Refer to Chapter 3 if you need a refresher on getting some real ETH or Ropsten Test ETH (rETH).

   WARNING

   Problems may arise on Remix if you have other Web3-enabled wallet browser extensions installed, such as the Dapper Legacy wallet. Using the upcoming steps, I recommend disabling these other extensions (and keeping only the MetaMask extension active) as you continue this step-by-step guide.

FIGURE 11-7: Accessing the MetaMask browser extension.

Follow these steps to temporarily disable potentially problematic browser extensions:

2a. Right click the icon of the extension you'd like to disable from your browser's toolbar.

A drop-down menu appears, as shown in Figure 11-8.

2b. Select the Manage Extension option.

A new browser tab appears, with options to manage the selected extension, as shown in Figure 11-9.

2c. Use the toggle button to switch the extension from on to off.

TIP

You can reactivate a disabled browser extension anytime. On the Chrome and Brave browsers, simply click the puzzle-shaped icon from your browser's toolbar and select the Manage Extensions option from the drop-down menu that appears (see Figure 11-10). Other browsers have similar icons embedded in the browser's toolbar to access and manage your browser extensions.

Yay! You can now turn your focus back to Remix to proceed to deploy your smart contract.

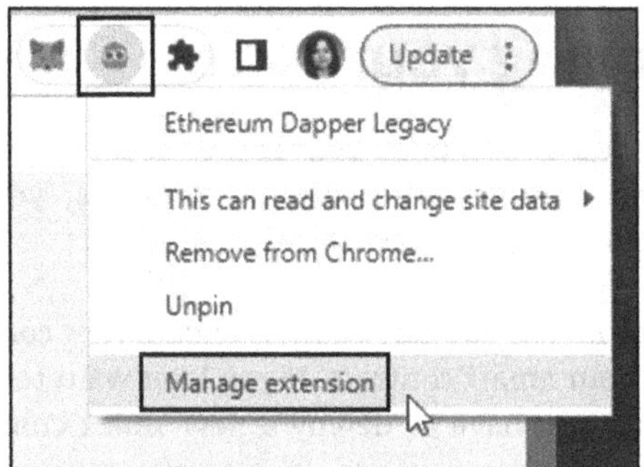

FIGURE 11-8: Drop-down menu to manage a specific browser extension.

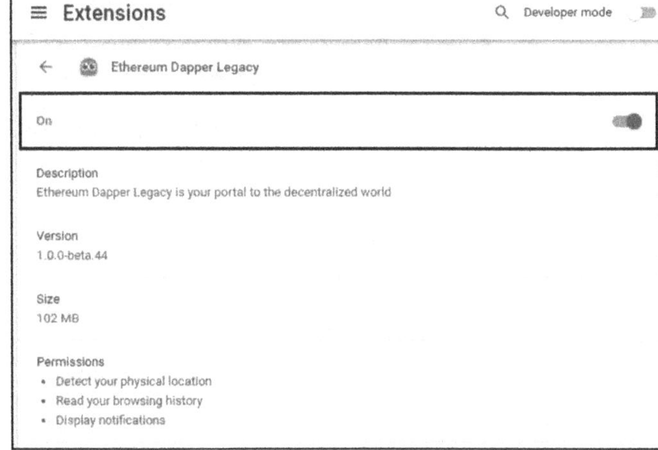

FIGURE 11-9: Details and options to manage the Dapper Legacy browser extension.

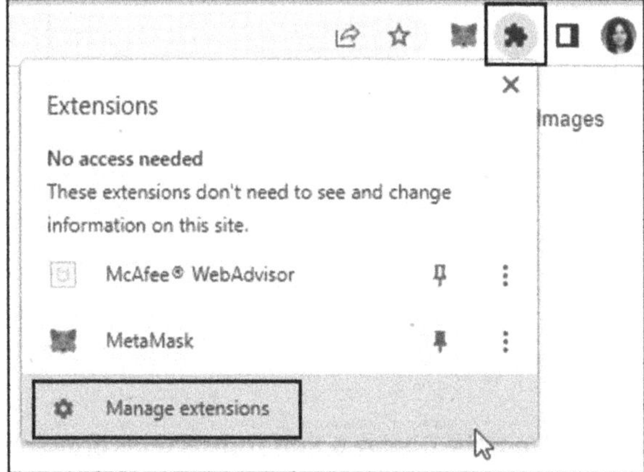

FIGURE 11-10: Drop-down menu to manage all browser extensions, both enabled and disabled.

Deploying your code

Now that you've compiled your source code, logged in to MetaMask, and disabled other Web3 extensions, you're ready to deploy your smart contract through Remix.

REMEMBER

Keep in mind that you can't edit or update your code after you've deployed your smart contract. If you later want to add or correct something, you have to deploy a new smart contract with the updated code.

Follow these steps to submit your bytecode to the EVM.

1. **From the Remix page, click the Ethereum icon in the navigation toolbar located on the far left.**

   The Deploy & Run Transactions page appears in the left browser pane, as shown in Figure 11-11.

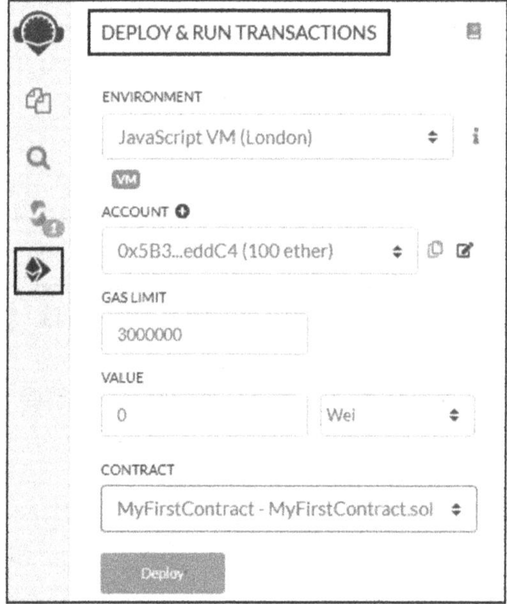

FIGURE 11-11: The Deploy & Run Transactions browser pane on Remix.

2. **From the Deploy & Run Transactions browser pane, select the Injected Web3 option from the Environment drop-down menu, as shown in Figure 11-12.**

A MetaMask pop-up notification window appears, as shown in Figure 11-13.

3. **Select the account(s) you'd like to use and click the Next button.**

   A confirmation page appears, as shown in Figure 11-14.

4. **Click the Connect button to allow Remix to connect to the account(s) in your MetaMask wallet.**

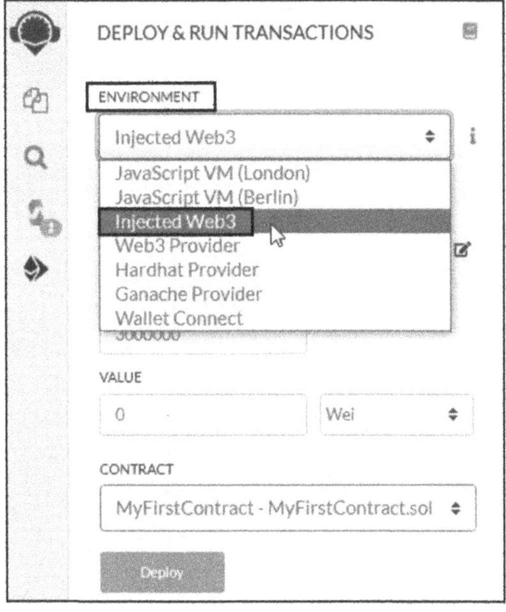

FIGURE 11-12: The Environment drop-down menu from the Deploy & Run Transactions browser pane on Remix.

Looking at the Deploy & Run Transactions browser pane alongside the MetaMask drop-down menu, as shown in Figure 11-15, you see the following:

- **The network to which you're now connected.** In my case, I am connected to the Ropsten Testnet.
- **Your selected account(s) under the Account drop-down menu in the Deploy & Run Transactions browser pane.** In my case, I am using my account with public address beginning with `0xC3D` and ending in `A0BC`, with a balance of approximately 1.0036 rETH.

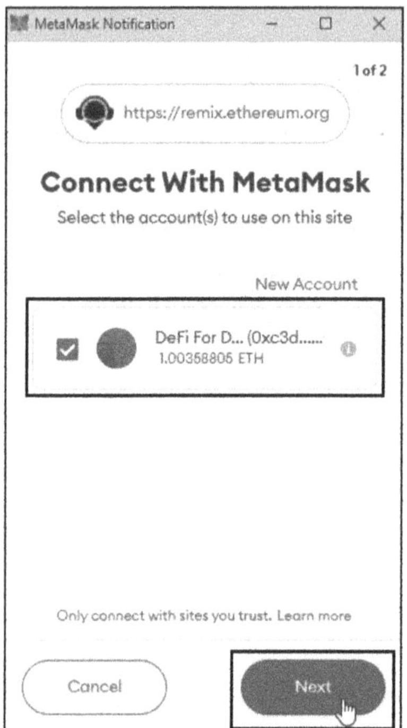

FIGURE 11-13: A MetaMask pop-up notification to select the account(s) you want to connect.

FIGURE 11-14: A MetaMask pop-up notification to confirm connecting to Remix.

FIGURE 11-15: Network and account connection details displayed on the Deploy & Run Transactions browser pane on Remix alongside the MetaMask dropdown window.

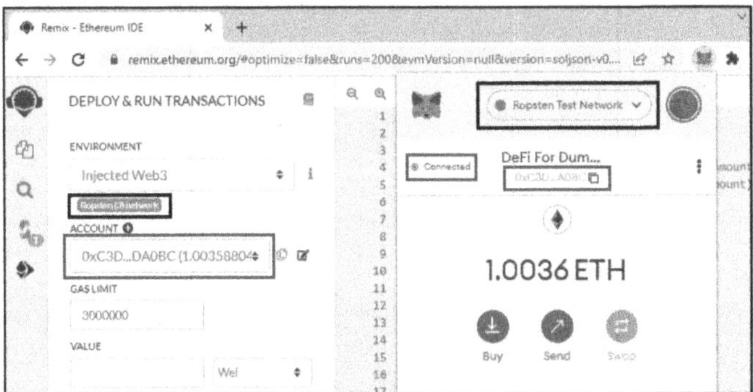

5. **Make sure you've selected the appropriate contract (`MyFirstContract`) and then click the Deploy button, as shown in Figure 11-16.**

   A MetaMask pop-up notification appears to confirm the transaction, as shown in Figure 11-17.

6. **Click the Confirm button in the bottom-right corner to continue.**

   Wait approximately one minute for your transaction to be mined. Be patient.

REMEMBER

Keep in mind that during times of high network volume, your transaction can even take 30 minutes or longer to be mined and included on the public blockchain.

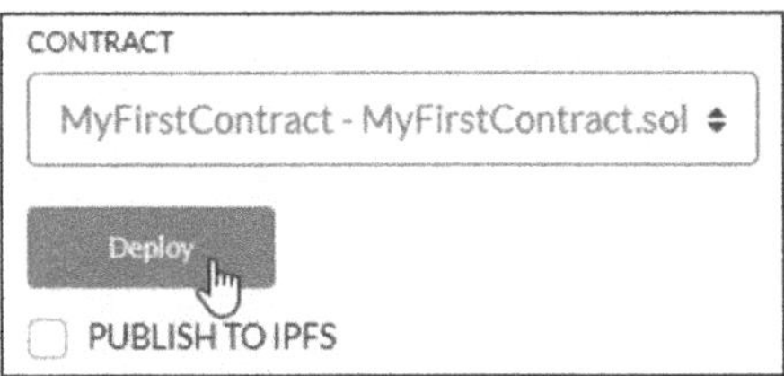

FIGURE 11-16: Deploying `MyFirstContract` through Remix.

When your transaction is complete, you'll be able to view and interact with this contract under "Deployed Contracts" located at the bottom of the Deploy & Run Transactions browser pane, as shown in Figure 11-18.

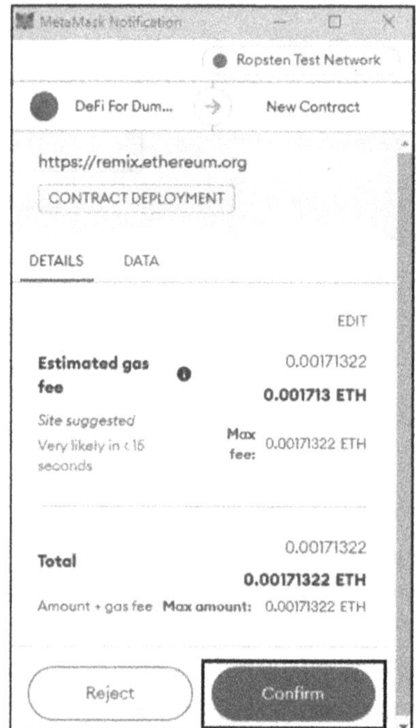

FIGURE 11-17: Confirming the transaction to deploy your contract onto the Ropsten Testnet.

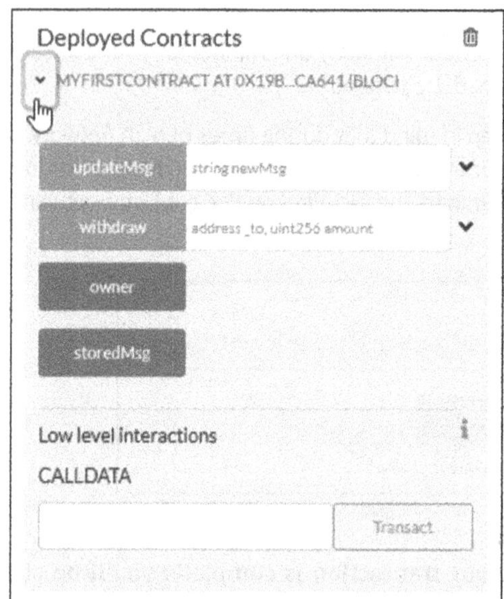

FIGURE 11-18: Interacting with your deployed contract via Remix.

TIP

You can click the downward arrow icons, which look like upside-down carets (^), to further expand or collapse functions contained in your contract.

Great work! `MyFirstContract` is now deployed and ready for action!

Accessing Your Smart Contract

Now that you have a functional smart contract up and running on a public blockchain, you'll want to see how to access your smart-contract functions and follow your smart contract's transaction logs.

Following your smart contract on a block explorer

When your smart contract is deployed to a public blockchain, all transactions associated with this smart-contract account are memorialized on the blockchain and publicly accessible to anyone who wants to track the activity associated with your smart contract.

Follow these steps to view your contract on a public block explorer:

1. **Under the Deployed Contracts section (at the bottom of the Deploy & Run Transactions browser pane), click the double-page icon to the right of your deployed contract to copy the contract account address, as shown in Figure 11-19.**

   My contract account address is: `0x19bc7cF3213Fb21f2319dB91323352fb09fcA641`.

   The public address of the (externally owned) account from which I launched this smart-contract account is: `0xC3Da0e-aB3D30C4a6a298467729B00F659daDA0BC`.

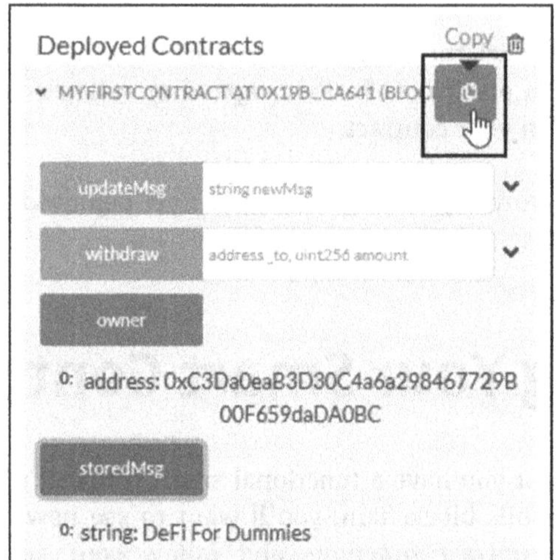

FIGURE 11-19: Copying a smart-contract account address.

2. **Open a new browser tab and go to** ropsten.etherscan.io.

   TIP

   Don't close your Remix browser tab yet. You'll return to Remix shortly to interact with your smart contract.

   REMEMBER

   I'm using a Ropsten block explorer because I've chosen to deploy my smart contract onto the Ropsten Testnet. Later, if you deploy your contract onto Mainnet, you'll need to use a Mainnet block explorer, which can be accessed at `www.etherscan.io`. Similarly, if you deploy on, say, the Goerli Testnet, you'll need to use a Goerli block explorer, which can be accessed at `goerli.etherscan.io`.

3. **Paste your smart-contract account address (copied in Step 1 of this step list) into the search bar on the Ropsten Testnet Explorer page, as shown in Figure 11-20, and then press Enter or click the search icon.**

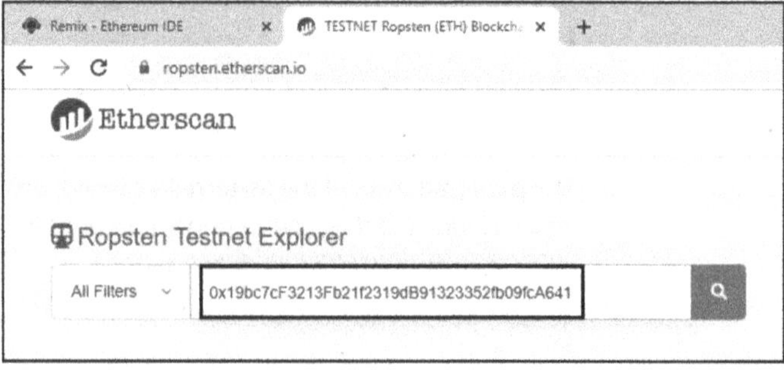

FIGURE 11-20: Finding your contract account on Etherscan's Ropsten Testnet Explorer.

A new page appears, providing details specific to your smart contract, as shown in Figure 11-21. A few things to note:

- You can see the contract account address at the top of the page. In my case, this address is `0x19bc7cF3213Fb21f2319dB91323352fb09fcA641`.
- You can also see the public address of the contract creator in the More Info box in the upper-right corner. In my case, this public address is `0xC3Da0eaB3D30C4a6a298467729B00F659daDA0BC`.
- This smart-contract account currently has a balance of 0 rETH (as you can see in the Contract Overview box in the upper-left corner). In the next section ("Interacting with your smart contract"), you can play around with sending and withdrawing rETH to and from your smart-contract account.
- Finally, note that currently only one transaction is associated with this smart-contract account — namely, the initial transaction that created this smart-contract account.

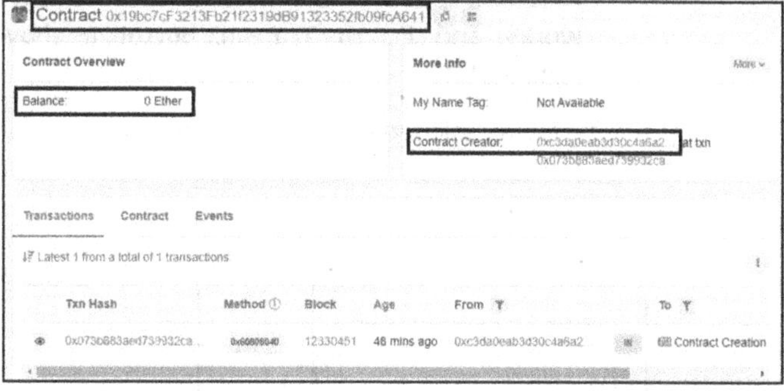

FIGURE 11-21: Details on the Ropsten Testnet Explorer for `MyFirstContract`.

Yay! Now that you know how to view your smart-contract records on a public block explorer, proceed to the next section to begin interacting with your smart contract.

Interacting with your smart contract

Follow these steps to view the values stored in your contract's state variables and to call the `updateMsg0` function to alter the `storedMsg` variable:

1. **Toggle back to your Remix browser tab, and return your focus to your newly deployed** `MyFirstContract`, **located under Deployed Contracts at the bottom of the Deploy & Run Transactions browser pane.**

   TIP

   Keep your Etherscan block explorer tab open so that you can switch back to view updates to your smart-contract records as you interact with your smart contract.

2. **Click the** `owner` **and** `storedMsg` **buttons.**

   You should see your (externally owned) account address as the owner of the smart contract, and the string `DeFi For Dummies` as the current value for `storedMsg`, as shown in Figure 11-22.

3. **Click the downward arrow to expand the** `updateMsg` **function, type in a new message to store (any message works), and click the Transact button, as shown in Figure 11-22.**

   A MetaMask pop-up notification appears to confirm this transaction.

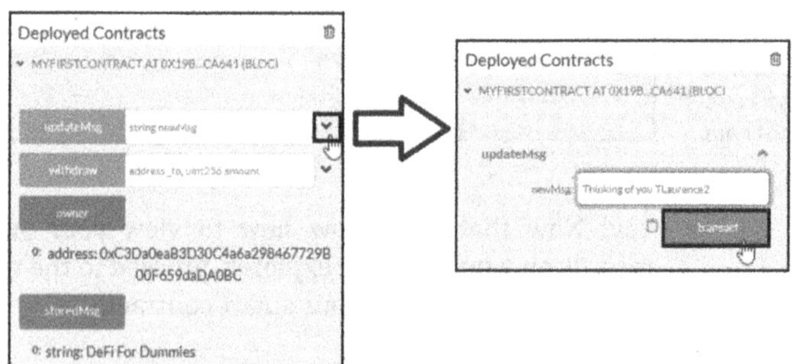

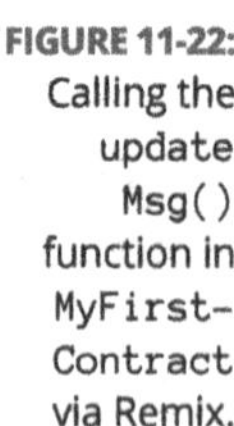

FIGURE 11-22: Calling the `updateMsg()` function in `MyFirstContract` via Remix.

4. **Click the Confirm button and wait for the transaction to be mined.**

When the transaction is complete, you can click the `storedMsg` button again to see the updated message in storage as part of your smart-contract data.

TIP

You can also toggle back to the Etherscan block explorer again to view your smart contract's updated records on the public blockchain. (Be sure to hit the Refresh button!) Here are a few things to note:

- The Transactions tab (see Figure 11-23) now shows two transactions associated with your smart contract: the originating transaction, and the transaction to call the `updateMsg()` function. (The act of viewing state variables, `owner` and `storedMsg`, do not count as transactions and do not cost gas.)
- The Events tab (see Figure 11-24) shows the logged `storedMsg` history (from the emitted `LogMsg` event defined in the `MyFirstContract` source code). The first stored message, `DeFi For Dummies`, was logged at contract origination. The subsequent stored message, `Thinking of you TLaurence2`, was logged when I called the `updateMsg()` function in Step 3 of this step list.

TIP

You can switch the display setting from hexadecimal format (Hex) to standard text (Text) by clicking the button under the Logs column to the left of the emitted information.

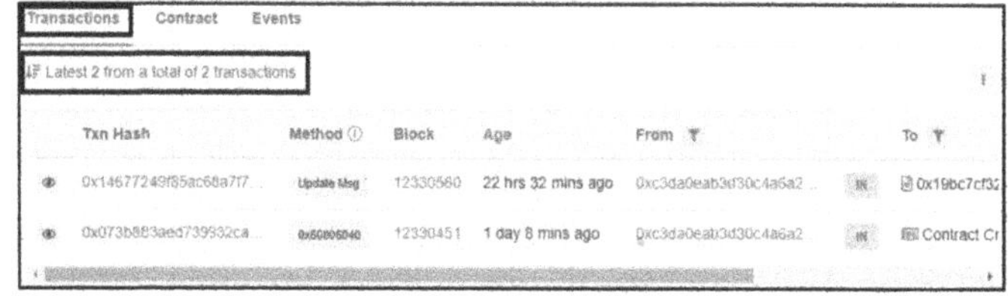

FIGURE 11-23: Updated transaction records on the Ropsten Testnet Explorer for `MyFirst-Contract`.

FIGURE 11-24: Updated event logs on the Ropsten Testnet Explorer for `MyFirst-Contract`.

Sending funds to your contract account

Next, follow these instructions to send rETH to your smart-contract account:

1. **Click the MetaMask fox icon in your browser's toolbar and click the Send button from the MetaMask drop-down window, as shown in Figure 11-25.**

   A new page appears in the MetaMask drop-down window with a text box prompt for the recipient's address, as shown in Figure 11-26.

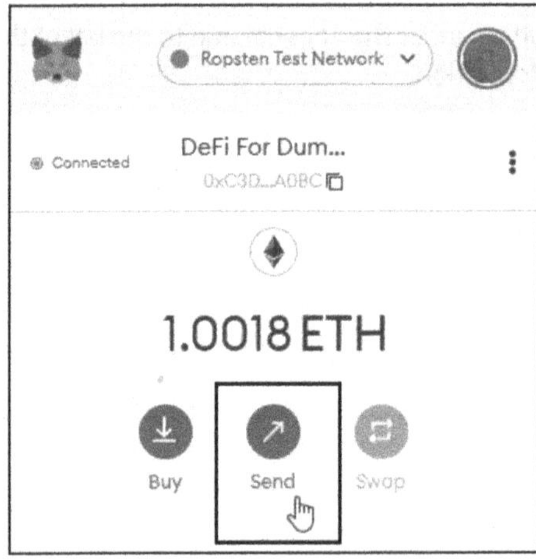

FIGURE 11-25: Sending funds through the MetaMask wallet.

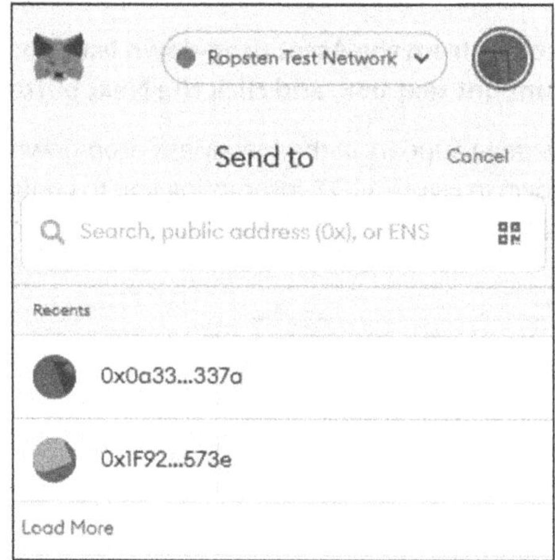

FIGURE 11-26: A text box prompt on MetaMask for a recipient's address.

2. **Paste in your contract account address.**

   (See Step 1 from the step list in the section on "Following your smart contract on a block explorer" for a refresher on copying your contract account address.)

   Two new fields appear below, as shown in Figure 11-27, to designate the asset and amount you want to send.

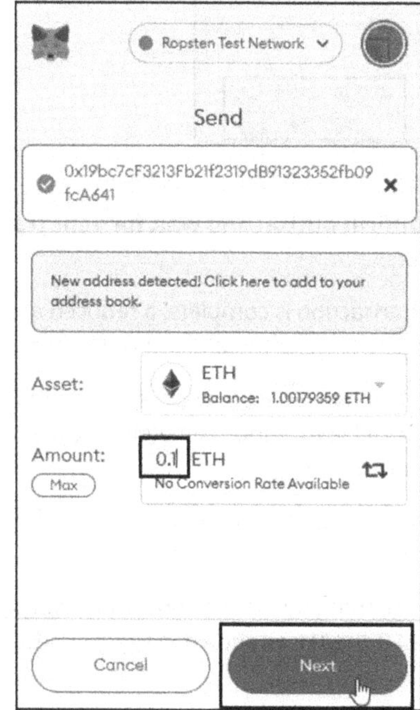

FIGURE 11-27: A text box prompt on MetaMask for the asset and quantity to send.

3. **Select ETH from the Asset drop-down list, type in `0.1` in the Amount text box, and click the Next button.**

   A new page appears in the MetaMask drop-down window, as shown in Figure 11-28, prompting you to confirm the transaction.

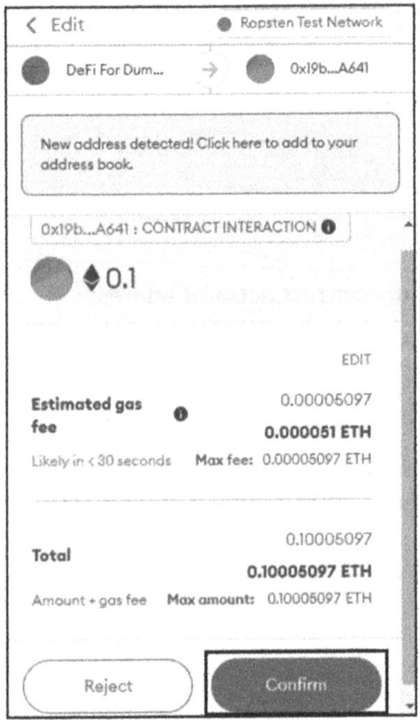

FIGURE 11-28: Confirming transaction to send 0.1 rETH.

4. **Click the Confirm button and wait for your transaction to be mined.**

   When your transaction is complete, a reduced account balance appears on your MetaMask home screen.

   My balance has declined from approximately 1.0018 rETH (refer to Figure 11-25) to approximately 0.9018 rETH, as shown in Figure 11-29.

   In addition, if you toggle back to the Etherscan block explorer:

   - You can see that your smart-contract account now has a balance of 0.1 rETH, as shown in Figure 11-30.

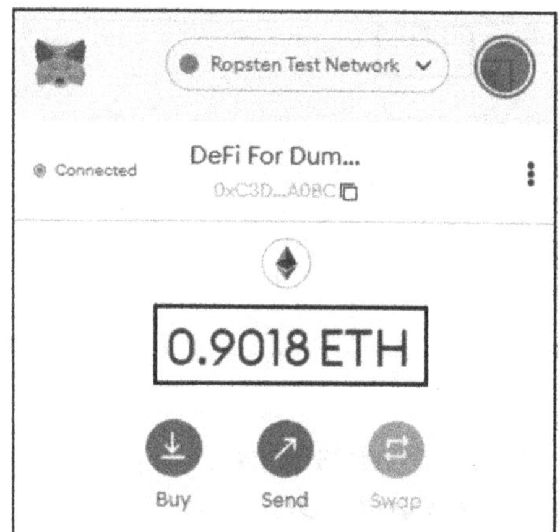

FIGURE 11-29: The reduced account balance after sending 0.1 rETH to `MyFirst-Contract`.

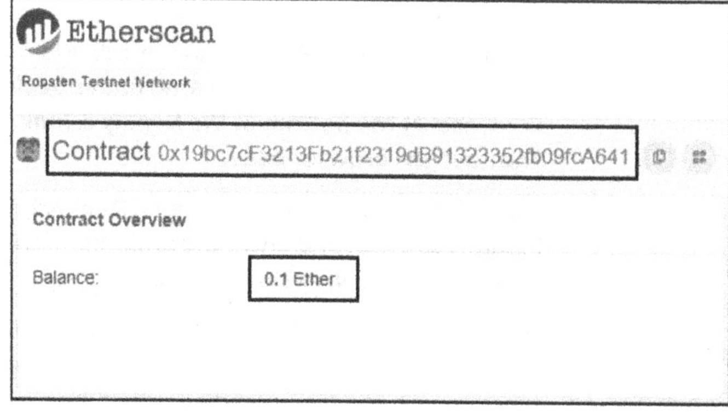

FIGURE 11-30: The updated contract account balance for `MyFirst-Contract` after receiving 0.1 rETH.

- You can also see that a new event has been logged under the Events tab, as shown in Figure 11-31, from the emitted `LogReceive` event to record the sender account address and the amount sent denoted in wei.

  In my case, the sender account address corresponds to the DeFi For Dummies account I created for this book: `0xC3Da0eaB3D30C4a6a298467729B00F659daDA0BC`. Also, the amount sent is `100,000,000,000,000,000` wei, which is equivalent to 0.1 ETH.

TIP

Notice that I've switched the settings here to display the first field as a hexadecimal address (Addr) and the second field as a number in decimal format (Num).

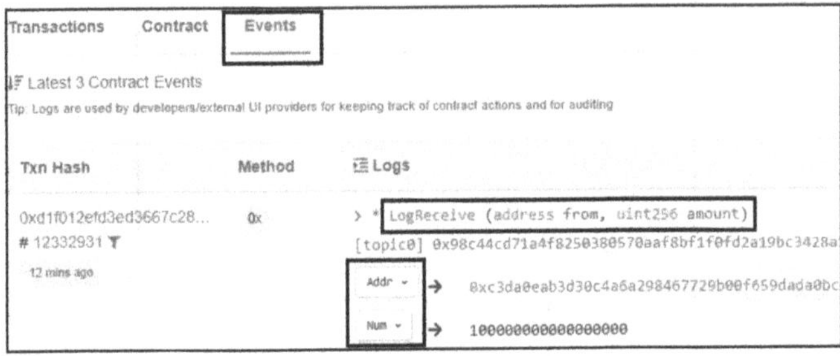

FIGURE 11-31: The LogReceive event log displaying the sender account address and amount sent denoted in wei.

Withdrawing funds from your contract account

Finally, follow these instructions to withdraw rETH from your smart-contract account:

1. **Toggle back to your Remix browser tab and return your focus to `MyFirstContract` located under Deployed Contracts at the bottom of the Deploy & Run Transactions browser pane.**
2. **Expand the `withdraw` function, specify a recipient account address, and enter the amount (in wei) you want to withdraw, as shown in Figure 11-32.**

REMEMBER

The `withdraw()` function includes the following line of code to prevent unauthorized accounts from accessing funds: `require(msg.sender == owner, "not the owner");`. Thus, a withdrawal transaction can be executed only from the original account that initiated the transaction to deploy the smart contract. Of course, any recipient can be specified. I've chosen to withdraw 50,000,000,000,000,000 wei (0.05 rETH) from my `MyFirstContract` contract account back to my original DeFi For Dummies account: `0xC3Da0eaB3D30C4a6a298467729B00F659daDA0BC`.

3. **Click the Transact button and then click the Confirm button on the MetaMask pop-up notification window that appears, and wait for your transaction to be mined.**

When your transaction is complete, you'll notice an increased account balance on your MetaMask home screen.

My balance has increased from approximately 0.9018 rETH (refer to Figure 11-29) to approximately 0.9517 rETH, as shown in Figure 11-33.

FIGURE 11-32: Calling the `withdraw()` function in `MyFirstContract` via Remix.

In addition, if you toggle back to the Etherscan block explorer:

- You see that your smart-contract account now has a reduced balance of 0.05 rETH, as shown in Figure 11-34.
- There's also another event logged under the Events tab, as shown in Figure 11-35, from the emitted `LogWithdraw` event to record the recipient account address and the amount withdrawn denoted in wei.

  In my case, the recipient account address corresponds to the DeFi For Dummies account I created for this book: `0xC3Da0eaB3D30C4a6a298467729B00F659daDA0BC`, and the amount withdrawn is `50,000,000,000,000,000` wei, which is equivalent to 0.05 ETH.

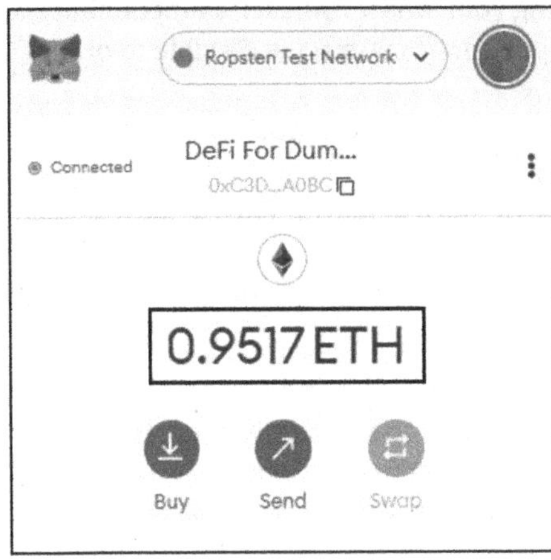

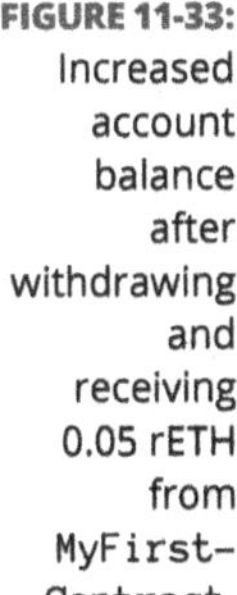

FIGURE 11-33: Increased account balance after withdrawing and receiving 0.05 rETH from `MyFirstContract`.

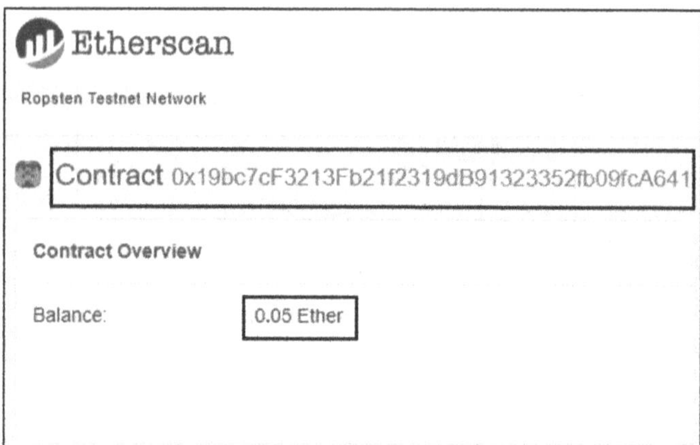

FIGURE 11-34: Decreased smart-contract account balance for `MyFirst-Contract` after withdrawing 0.05 rETH.

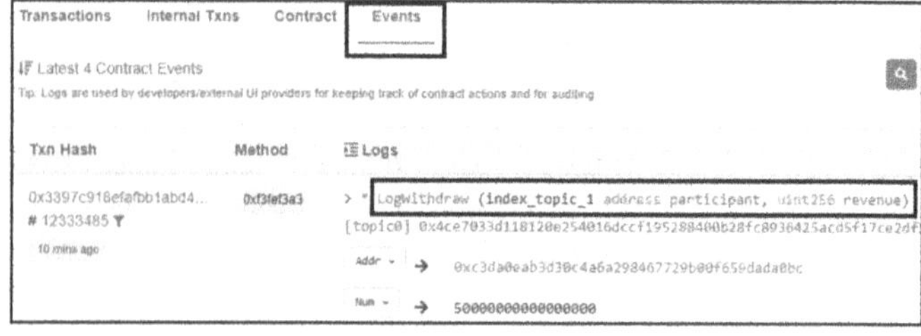

FIGURE 11-35: `LogWithdraw` event log displaying the recipient account address and amount withdrawn/sent from `MyFirst-Contract`.

Allowing others to interact with your smart contract

After testing your smart contract's functionality, the next step is to make your smart contract accessible to others.

To start, you need to make your source code publicly available, specifically by adding it to your smart contract's "profile" on the Etherscan block explorer. Follow these steps:

1. **Toggle to the Contract tab on the Etherscan block explorer.**

TIP

If you copied my code verbatim (from the earlier section "Entering your code"), you'll likely see that this contract code has already been verified and published, as shown in Figure 11-41. If this is the case, you can skip straight ahead to Step 7.

2. **On the Contract tab, click the Verify and Publish link, as shown in Figure 11-36.**

   A new page appears, as shown in Figure 11-37, prompting you to confirm the Contract Address, Compiler Type, and Open Source License Type.

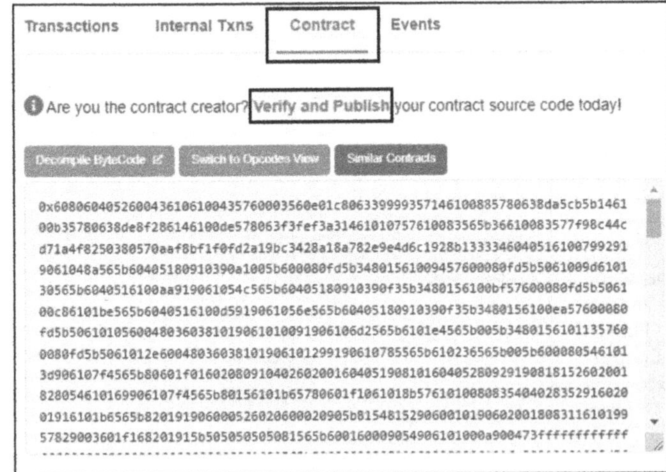

FIGURE 11-36: Viewing `MyFirst-Contract` code details from the Contract tab.

3. **Make the following selections, as shown in Figure 11-38:**

   a. **Select** Solidity (Single File) **as the Compiler Type to make a drop-down menu appear in which to specify the Compiler Version.**

   b. **Select** v0.8.14+commit.80d49f37 **as the Compiler Version.**

   c. **Select** 2) The Unlicense (Unlicense) **as the Open Source License Type.**

   d. **Agree to the terms of service and click the Continue button to proceed.**

   A new page appears, prompting you to enter your Solidity Contract Code.

4. **Copy and paste in the exact** MyFirstContract.sol **Solidity source code you compiled on Remix, as shown in Figure 11-39. You can ignore the rest of the items on this page.**

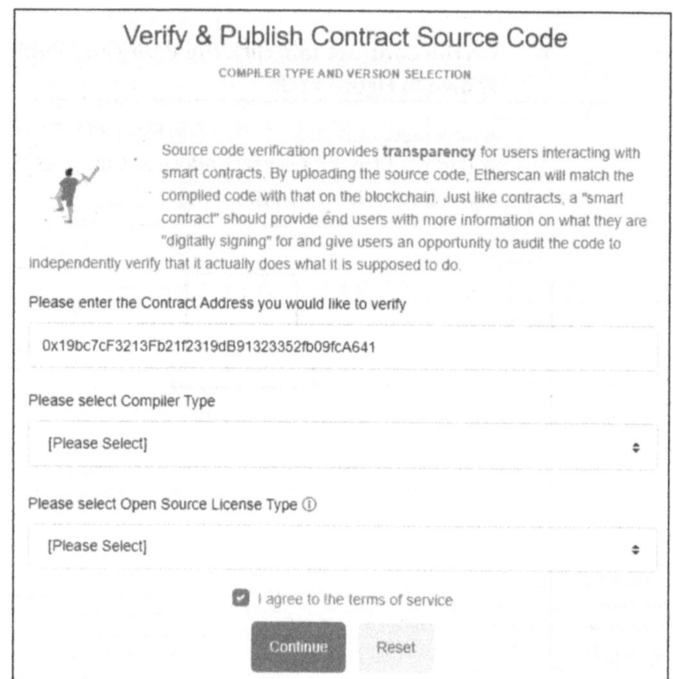

FIGURE 11-37: Etherscan's Verify & Publish Contract Source Code form.

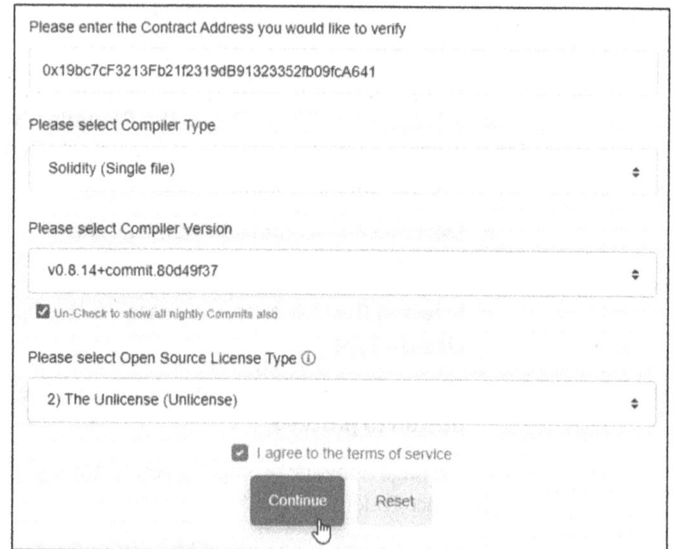

FIGURE 11-38: Completed selections on the Verify & Publish Contract Source Code form.

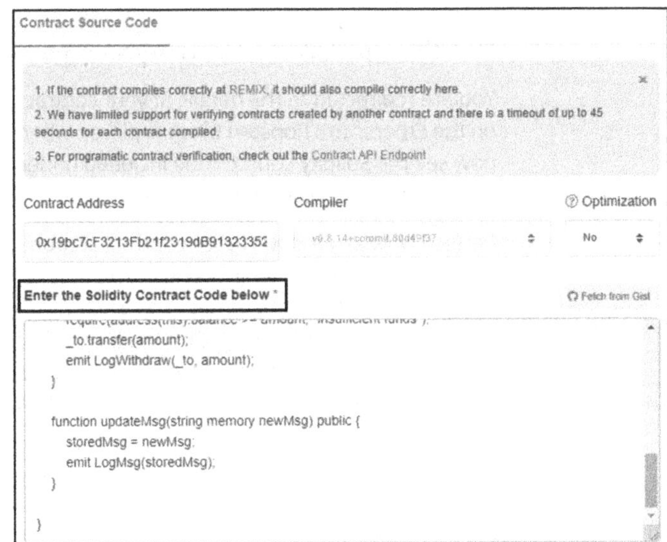

FIGURE 11-39: Entering source code on the Verify & Publish Contract Source Code form.

5. **Scroll down and click the Verify and Publish button.**

   After your source code has been compiled, a new Compiler Output tab appears, providing the final details, as shown in Figure 11-40.

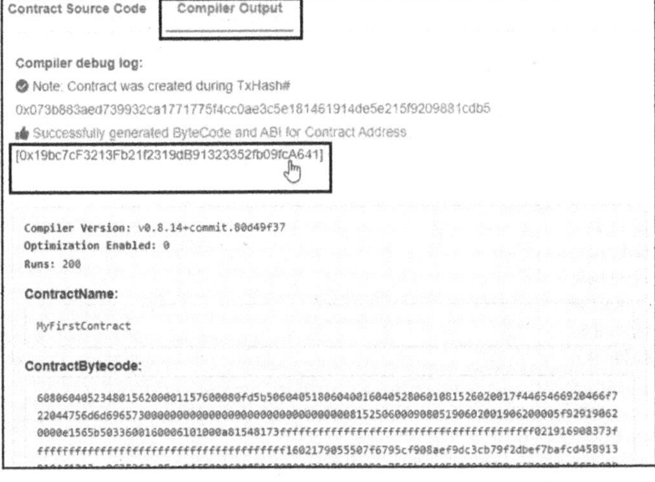

FIGURE 11-40: Final output from successful compilation and completion of the Verify & Publish Contract Source Code form.

6. **Click the hyperlinked address to your contract account.**

   You are redirected to the details of your contract account on the Etherscan's Ropsten block explorer, where you can now see the Solidity source code included under the Contract tab, as shown in Figure 11-41.

   Perfect! Now anyone with your contract account address can interact with your smart contract via `ropsten.etherscan.io` (or, say, `goerli.etherscan.io` if you deployed your contract onto the Goerli Testnet, or `www.etherscan.io` if you deployed your contract onto Mainnet). To see how this works, continue on to the following steps:

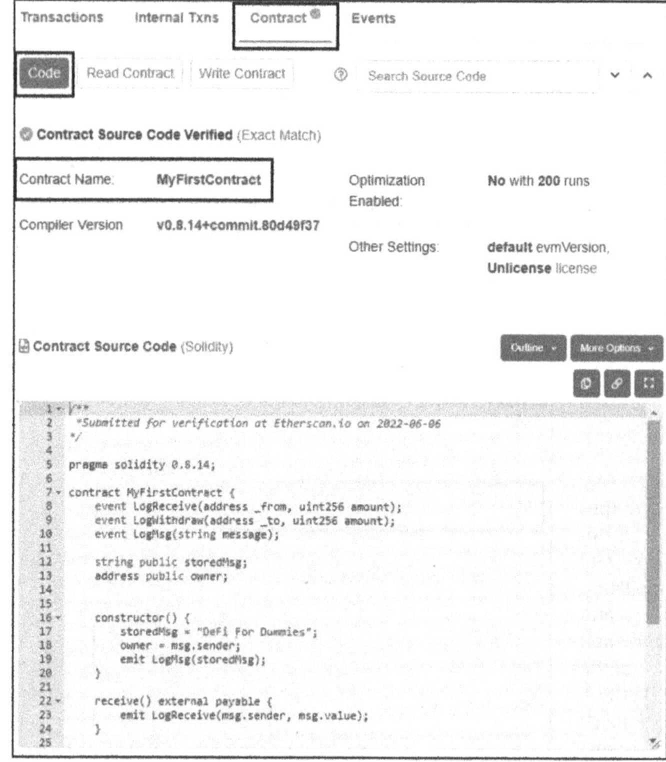

FIGURE 11-41: The `MyFirstContract` source code is now available under the Contract tab.

7. **From the Contract tab, click the Read Contract button.**

   A new page appears, displaying the values stored in the state variables defined in your smart contract, as shown in Figure 11-42.

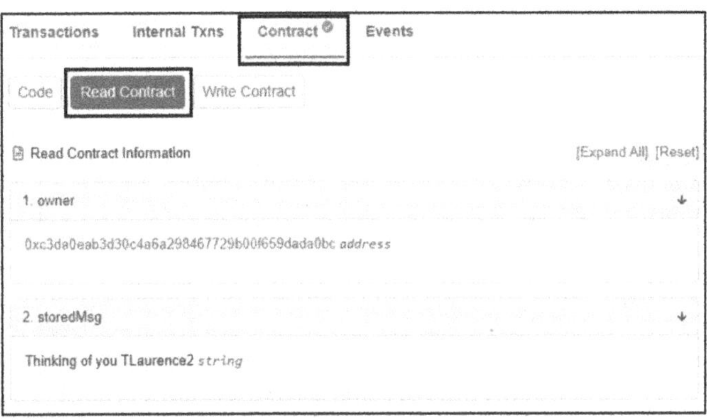

FIGURE 11-42: Viewing values stored in the `owner` and `storedMsg` state variables housed in `MyFirstContract`.

8. **Click the Write Contract button.**

   A new page appears, allowing you to call the functions defined in your smart contract, as shown in Figure 11-43.

9. **Click the Connect to Web3 button.**

   A pop-up window appears, allowing you to select a Web3-enabled wallet, as shown in Figure 11-44.

10. **Select the MetaMask option. Then click the Next button on the MetaMask pop-up notification that appears, and then the click the Connect button that appears on the next page of the pop-up notification.**

WARNING

After these steps, you may need to click the Connect to Web3 button again (from the preceding Step 9) and follow the prompts a second time before you're actually connected.

You know you're connected when the red dot next to the Connect to Web3 button (refer back to Figure 11-43) turns into a green dot with the word *Connected,* as shown in Figure 11-45.

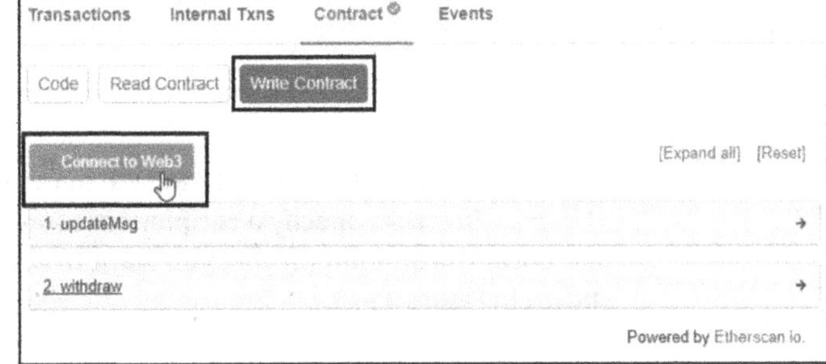

FIGURE 11-43: Accessing functions defined in `MyFirstContract`.

FIGURE 11-44: The pop-up window to select a Web3-enabled wallet to connect to the Etherscan site.

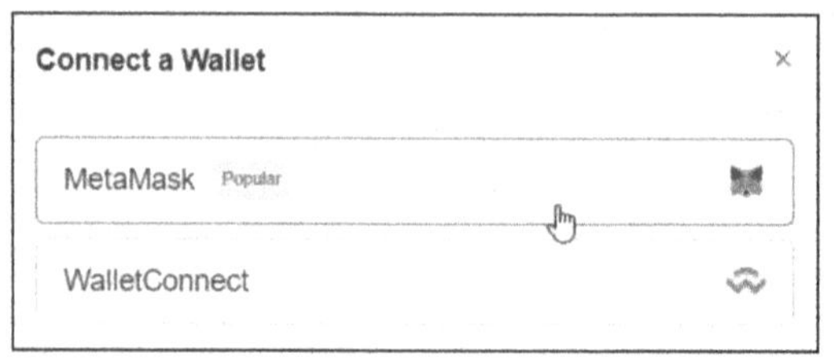

11. **After you're connected, expand the** `updateMsg` **function, enter a new message, and click the Write button, as shown in Figure 11-45.**

    A MetaMask pop-up notification appears to confirm the transaction.

12. **Click the Confirm button and wait for the transaction to be mined.**

    When the transaction is complete, you can toggle back to the Read Contract mode and view the updated value in the `storedMsg` state variable, as shown in Figure 11-46.

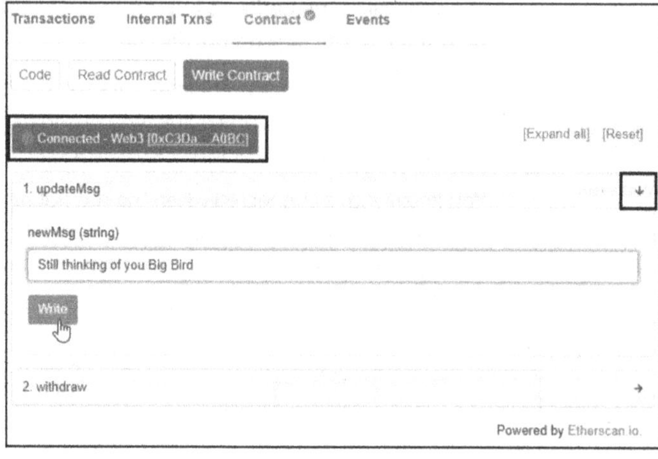

FIGURE 11-45: Calling the `updateMsg()` function in `MyFirstContract.` via Etherscan.

13. **Back under the Write Contract mode, expand the** `withdraw` **function, specify a recipient account address, and enter the amount (in wei) you want to withdraw, as shown in Figure 11-47.**

FIGURE 11-46: Viewing updated `storedMsg` value housed in `MyFirstContract`.

REMEMBER

To successfully execute a withdrawal, you need to initiate this transaction from the original account you used to deploy your smart contract (though, of course, you can specify any recipient). I've chosen to withdraw 25,000, 000,000,000,000 wei (0.025 rETH) back to my original DeFi For Dummies account: `0xC3Da0eaB3D30C4a6a298467729B00F659daDA0BC`.

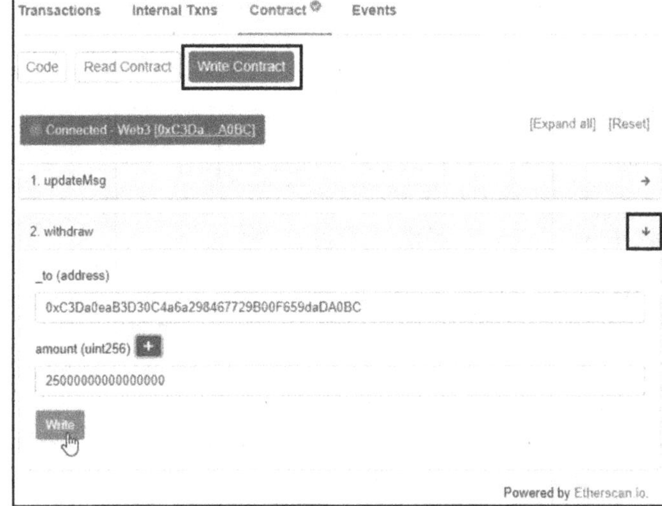

FIGURE 11-47: Calling the `withdraw()` function in `MyFirstContract` via `ropsten.etherscan.io`.

14. Click the Write button, and then click the Confirm button on the MetaMask pop-up notification window that appears, and wait for your transaction to be mined.

After your transaction is complete, you can see an increased account balance on your MetaMask home screen. In my case, you can see that my balance has increased from approximately 0.9517 rETH (refer back to Figure 11-33) to approximately 0.9766 rETH, as shown in Figure 11-48.

In addition, from the Etherscan block explorer, your smart-contract account now displays a (further) reduced balance from 0.05 rETH (refer back to Figure 11-34) to 0.025 rETH, as shown in Figure 11-49.

Congratulations! You have a fully functional smart contract that is now part of the DeFi ecosystem. Keep in mind that this contract account can collect only rETH because it was deployed onto the Ropsten Testnet. When you're feeling sufficiently comfortable and confident, you'll want to deploy your smart contract(s) onto the Ethereum Mainnet (or some other smart-contract platform).

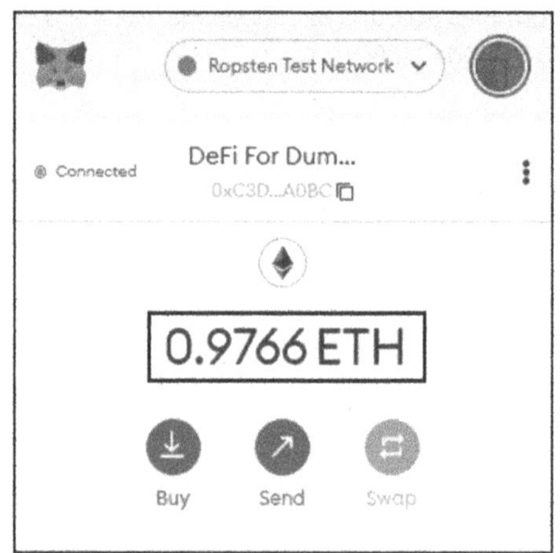

FIGURE 11-48: Further increased account balance after withdrawing and receiving 0.025 rETH from `MyFirstContract`.

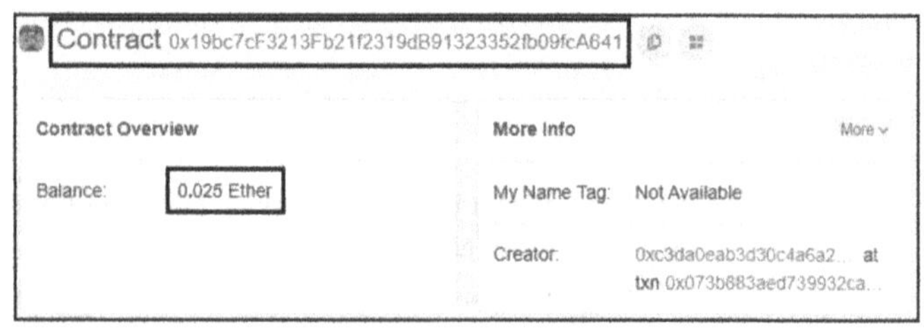

FIGURE 11-49: Further decreased smart-contract account balance after withdrawing 0.025 rETH from `MyFirstContract`.

IN THIS CHAPTER

» Configuring network connections in MetaMask

» Deploying your smart contract on Binance Smart Chain and other EVM-compatible smart-contract platforms

» Using a block explorer to track and interact with your smart contract after deployment

Chapter 12

Launching a Smart Contract on the Binance Smart Chain

This chapter walks you through how to deploy and subsequently interact with your smart contract on the Binance Smart Chain (BSC). BSC is EVM-compatible, which means you can reuse the same source code written for smart contracts on Ethereum. You can also connect to BSC using MetaMask, and you can use the Remix IDE to compile and deploy your smart contracts onto BSC.

TIP

If you haven't already done so, I highly recommend reading the section on understanding smart contracts in Chapter 11. That said, Chapter 11 is not a necessary prerequisite to successfully dive into the step-by-step instructions in this chapter.

REMEMBER

However, you will need to have installed the MetaMask browser extension (see Chapter 3).

Testing the Waters: How to Navigate the BSC Testnet

As in previous chapters, I carry out my main instructions on a test network to allow for plenty of trial and error without the pain of losing actual tokens (and actual money!).

If you've already deployed a smart contract onto one of Ethereum's testnets (or Mainnet itself), you'll notice that the steps to deploying a smart contract onto the BSC Testnet are very similar after you've configured your MetaMask wallet accordingly.

Configuring MetaMask

Follow these steps to add the BSC Testnet to the Networks menu:

1. **Click the MetaMask fox icon in your browser's toolbar and sign in to your account.**

   REMEMBER

   Refer to Chapter 3 if you need a refresher on navigating MetaMask.

2. **Click the colorful circle in the upper-right corner; then select the Create Account option, as shown in Figure 12-1, to create a new account.**

   TIP

   Although you can use the same account you created in Chapter 3, I recommend creating another account for your BSC activity. I've chosen to name my new account "BSC Test Account."

3. **Click the Networks drop-down menu and then click the Add Network button, as shown in Figure 12-2.**

   A new browser tab appears, prompting you to provide details of the network you want to add, as shown in Figure 12-3.

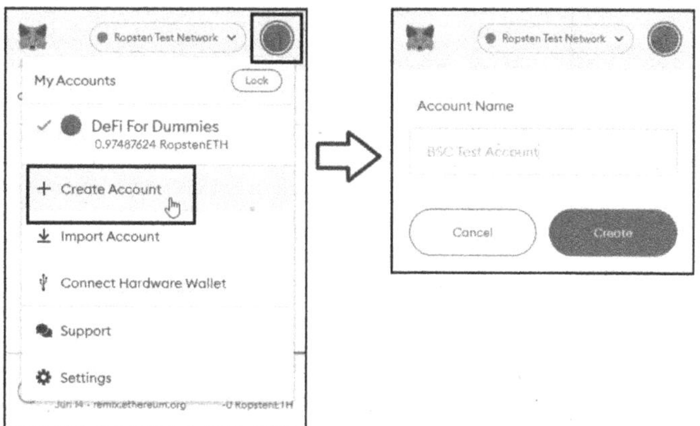

FIGURE 12-1: Creating a new account in your MetaMask wallet.

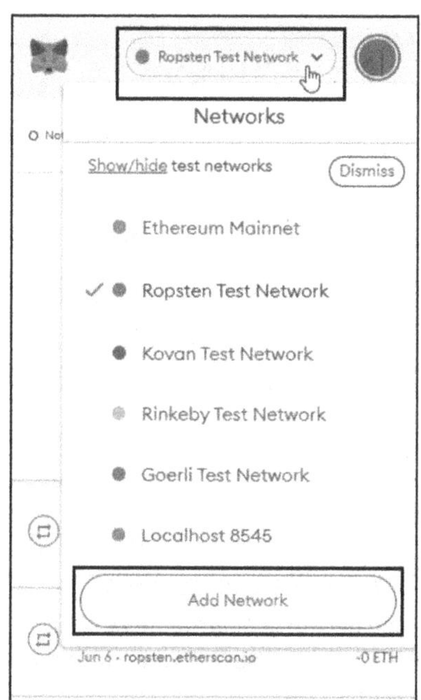

FIGURE 12-2: The Networks drop-down menu on MetaMask.

4. **Enter the following information and then click the Save button.**

   - **Network Name:** `Smart Chain - Testnet`
   - **New RPC URL:** `https://data-seed-prebsc-1-s1.binance.org:8545/`
   - **ChainID:** 97

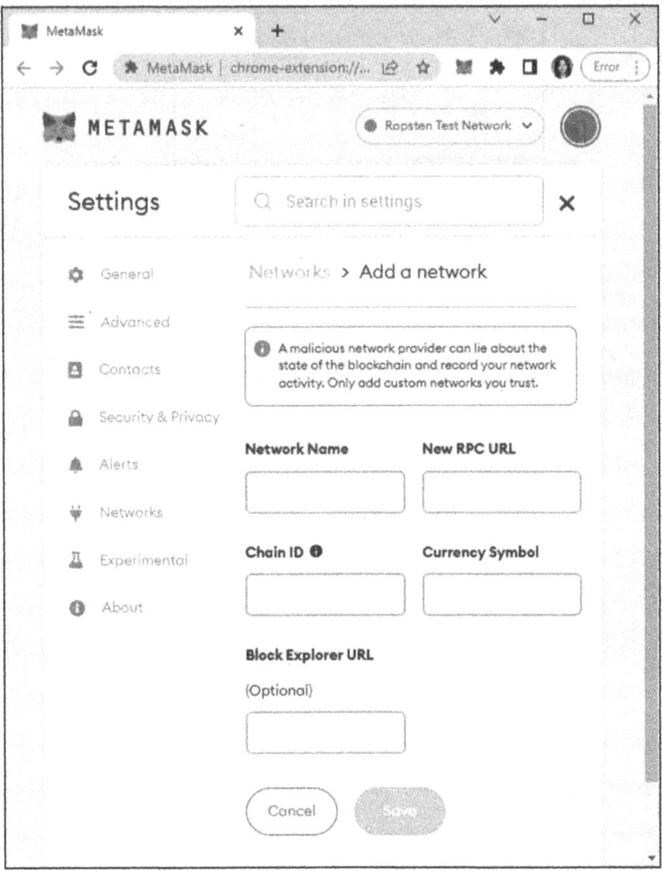

FIGURE 12-3: Adding new network information on MetaMask.

- **Symbol:** BNB
- **Block Explorer URL:** `https://testnet.bscscan.com`

REMEMBER

You can change networks at any time by clicking the network name to access the Networks drop-down menu, as shown in Figure 12-4.

Now that you're connected to the BSC Testnet, follow these steps to fund your account with some test BNB, which is the native token that fuels transactions on the BSC Testnet.

5. **From the main MetaMask drop-down menu, click your account name to copy your public address, as shown in Figure 12-5.**

   In my case, my BSC Test Account's public address is `0xd4Dd8745Bf85C1F93A5B6c02E125Ae6264F37368`.

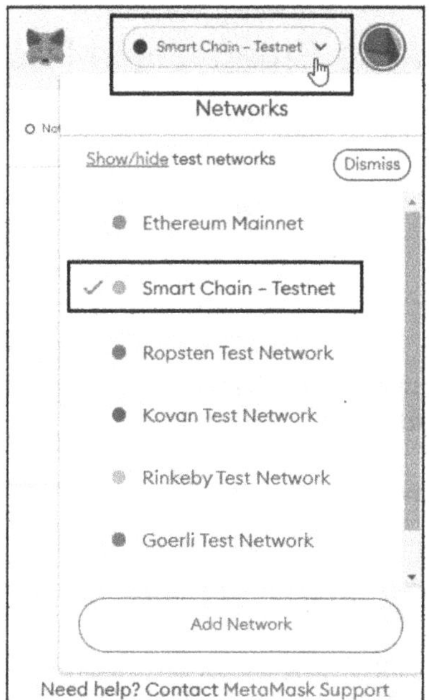

FIGURE 12-4: Revisiting the Networks drop-down menu on MetaMask, which now includes the BSC Testnet as an option.

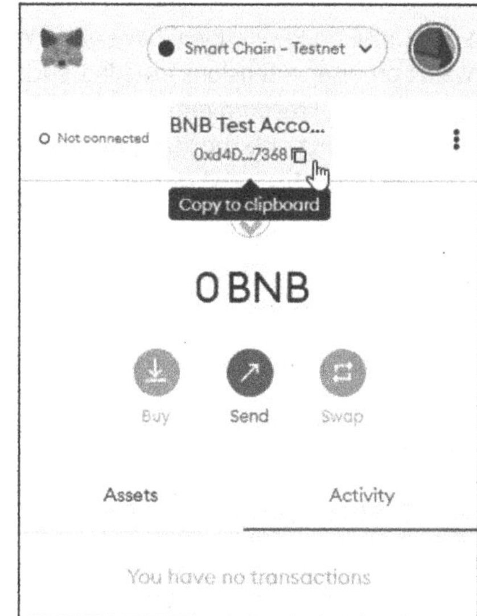

FIGURE 12-5: Copying BSC Test Account address from MetaMask.

6. **Point your browser to** `https://testnet.binance.org/faucet-smart` **to access the Binance Smart Chain Faucet, as shown in Figure 12-6.**

FIGURE 12-6: The Binance Smart Chain Faucet.

7. **Paste in your account address and then click the Give Me BNB button.**

Yay, you now have some test BNB!

Launching your smart contract

Now that you're connected to the BSC Testnet and armed with some test funds, follow these steps to deploy your smart contract:

1. **Point your browser to** `https://remix.ethereum.org/`.

   WARNING

   Problems may arise on Remix if you have other Web3-enabled wallet browser extensions installed, such as the Dapper Legacy wallet. I recommend disabling these other extensions (and keeping only the MetaMask extension active) as you continue this step-by-step guide.

   TIP

   Refer to the sections about using the Remix IDE and pre-launch preparations in Chapter 11 for more detailed instructions and accompanying figures.

2. **From the Remix IDE home page, click the New File link.**

   A new, unnamed file appears in the File Explorer browser pane to the left.

3. **In the text input box, type** MyFirstContract.sol **and press Enter to name your new file.**

   A new tab labeled MyFirstContract.sol appears in the main browser pane to the right. This tab is where you'll enter your source code.

4. **Open a new browser tab and point your browser to** `https://www.seoyoungkim.com/defifd/MyFirstContract.sol` **to copy the smart-contract source code.**

TIP

Refer to the section about writing your code in Chapter 11 for a chunk-by-chunk explanation of the provided code.

5. **Toggle back to the Remix browser tab and paste the copied source code into the MyFirstContract.sol tab of the main browser pane to the right.**

6. **Click the Solidity Compiler icon in the navigation toolbar located on the far left.**

   The Solidity Compiler page appears in the left browser pane, as shown in Figure 12-7.

7. **Click the Compile MyFirstContract.sol button.**

   Compilation details appear at the bottom of the Solidity Compiler browser pane.

   Great work! Now you're ready to deploy!

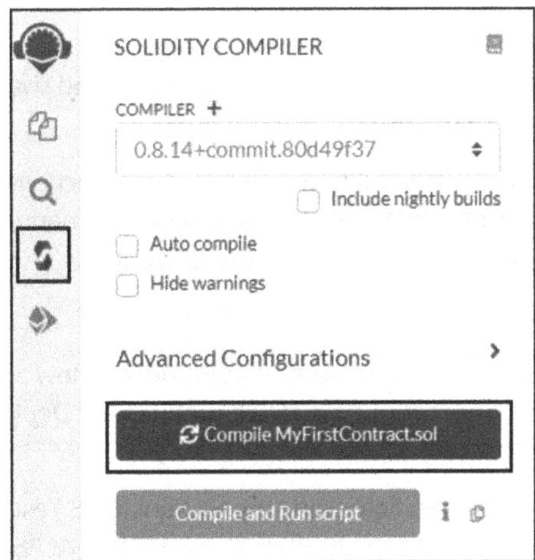

FIGURE 12-7: The Solidity Compiler browser pane on Remix.

8. **Click the Ethereum icon in the navigation toolbar located on the far left.**

   The Deploy & Run Transactions page appears in the left browser pane, as shown in Figure 12-8.

9. **Select the Injected Web3 option on the Environment drop-down menu, as shown in Figure 12-9.**

   A MetaMask pop-up notification window appears, allowing you to select the accounts you'd like to connect to the Remix IDE.

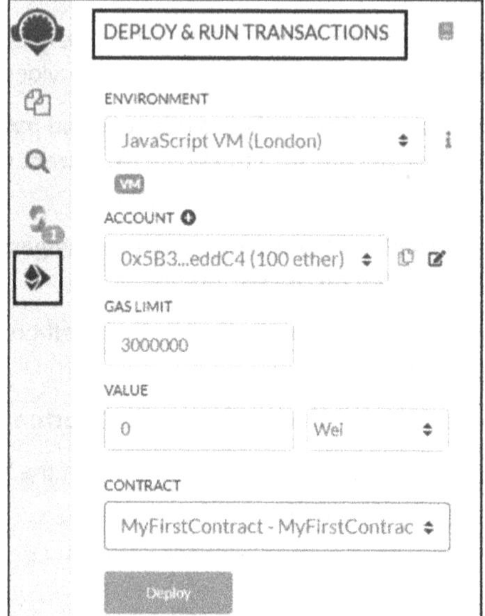

FIGURE 12-8: The Deploy & Run Transactions browser pane on Remix.

10. **Confirm the account you'd like to use and then click the Connect button.**

    If you look now at the Deploy & Run Transactions browser pane alongside the MetaMask drop-down menu, as shown in Figure 12-10, you'll notice the following:

    - You're connected to the BSC Testnet.
    - Your selected account or accounts are now accessible on the Account drop-down menu in the Deploy & Run Transactions browser pane.

    In my example, I am using my account (BNB Test Account) with public address `0xd4Dd8745Bf85C1F93A5B6c02E-125Ae6264F37368`.

11. **Return your focus to the Deploy & Run Transactions browser pane, make sure you've selected the appropriate contract (`MyFirstContract`) and then click the Deploy button.**

    A MetaMask pop-up notification appears, prompting you to confirm the transaction.

    Great work! You'll now notice `MyFirstContract` under Deployed Contracts located at the bottom of the Deploy & Run Transactions browser pane.

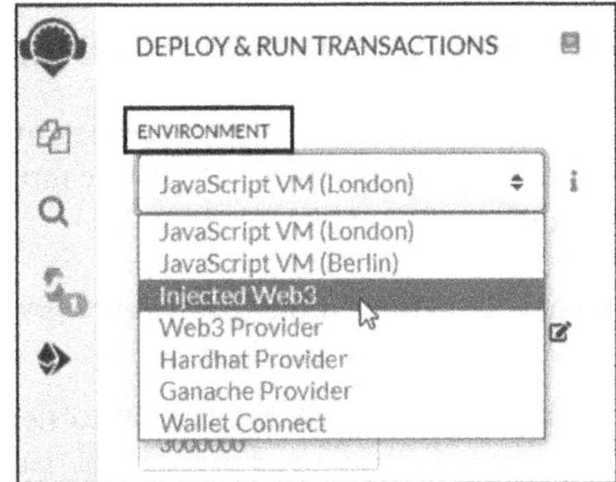

FIGURE 12-9: The Environment drop-down menu from the Deploy & Run Transactions browser pane on Remix.

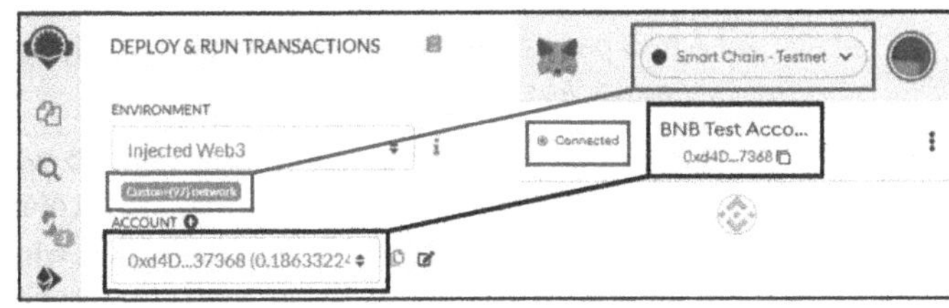

FIGURE 12-10: The Deploy & Run Transactions browser pane on Remix alongside the MetaMask drop-down window.

12. **Finally, click the double-page icon to the right of your deployed contract to copy your contract account address, as shown in Figure 12-11.**

    You'll need this contract account address to follow and interact with your contract in the next section. As for me, my contract's address is `0x61B36cb042D368A232A62f-517bbed86b82b7acc3`.

FIGURE 12-11: Copying the `MyFirstContract` contract account address from the Deploy & Run Transactions browser pane on Remix.

Accessing your smart contract

Now that you have your smart contract up and running on the BSC Testnet, follow these steps to view your contract and interact with its functions:

1. **Open a new browser tab, and point your browser to** `https://testnet.bscscan.com/`**.**

TIP

Don't close your Remix browser tab yet. You'll need to access your smart-contract source code again later.

2. **Paste your smart-contract account address into the search bar, as shown in Figure 12-12, and then press Enter or click the search icon.**

   A new page appears, providing details specific to your smart contract, as shown in Figure 12-13.

   Notice that you begin on the Transactions tab, which displays all transactions involving this smart-contract account. So far, there is only one transaction, which is the transaction that originated this smart-contract account.

FIGURE 12-12: Finding your contract account on the BSC Testnet Explorer.

3. **Toggle to the Contract tab.**

TIP

If you copied my code verbatim, you'll likely see that this contract code has already been verified and published, as shown in Figure 12-17. If this is the case, you can skip straight ahead to Step 9.

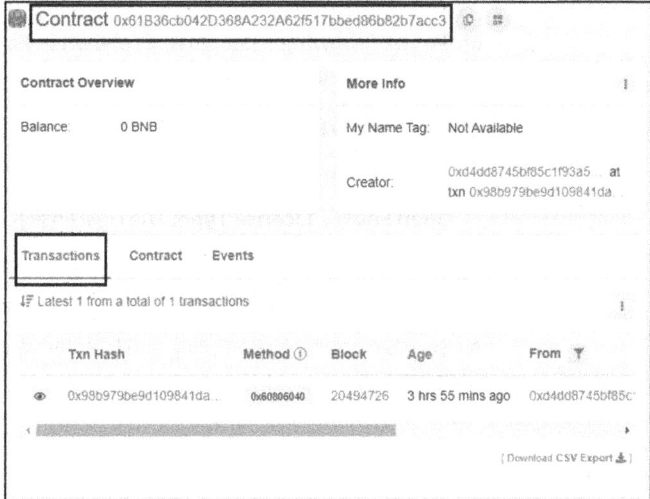

FIGURE 12-13: Details on the BSC Testnet Explorer for my contract account (`MyFirst-Contract`).

4. **On the Contract tab, click the Verify and Publish link, as shown in Figure 12-14.**

   A new page appears, prompting you to confirm the Contract Address, Compiler Type, and Open Source License Type.

REMEMBER

If you don't see the Verify and Publish link, you can skip straight ahead to Step 9.

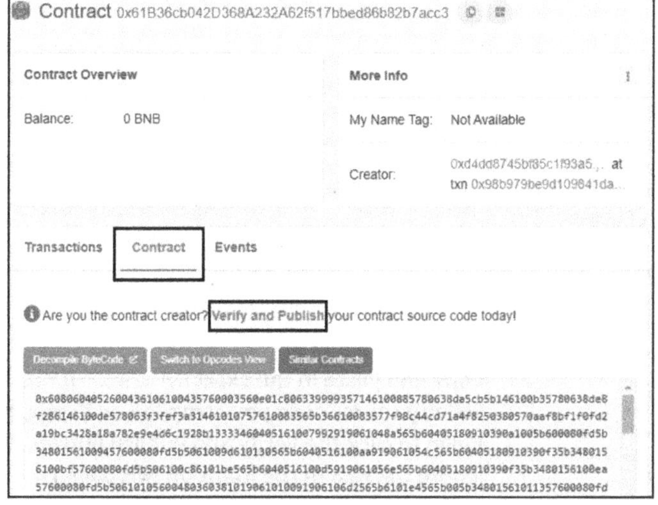

FIGURE 12-14: Viewing `MyFirst-Contract` code details from the Contract tab on the BSC Testnet Explorer.

5. **Make the following selections, as shown in Figure 12-15, and then click the Continue button.**
   - **Compiler Type:** Solidity (Single file)
   - **Compiler Version:** v0.8.14+commit.80d49f37
   - **Open Source License Type:** The Unlicense (Unlicense)

6. **Agree to the terms of service, and then click the Continue button to proceed.**

   A new page appears, prompting you to enter your Solidity Contract Code.

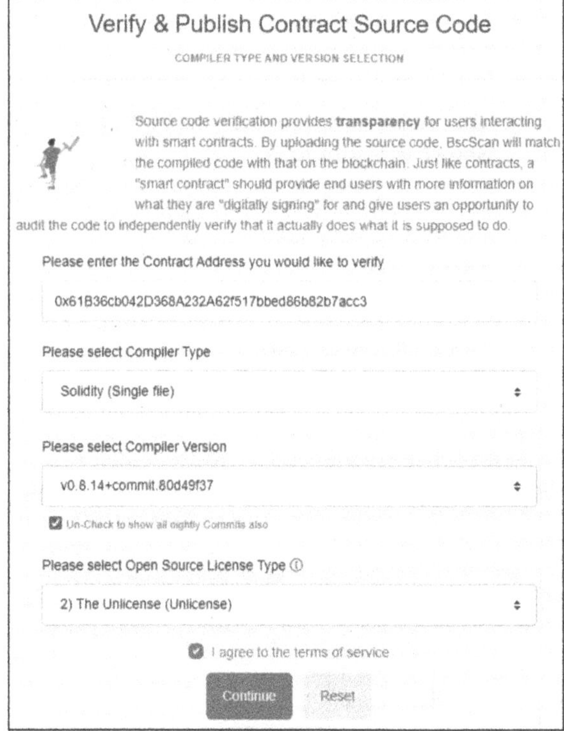

FIGURE 12-15: Completed selections on the Verify & Publish Contract Source Code form.

7. **Copy and paste in the exact `MyFirstContract.sol` Solidity source code you compiled on Remix; then scroll down to click the Verify and Publish button. (You can ignore the rest of the items on this page.)**

After your source code has been compiled, a new Compiler Output tab appears, providing the final details, as shown in Figure 12-16.

8. **Click the hyperlinked address to your contract account.**

   You'll be redirected to the details of your contract account on the BSC Testnet Explorer, where you'll now be able to see the Solidity source code included under the Contract tab, as shown in Figure 12-17.

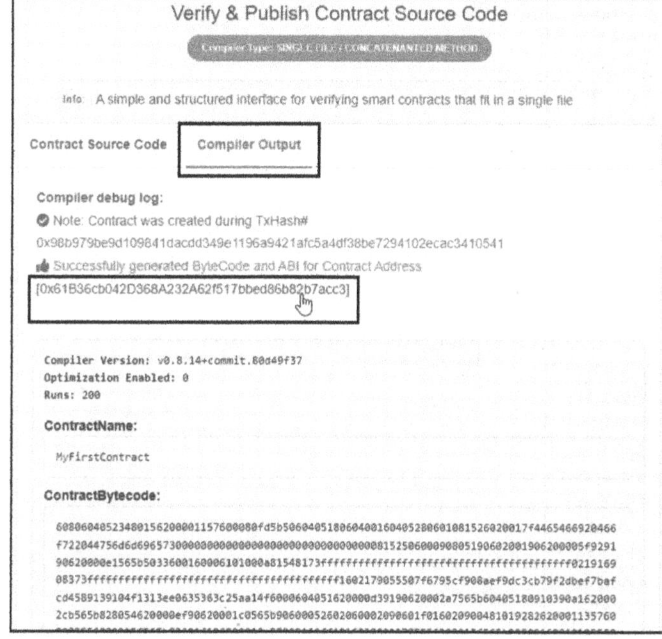

FIGURE 12-16: Final output from successful compilation and completion of the Verify & Publish Contract Source Code form.

9. **On the Contract tab, click the Read Contract button.**

   A new page appears, displaying the values stored in the state variables defined in your smart contract, as shown in Figure 12-18.

10. **Click the Write Contract button.**

    A new page appears, allowing you to call the functions defined in your smart contract, as shown in Figure 12-19.

FIGURE 12-17: `MyFirstContract` source code now available on the BSC Testnet Explorer under the Contract tab.

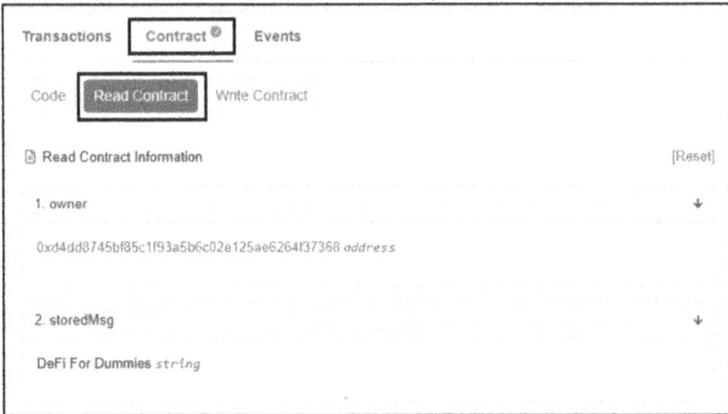

FIGURE 12-18: Viewing values stored in the `owner` and `storedMsg` state variables housed in `MyFirstContract`.

11. **Click the Connect to Web3 button.**

    A pop-up window appears, allowing you to select a Web3-enabled wallet.

12. **Select the MetaMask option; then follow the prompts in the MetaMask pop-up notification to connect your BSC Test Account.**

After these steps, you may need to click the Connect to Web3 button again (from Step 11 in this list) and follow the prompts a second time before you're actually connected.

You'll know you're connected when the red dot next to the Connect to Web3 button (refer to Figure 12-19) turns into a green dot with the word Connected alongside the connected account's address, as shown in Figure 12-20.

FIGURE 12-19: Accessing functions defined in `MyFirstContract`.

13. **When you're connected, type a few words into the `newMsg` text box (under the** `updateMsg` **function header) and click the Write button, as shown in Figure 12-20.**

    A MetaMask pop-up notification appears, prompting you to confirm the transaction.

    After the transaction is complete, click the Read Contract button to view the updated value in the `storedMsg` state variable, as shown in Figure 12-21.

    Great, you've now tested and verified the `updateMsg()` function. Next, before you can test the `withdraw()` function, you first need to send some test BNB to your `MyFirstContract` contract account.

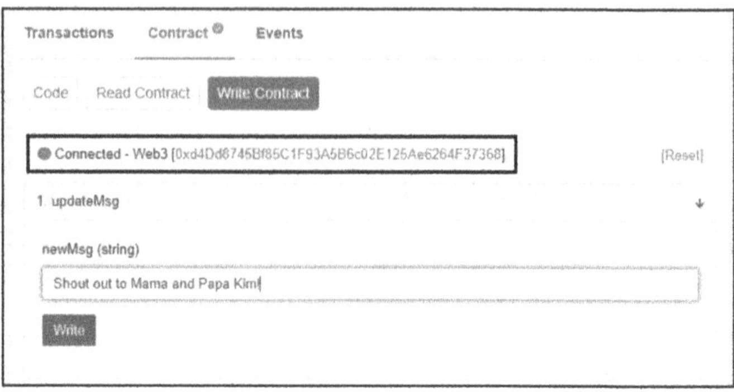

FIGURE 12-20: Calling the update Msg() function in MyFirst Contract on the BSC Testnet Explorer.

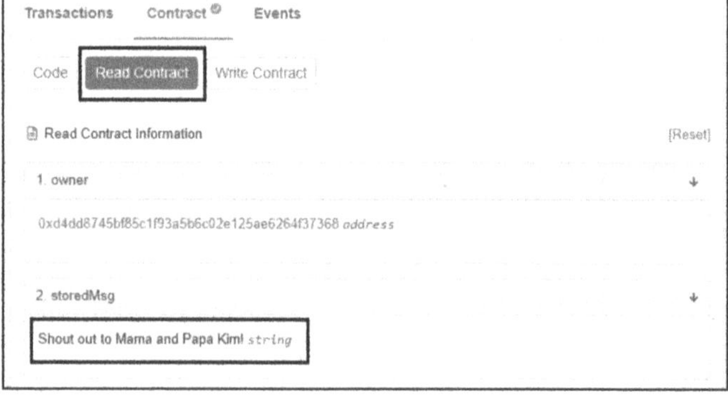

FIGURE 12-21: Viewing the updated storedMsg value housed in MyFirst-Contract.

WARNING

Do *not* send actual BNB to this contract account. Because this smart contract was deployed onto the BSC Testnet, it can accept only test BNB. Also, keep in mind that not all smart-contract accounts can receive funds. The `receive()` function, implemented in lines 18 to 20 of the `MyFirstContract` source code, specifically enables this feature.

14. **Click the MetaMask fox icon in your browser's toolbar, and click the Send button from the main drop-down menu.**

15. **Paste in your contract account address, enter the amount of test BNB you want to send, and then click the Next button, as shown in Figure 12-22.**

    I've chosen to send 0.5 test BNB to my contract account.

    When the transaction is complete, you'll be able to see the updated balance for your contract account on the BSC Testnet Explorer, as shown in Figure 12-23. (***Note:*** You may need to click your browser's refresh button.)

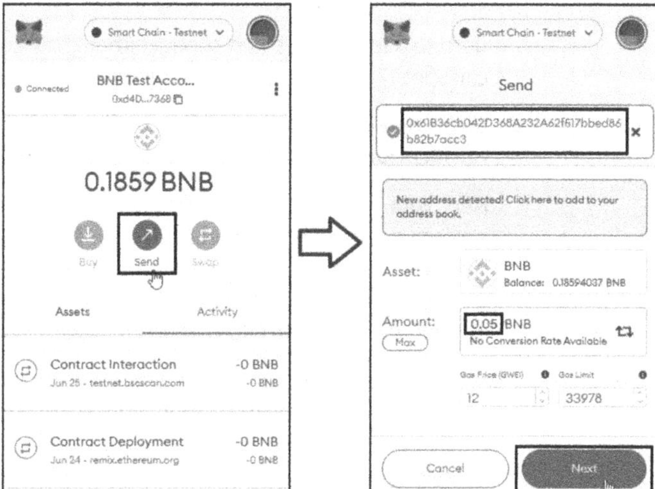

FIGURE 12-22: Sending 0.05 test BNB from BNB Test Account to `MyFirst-Contract` contract account via MetaMask.

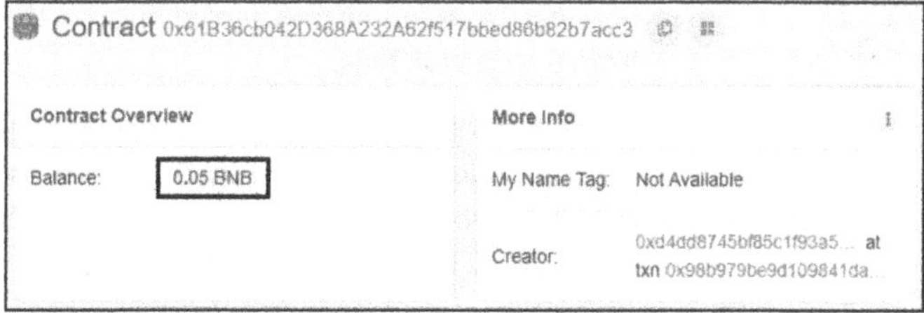

FIGURE 12-23: Updated account balance for `MyFirst-Contract` contract account as shown on the BSC Testnet Explorer.

16. **Return to the Write Contract mode (under the Contract tab).**
17. **Under the `withdraw` function header, specify a recipient account address and then enter the amount (in wei) that you want to withdraw, as shown in Figure 12-24.**

    I've chosen to withdraw 40,000,000,000,000,000 wei (0.04 test BNB) and send it back to my original BSC Test Account: `0xd4Dd8745Bf85C1F93A5B6c02E125Ae6264F37368`.

REMEMBER

At contract initiation, the `owner` variable was set to the originating account's address (in line 14 within the `constructor()` function of the `MyFirstContract` source code). Thus, to successfully execute a withdrawal, you need to initiate this transaction from the original account you used to deploy your smart contract (though, of course, you can specify any recipient account address).

18. **Click the Write button and follow the MetaMask pop-up notifications to confirm your transaction request.**

    After your transaction is complete, you'll notice an increased account balance on your MetaMask home screen and a decreased account balance for your smart-contract account on the BSC Testnet Explorer, as shown in Figure 12-25. Specifically, here's the information you'll see:

    - My BNB Test Account balance on MetaMask, for example, has gone from approximately 0.1859 (refer to Figure 12-22) to 0.1359 (after sending 0.05 test BNB to `MyFirstContract`) to a final balance of 0.1753 (after receiving 0.04 test BNB back from `MyFirstContract` in Step 17).

REMEMBER

      The account balances following each transaction reflect not only the amounts transferred but also the slippage from transaction fees.

    - In addition, `MyFirstContract`'s account balance on the BSC Testnet Explorer has gone from 0.00 (refer to Figure 12-13) to 0.05 (refer to Figure 12-23) to a final balance of 0.01 (after withdrawing 0.04 test BNB in Step 17).

FIGURE 12-24: Calling the `withdraw()` function in `MyFirstContract` on the BSC Testnet Explorer.

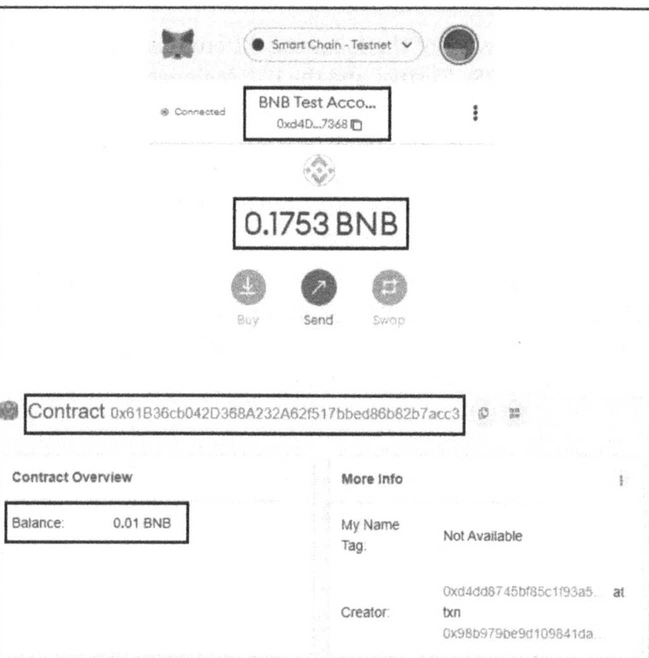

FIGURE 12-25: Final account balances for BNB Test Account on MetaMask and `MyFirst-Contract` contract account on the BSC Testnet Explorer.

Feeling Ready for Mainnet?

If you're prepared to spend some real BNB and deploy your smart contract onto the BSC Mainnet, you can enter the following network details on MetaMask:

- **Network Name:** `Smart Chain`
- **New RPC URL:** `https://bsc-dataseed.binance.org/`
- **ChainID:** 56
- **Symbol:** BNB
- **Block Explorer URL:** `https://bscscan.com`

After you're connected to the BSC Mainnet, you'll need to fund your account with some real BNB. The quickest way is to use the Buy function from the MetaMask wallet, as shown in Figure 12-26.

Be aware of the following differences between being connected to the BSC Testnet and the BSC Mainnet:

REMEMBER

- The Buy button on the MetaMask main menu is now active because I've connected to the BSC Mainnet (in contrast to when I was connected to the BSC Testnet, as shown previously in Figure 12-25).
- My BNB Test Account now reflects a balance of 0 BNB, because the BSC Mainnet doesn't recognize the test BNB in my account. My account will once again reflect the prior balance when I toggle back to the BSC Testnet.

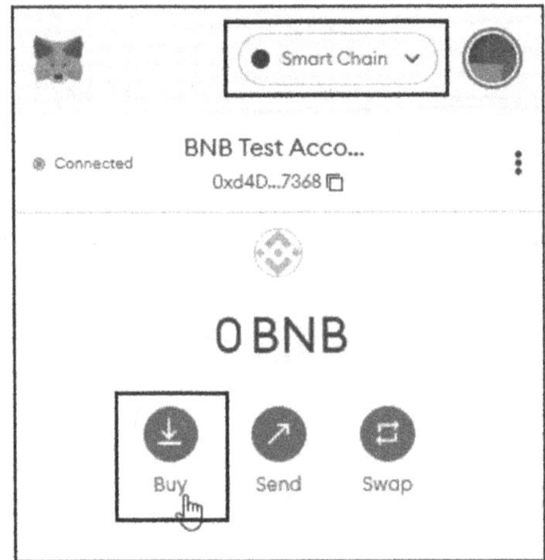

FIGURE 12-26: Buying BNB via the MetaMask wallet.

Alternatively, you can purchase BNB on Binance's crypto exchange, accessed at `https://binance.us` (for U.S. customers) or `https://binance.com` (for non-U.S. customers). BNB is currently not available to trade on the three largest U.S. crypto exchanges: Coinbase, Gemini, or Kraken.

Deploying onto Other EVM-Compatible Platforms

Now that you've successfully deployed a smart contract onto the BSC Testnet (or Mainnet), you can follow the same process to deploy onto any EVM-compatible blockchain. Simply configure your MetaMask wallet to connect to the appropriate network, and repeat the step-by-step instructions provided in this chapter. Yes, the blockchain world is your oyster!

REMEMBER

Keep in mind that in this rapidly developing space, network coordinates may change, test faucets may go dry, and entire networks may be deprecated by the time you read this section. When in doubt, check the developers' documentations provided by the respective platforms.

Avalanche

To connect to the Avalanche Mainnet, enter the following network details:

- **Network Name:** `Avalanche Mainnet C-Chain`
- **New RPC URL:** `https://api.avax.network/ext/bc/C/rpc`
- **Chain ID:** `0xa86a`
- **Currency Symbol:** AVAX
- **Block Explorer URL:** `https://snowtrace.io`

To connect to Avalanche's FUJI Testnet, enter the following network details:

- **Network Name:** `Avalanche Testnet C-Chain`
- **New RPC URL:** `https://api.avax-test.network/ext/bc/C/rpc`
- **Chain ID:** `0xa869`
- **Currency Symbol:** AVAX
- **Block Explorer URL:** `https://testnet.snowtrace.io`

You can obtain Fuji-compatible AVAX test tokens from Avalanche's faucet, accessed at `https://faucet.avax.network/`.

Polygon

To connect to the Polygon Mainnet, enter the following network details:

- **Network Name:** Polygon Mainnet
- **New RPC URL:** https://polygon-rpc.com/
- **Chain ID:** 137
- **Currency Symbol:** MATIC
- **Block Explorer URL:** https://polygonscan.com

To connect to the Polygon's Mumbai Testnet, enter the following network details:

- **Network Name:** Matic Mumbai
- **New RPC URL:** https://rpc-mumbai.maticvigil.com/
- **Chain ID:** 80001
- **Currency Symbol:** MATIC
- **Block Explorer URL:** https://mumbai.polygonscan.com/

You can obtain Mumbai MATIC test tokens from Polygon's faucet, accessed at https://faucet.polygon.technology/.

Cronos

To connect to the Cronos Mainnet, enter the following network details:

- **Network Name:** Cronos
- **New RPC URL:** https://evm.cronos.org
- **Chain ID:** 25
- **Currency Symbol:** CRO
- **Block Explorer URL:** https://cronoscan.com

To connect to the Cronos Testnet, enter the following network details:

- **Network Name:** Cronos testnet
- **New RPC URL:** https://evm-t3.cronos.org
- **Chain ID:** 338
- **Currency Symbol:** tCRO
- **Block Explorer URL:** https://testnet.cronoscan.com

You can obtain CRO test tokens from the Cronos TCRO Faucet, accessed at https://cronos.org/faucet.

Fantom

To connect to the Fantom Mainnet, enter the following network details:

- **Network Name:** Fantom Opera
- **New RPC URL:** https://rpc.ftm.tools/
- **Chain ID:** 250
- **Currency Symbol:** FTM
- **Block Explorer URL:** https://ftmscsan.com/

To connect to the Fantom Testnet, enter the following network details:

- **Network Name:** Fantom testnet
- **New RPC URL:** https://rpc.testnet.fantom.network/
- **Chain ID:** 0xfa2
- **Currency Symbol:** FTM
- **Block Explorer URL:** https://testnet.ftmscsan.com/

You can obtain FTM test tokens from Fantom's Testnet Opera Faucet, accessed at https://faucet.fantom.network/.

Arbitrum

To connect to the Arbitrum Mainnet, enter the following network details:

- **Network Name:** `Arbitrum Mainnet Beta`
- **New RPC URL:** `https://arb1.arbitrum.io/rpc`
- **Chain ID:** `42161`
- **Currency Symbol:** `ETH`
- **Block Explorer URL:** `https://arbiscan.io`

To connect to the Arbitrum Rinkeby Testnet, enter the following network details:

- **Network Name:** `Arbitrum Testnet`
- **New RPC URL:** `https://rinkeby.arbitrum.io/rpc`
- **Chain ID:** `421611`
- **Currency Symbol:** `ETH`
- **Block Explorer URL:** `https://testnet.arbiscan.io/`

As a layer 2 rollup built on top of and secured by Ethereum, the Arbitrum Mainnet (sort of) uses ETH, and the Arbitrum Rinkeby Testnet (sort of) uses Rinkeby test ETH. You can obtain Rinkeby test tokens from the Rinkeby Authenticated Faucet, accessed at `https://faucet.rinkeby.io/`, or from Alchemy's Rinkeby Faucet, accessed at `https://rinkebyfaucet.com/`.

WARNING

You can't directly use your ETH on the Arbitrum Mainnet. You must first send your ETH to an Arbitrum bridge contract account on Ethereum, which will create Arbitrum-compatible ETH for you to use on the Arbitrum Mainnet. Likewise, you must send your Rinkeby test ETH to an Arbitrum bridge contract on the Rinkeby test network, which will create compatible test tokens for you to use on the Arbitrum Rinkeby Testnet. See Chapter 10 for more details on layer 2 rollups and bridges.

Huobi ECO (HECO)

To connect to the HECO Mainnet, enter the following network details:

- **Network Name:** `Heco-Mainnet`
- **New RPC URL:** `https://http-mainnet.hecochain.com`
- **Chain ID:** `128`
- **Currency Symbol:** `HT`
- **Block Explorer URL:** `https://hecoinfo.com`

To connect to the Heco Testnet, enter the following network details:

- **Network Name:** `Heco-Testnet`
- **New RPC URL:** `https://http-testnet.hecochain.com`
- **Chain ID:** `256`
- **Currency Symbol:** `HT`
- **Block Explorer URL:** `https://testnet.hecoinfo.com`

You can obtain HT test tokens from the Huobi ECO Chain Test Faucet, accessed at `https://scan-testnet.hecochain.com/faucet`.

Celo

To connect to the Celo Mainnet, enter the following network details:

- **Network Name:** `Celo (Mainnet)`
- **New RPC URL:** `https://forno.celo.org`
- **Chain ID:** `42220`
- **Currency Symbol:** `CELO`
- **Block Explorer URL:** `https://explorer.celo.org`

To connect to Celo's Alfajores Testnet, enter the following network details:

- **Network Name:** `Celo (Alfajores Testnet)`
- **New RPC URL:** `https://alfajores-forno.celo-testnet.org`
- **Chain ID:** `44787`
- **Currency Symbol:** `CELO`
- **Block Explorer URL:** `https://alfajores-blockscout.celo-testnet.org`

You can obtain Alfajores-compatible CELO test tokens from Celo's faucet, accessed at `https://celo.org/developers/faucet`.

IN THIS CHAPTER

» Drafting your proof of concept

» Preparing for full-stack development

» Leveraging smart-contract libraries

» Integrating your back-end smart contract with your front-end web app

Chapter 13

Launching Your First DeFi Product

This chapter is not for the faint of heart. It entails a more complex combination of steps to prepare your development environment and ultimately create a nice interface for users.

In this chapter, I walk you through how to build out a full dApp. You first see an overview of the stages and considerations in fleshing out your DeFi proof of concept. Then, in the step-by-step instructions that follow, the chapter guides you through full-stack development, starting with the back-end smart contract and ending with the front-end web application for end users of your DeFi product.

To follow the hands-on instructional portion of this chapter, you will need to have completed some key steps in advance. I assume that you have already installed the MetaMask browser extension and set up a funded account, all covered in Chapter 3.

TIP

If you're feeling antsy for action, you can head straight down to the section on "Preparing Your Development Stack." In fact, if you're feeling extra antsy and don't plan to subsequently build out the front-end web application, you can even skip straight down to the section on "Implementing the Back End of your DApp."

However, if you do later want to complete the final component in the section on "Creating the Front-End User Interface," you'll need to circle back to complete the section on "Preparing Your Development Stack" to have the necessary accounts and IDEs for that additional stage.

In any case, if you haven't already done so, I highly recommend reading the section about understanding smart contracts in Chapter 11 as well as completing the hands-on guides in that chapter on how to launch and access your smart contract. However, these aren't necessary prerequisites to successfully complete this current chapter.

Proving Your Proof of Concept

In developing your DeFi proposal, you need to answer the following key questions:

- » What is the market pain you want to address?
- » Who is your target audience?
- » What services and products already exist, and how does yours differ?
- » What is the overarching value proposition here?
- » How will you implement your idea?

Overall, the goal is to pull people into your product rather than simply pushing it onto them.

I go through a simple example with these key questions in mind to flesh out the idea of a DeFi Crowdfund DApp Service that will provide quick yet customized blockchain-based crowdfunding solutions, complete with an easy front-end web interface.

Identifying the market pain

Suppose you have a great idea for a new book, but you don't have enough capital to execute your idea. How might you raise the money you need?

- You could borrow money from your bank, but as a small player, the loan would be rather expensive.
- You could ask a friend to invest in the idea as your business partner, but then you could lose a lot of creative control and it might hurt your friendship.
- Or, perhaps, you could crowdfund the money from thousands of people who are interested in seeing your new book come out.

Then, once your book is complete, each contributor would receive a copy (or multiple copies, depending on how much they contributed). So how do you go about raising money in this way? Cue the DeFi Crowdfund DApp Service!

Assessing the competition

In the CeFi-verse, Kickstarter and Indiegogo are two widely used platforms for crowdfunding projects. Both services are trusted and easy to use. However, they are quite expensive. Neither service charges any money up front, but the back-end fee is 5 percent of the total funds raised. Contributors are also charged a 3 percent processing fee (plus an additional $0.20 per contribution).

Thus, from $100,000 worth of contributions, $97,000 makes its way to the fundraising pot, and $92,150 ultimately goes to the entrepreneur.

In addition, these contributions and corresponding claims lack liquidity. Contributors who are no longer interested in receiving a copy of your book can't quickly and easily transfer their book claims.

In the DeFi-verse, you can deploy an ERC-20–compliant smart contract on Ethereum for fundraising purposes, and then create a website with the relevant information. Contributors can rest assured in the trustless security provided by Ethereum's decentralized recordkeeping system.

The gas fees required for you to launch this contract, and, subsequently, for contributors to send you ETH are far lower than the fees charged by established crowdfunding platforms like Kickstarter and Indiegogo.

Moreover, these contributions and corresponding claims are much more liquid and easy to transfer. However, deploying a smart contract can be a rather daunting task for those who are less technically savvy.

Solidifying the value proposition

Overall, the DeFi Crowdfund DApp Service provides an approachable middle ground by quickly generating and deploying a customized smart contract for your project that is integrated with a web application. This service provides a cheaper and no-frills solution for creators and entrepreneurs who aren't tech savvy.

Of course, after you've outlined the value provided by the DeFi Crowdfund DApp Service, you have to decide how much to charge for the service and what the fee structure should look like. You'll also need to come up with a cool tagline.

Finally, you need to build a test product to demonstrate that your idea is feasible.

Preparing Your Development Stack

Building out a full-blown dApp entails connecting your back-end smart contract to a more palatable front-end user interface (UI), with (hopefully!) a streamlined user experience (UX). Naturally, the inherent complexities in implementing a dApp require additional components to your development environment.

To fully execute the `Crowdfund` dApp presented in this chapter, your full stack requires the following:

- The MetaMask browser extension, with funded account(s); and the Remix IDE, an integrated development environment for Solidity, for back-end development.
- An Etherscan account with Etherscan API Keys; and RStudio, an integrated development environment for R, to create the front-end wrapper.

The following sections walk you through the latter components required for front-end integration.

Setting up necessary accounts

To successfully complete this chapter, you need the following accounts:

- A MetaMask account and an Ethereum account funded with ETH (or test ETH for your chosen test network), which I assume you already have.
- An account on Etherscan, which you need for the API keys that will allow your website to communicate with Etherscan.

Follow these steps to create an Etherscan account and generate an API key:

1. **Go to** `https://etherscan.io/`**.**
2. **Click the Sign In link located in Etherscan's navigation toolbar.**

   A sign-in page appears, as shown in Figure 13-1.
3. **Click the Click to Sign Up link, located below the text prompts for your username and password.**

   A new page appears, allowing you to register a new account, as shown in Figure 13-2.
4. **Complete the form and click the Create an Account button.**

Etherscan
Eth: $1,203.83 (-2.88%) | 49 Gwei
All Filters
Search by Address / Txn Hash / Block / Token / Ens
Home
Blockchain
Tokens
Resources
More
Sign In
Welcome back
Login to your account
Username
Username
Password
Forgot your password?
Password
Remember & Auto Login
I'm not a robot
reCAPTCHA
Privacy - Terms
Don't have an account?
Click to sign up
LOGIN

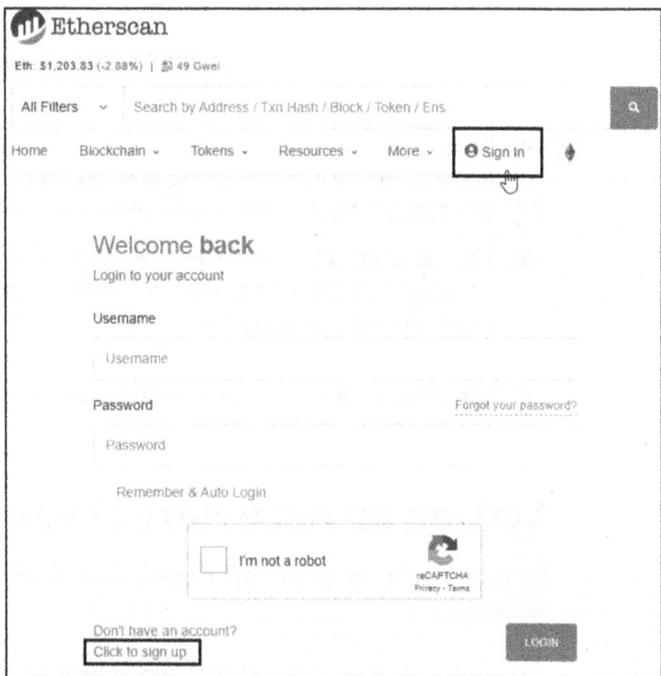

FIGURE 13-1: Account sign-in page on Etherscan.

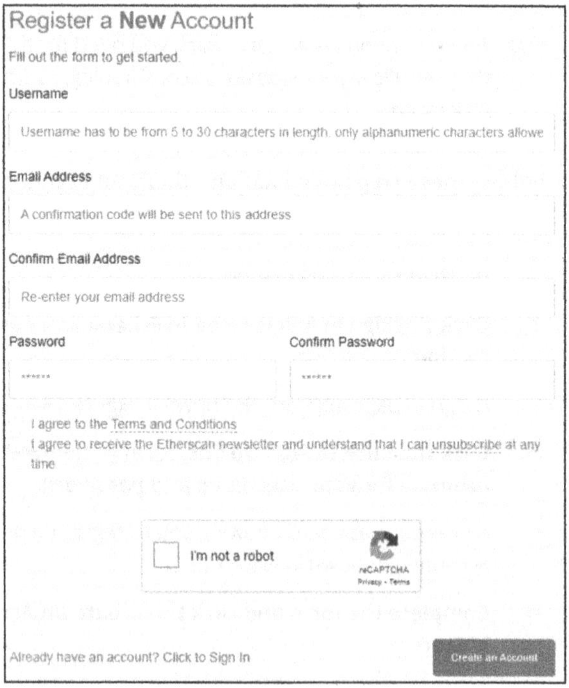

Register a New Account
Fill out the form to get started.
Username
Username has to be from 5 to 30 characters in length, only alphanumeric characters allowe
Email Address
A confirmation code will be sent to this address
Confirm Email Address
Re-enter your email address
Password
Confirm Password
I agree to the Terms and Conditions
I agree to receive the Etherscan newsletter and understand that I can unsubscribe at any time
I'm not a robot
reCAPTCHA
Privacy - Terms
Already have an account? Click to Sign In
Create an Account

FIGURE 13-2: Registering a new account on Etherscan.

5. **Log in to the email address you provided to create your Etherscan account, and click the confirmation link in the email sent to you by Etherscan.**

   You'll be redirected back to Etherscan, now with a successfully verified account, as shown in Figure 13-3.

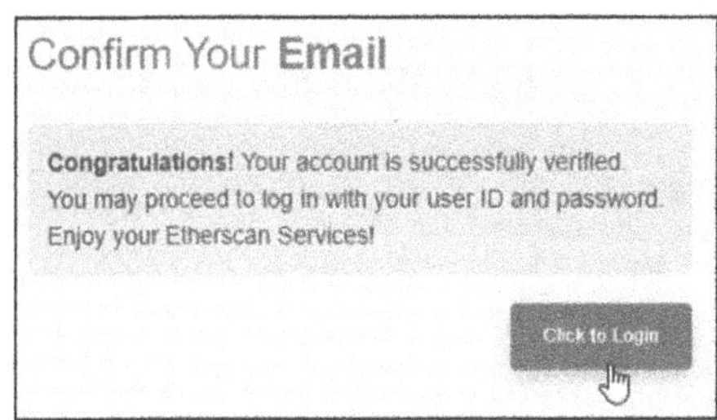

FIGURE 13-3: Verifying successful creation of your new account on Etherscan.

6. **Click the Click To Login button, and then follow the prompts to log in to your newly created account.**

   You'll be brought to the Account Overview page, as shown in Figure 13-4.

7. **Click the hyperlink to the right of the API Key Usage field, located in the Overview Usage information box.**

   You'll be brought to a page showing your active API keys, as shown in Figure 13-5.

8. **Click the + Add button and follow the prompts to name your new API key.**

   Etherscan allows you to create up to three API keys with your free account. Each API key is restricted to five API calls per second.

9. **Finally, copy your API Key Token.**

   You'll need this later when writing the code to issue API calls to Etherscan for the front-end UI of your dApp.

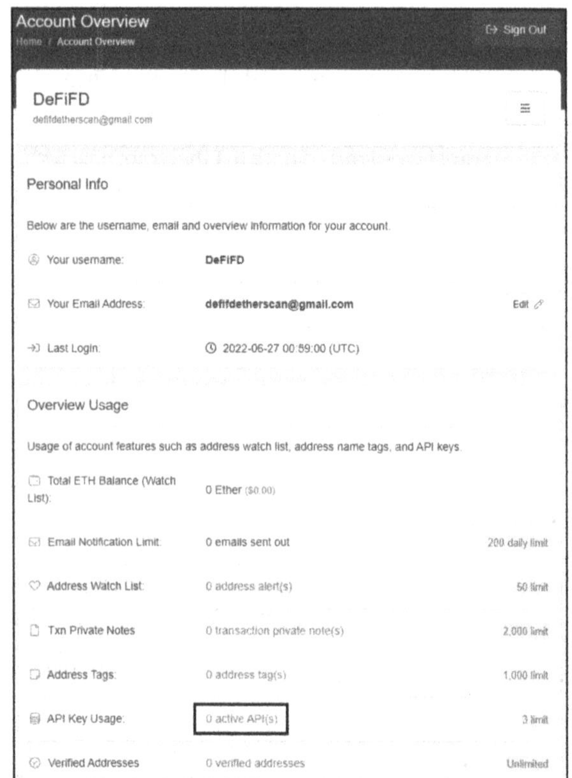

FIGURE 13-4: Account Overview page on Etherscan.

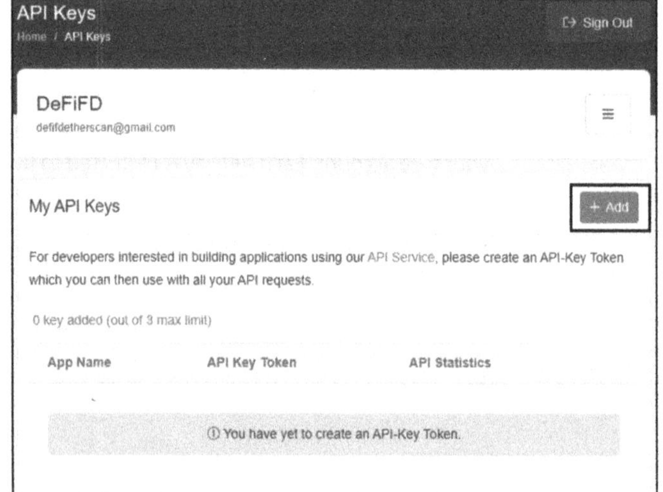

FIGURE 13-5: Viewing API keys associated with your account on Etherscan.

Setting up necessary IDEs

To successfully complete this chapter, you'll use the following ready-made IDEs:

- The Remix IDE, which can be accessed at `https://remix.ethereum.org`.
- The RStudio IDE, which you'll need to download and install.

You'll use the Remix IDE to develop and deploy the smart contract that will serve as the back-end logic for your dApp. Then, you'll use the RStudio IDE to develop the front-end wrapper for the end user.

Follow these steps to set up the Rstudio IDE onto your desktop machine:

1. **Go to** `https://cran.rstudio.com/` **to download and install R.**
2. **Go to** `https://www.rstudio.com/products/rstudio/download` **to download and install Rstudio Desktop.**

Implementing the Back End of Your DApp

In this section, I walk you through the code logic and ultimate deployment for the smart contract that will serve as the back-end logic for your dApp.

Entering your code

First, I present the source code, which can be directly copied from `https://www.seoyoungkim.com/defifdcode.html` with fewer formatting constraints. I also provide a chunk-by-chunk explanation of this code.

If you're feeling antsy to continue with the active, hands-on implementation, you can simply copy the code and skip straight down to the section on "Deploying your `Crowdfund` contract."

Code, uninterrupted

```
pragma solidity 0.8.14;

import
           "@openzeppelin/contracts@4.6.0/token/
  ERC20/ERC20.sol";

contract Crowdfund is ERC20 {
    event LogReceive(address _from, uint256 amount);
    event LogWithdraw(address _to, uint256 amount);

    address public founder;
    uint256 public constant rate = 100;

    constructor() ERC20(
            "DeFi For Dummies",
            "DEFIFD")
    {
            founder = msg.sender;
            _mint(founder,
   1000*1000000000000000000);
    }

    receive() external payable {
            emit LogReceive(msg.sender, msg.value);
            _mint(msg.sender, msg.value * rate);
    }

    function withdraw(
            address payable _to,
            uint256 amount
    )
            public
    {
            require(
             msg.sender == founder,
             "not the founder"
            );
            require(
             address(this).balance >= amount,
             "insufficient funds"
            );
```

```
            _to.transfer(amount);
            emit LogWithdraw(_to, amount);
    }

}
```

The play-by-play guide

Here, I provide a chunk-by-chunk overview of how the source code works.

TIP

To allow you greater autonomy in you DeFi journey, I also include tips below as to what cosmetic changes can easily be made without breaking the code.

```
pragma solidity 0.8.14;
```

This first line of code is the Solidity version pragma, which specifies that this source code should only be compiled under version 0.8.14.

REMEMBER

Recall that statements in Solidity are delimited by semicolons.

```
Import "@openzeppelin/contracts@4.6.0/token/
  ERC20/ERC20.sol";
```

This next line of code imports the `ERC20.sol` source code from OpenZeppelin's smart-contract library. OpenZeppelin provides an overview of the interfaces and contracts for the ERC-20 token standard at `https://docs.openzeppelin.com/contracts/4.x/api/token/erc20`. You can view OpenZeppelin's full `ERC20.sol` source code at `https://github.com/OpenZeppelin/openzeppelin-contracts/blob/v4.6.0/contracts/token/ERC20/ERC20.sol`. You'll notice that `ERC20.sol` itself imports code from additional source files in the OpenZeppelin library.

REMEMBER

Solidity supports multiple inheritance, both directly and indirectly, from numerous base contracts (also known as parent contracts).

```
contract Crowdfund is ERC20 {
```

This statement begins defining the contract, `Crowdfund`. Notice that through the keyword, `is`, `Crowdfund` is derived from a base contract, `ERC20`, which is implemented in the `ERC20.sol` source file imported in the prior line of code. Because `ERC20` itself inherits from other base contracts, `Crowdfund` ultimately inherits from OpenZeppelin's `ERC20`, `IERC20`, `IERC20metadata`, and `Context` contracts.

TIP

You can use a different name for your contract, other than Crowdfund, without having to alter anything else in the code to conform with the alternative contract name you designate.

REMEMBER

Finally, recall that Solidity uses curly brackets to begin and end blocks of code.

```
event LogReceive(address _from, uint256 amount);
event LogWithdraw(address _to, uint256 amount);
```

These lines define two separate events: `LogReceive` and `LogWithdraw`. When emitted, these events are designed to record the values of the specified arguments to the blockchain's ledger as part of an event log associated with this smart-contract account.

```
address public founder;
uint256 public constant rate = 100;
```

These lines declare two public state variables to be retained in contract storage: `founder`, which is an account address, and `rate`, which is a constant unsigned integer. The `founder` variable will be used to determine who has the right to withdraw funds from this contract account. The `rate` variable will be used to determine how many ERC-20 tokens to issue to a contributor per unit of ETH contributed.

TIP

You can replace `rate = 100` with any integer value you prefer without having to worry about any other changes in the code.

```
constructor() ERC20(
    "DeFi For Dummies",
     "DEFIFD")
```

The next block of code defines the special `constructor()` function to be executed only at contract initiation. The additional portion of the function header, `ERC20("DeFi For Dummies, "DEFIFD")`, allows you to specify the token name and ticker, respectively, which will be passed to the constructor function defined in the `ERC20` base contract.

You can customize the name and ticker above by simply replacing "DeFi For Dummies" with your desired name and "DEFIFD" with your desired ticker.

```
{
    founder = msg.sender;
    _mint(founder, 1000*1000000000000000000);
  }
```

Turning to the contents of the `constructor()` function, the first line initializes the `founder` variable to the address of the originating account of this smart contract. The second line calls the `_mint()` function inherited from the `ERC20` base contract. Specifically, at initiation, 1,000 `DEFIFD` tokens will be generated and given to the `founder` account.

You can change this initial 1,000-token founder's bounty to any integer.

The reason I multiply the desired quantity value of 1,000 with 10^{18} is that the `ERC20` base contract sets the default value for `decimals` to 18, following the convention in Ethereum where the smallest possible denomination of ETH is the wei, which equals 10^{-18} = 0.000000000000000001 ETH. Thus, if I simply specified `1000` in the code above, without multiplying by 10^{18}, the end result would be to mint and bestow 1,000 * 10^{-18} = 10^{-15} = 0.000000000000001 `DEFIFD` (and not 1,000 `DEFIFD`!) to the `founder` account.

```
receive() external payable {
    emit LogReceive(msg.sender, msg.value);
    _mint(msg.sender, msg.value * rate);
  }
```

The receive() function enables the contract account to receive funds. In addition, the receive() function has been defined to emit the LogReceive event and to call the _mint() function to create and bestow DEFIFD tokens at a 100:1 ratio (as specified by the rate variable) of ETH contributed.

```
function withdraw(
    address payable _to,
    uint256 amount
)
      public
```

This block of code declares a public function, withdraw(), that accepts two arguments: the address of the account to receive withdrawn funds (_to) and the amount to be withdrawn from the smart contract account (amount).

```
{
    require(
            msg.sender == founder,
            "not the founder"
    );
    require(
            address(this).balance >= amount,
            "insufficient funds"
    );
    _to.transfer(amount);
    emit LogWithdraw(_to, amount);
  }
```

Within the block of code defining the withdraw() function, the first two statements ensure that only the founder account can submit a request to withdraw funds and that the requested withdrawal doesn't exceed the account balance.

If the required conditions are met, the next two statements execute the transfer and emit the event to be logged.

```
  }
```

Finally, a closing curly bracket marks the end of the entire block of contract code!

Deploying your `Crowdfund` contract

Follow these steps to deploy your smart contract:

1. **Click the MetaMask fox icon in your browser's toolbar, and sign in to your account.**

   I proceed on the Ropsten Testnet with my DeFi For Dummies EOA (`0xC3Da0eaB3D30C4a6a298467729B00F-659daDA0BC`), as shown in Figure 13-6, throughout this instructional guide. I assume you're also on the Ropsten Testnet (and funded with rETH) or can now expertly toggle and follow in parallel on your desired network.

   REMEMBER

   Refer to the section on setting up your wallet in Chapter 3 for a refresher on navigating MetaMask.

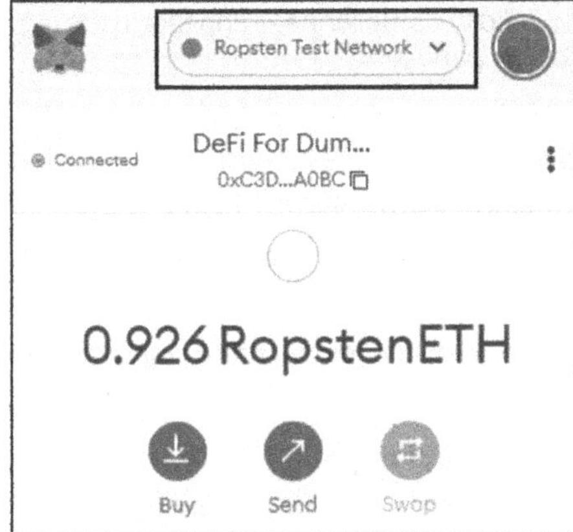

FIGURE 13-6: Connected to the Ropsten Testnet via MetaMask.

2. **Go to** `https://remix.ethereum.org/`.

   WARNING

   If you haven't already done so, I recommend disabling other Web3-enabled browser extensions (and keeping only the MetaMask extension active) as you continue this step-by-step guide.

   TIP

   Refer to Chapter 11 for more detailed instructions and accompanying figures.

3. **Create a new source file and enter the `Crowdfund` contract code provided in the prior section.**

   a. **From the Remix home page, click the New File link.**

      A new, unnamed file appears in the File Explorer browser pane to the left.

   b. **Type** Crowdfund.sol **and press Enter.**

      A new tab labeled "Crowdfund.sol" appears in the main browser pane to the right.

   c. **Enter the `Crowdfund` source code provided earlier. Recall that you can copy and paste this code directly from** `https://www.seoyoungkim.com/defifd/crowdfund.sol`.

4. **Compile your source code by following these steps:**

   a. **Click the Solidity Compiler icon in the navigation toolbar.**

      The Solidity Compiler page appears in the left browser pane.

   b. **From the Compiler drop-down menu, select the 0.8.14commit.80d49f37 option; then click the Compile Crowdfund.sol button.**

      Compilation details appear at the bottom of the Solidity Compiler browser pane.

5. **Deploy your smart contract and copy the contract account address by following these steps:**

   a. **Click the Deploy & Run Transactions (Ethereum) icon in the navigation toolbar located on the far left.**

      The Deploy & Run Transactions page appears in the left browser pane.

   b. **Select the Injected Web3 option from the Environment drop-down menu.**

      If you're not already connected, a MetaMask pop-up notification window appears, allowing you to select the accounts you'd like to connect to the Remix IDE.

   c. **Make sure you've selected the correct contract, `Crowdfund`, and click the Deploy button.**

      After following the pop-up prompts to confirm your transaction request, you can see the `Crowdfund` contract under Deployed Contracts at the bottom of the Deploy & Run Transactions browser pane, as shown in Figure 13-7.

REMEMBER

Be patient. During times of high network volume, your transaction can take quite a while to be mined and included on the public blockchain.

TIP

For a refresher on how to read and write to your smart contract from the Remix browser, refer to Chapter 11.

d. **Click the double-page icon to the right of your contract's name/address to copy your contract account address.**

In my case, the addresses to my contract account and originating EOA are as follows:

- Contract account address: `0xc325b0C0e7fC36e227C88b0a9e18cfA6809f68b6`
- Originating account address: `0xC3Da0eaB3D30C4a6a298467729B00F659daDA0BC`

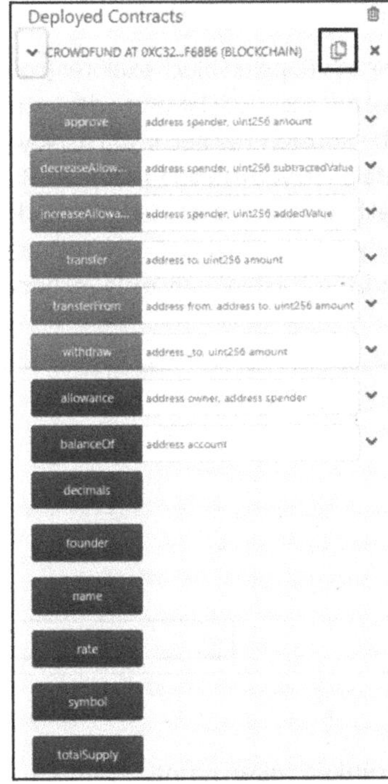

FIGURE 13-7: Deployed Crowdfund contract details from the Deploy & Run Transactions browser pane on Remix.

Following your `Crowdfund` contract

After successfully deploying your smart contract (see the preceding section for help with doing that), you can follow your smart contract on the Ropsten block explorer by taking these steps:

1. **Open a new browser tab, go to** `https://ropsten.etherscan.io`**, and enter your** `Crowdfund` **contract account address into the search bar.**

   In my case, I entered `0xc325b0C0e7fC36e227C88b0a9e18cfA6809f68b6`.

   A new page appears with basic contract details, as shown in Figure 13-8. Notice that a Token Tracker feature now appears, displaying the name (`DeFi For Dummies`) and ticker (`DEFIFD`) for your ERC-20 token.

TIP

   Don't close your Remix browser tab just yet. You'll need to return to Remix to complete the upcoming section, "Verifying your `Crowdfund` contract."

REMEMBER

   I'm using Etherscan's Ropsten block explorer (`ropsten.etherscan.io`) because I've chosen to deploy my smart contract onto the Ropsten Testnet. If you deploy your contract onto Mainnet, you'll need to access a Mainnet block explorer (`www.etherscan.io`). Similarly, if you deploy on a different test network, such as the Goerli Testnet you'll need to access a Goerli block explorer (`goerli.etherscan.io`).

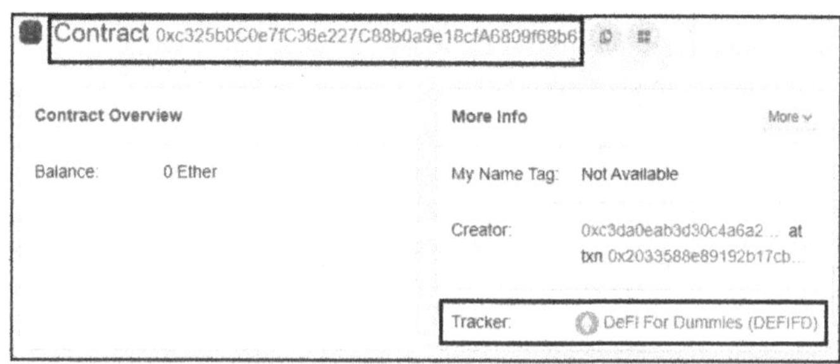

FIGURE 13-8: The `Crowdfund` contract account displayed on Etherscan's block explorer.

2. **Click the hyperlinked token name.**

   The token-tracker mode for your ERC-20 token appears, as shown in Figure 13-9.

The Token Tracker provides a convenient interface to view ERC-20 token-specific information. For instance, notice the following elements in the main dashboard for the `DeFi For Dummies` token:

- The Total Supply is currently 1,000 `DEFIFD`, which was generated at contract origination (in line 14 of the `Crowdfund` contract source code).
- There is currently only one account holding `DEFIFD` tokens, which is the `founder` account that was given these 1,000 tokens at origination (also in line 14 of the `Crowdfund` contract source code).

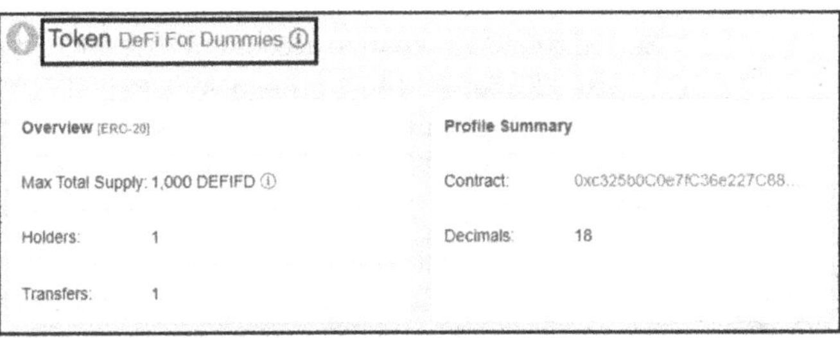

FIGURE 13-9: The `DeFi For Dummies` (`DEFIFD`) ERC-20 token on Etherscan's Token Tracker.

3. **Toggle to the Holders tab.**

   A page displaying all `DEFIFD` token holders appears, as shown in Figure 13-10.

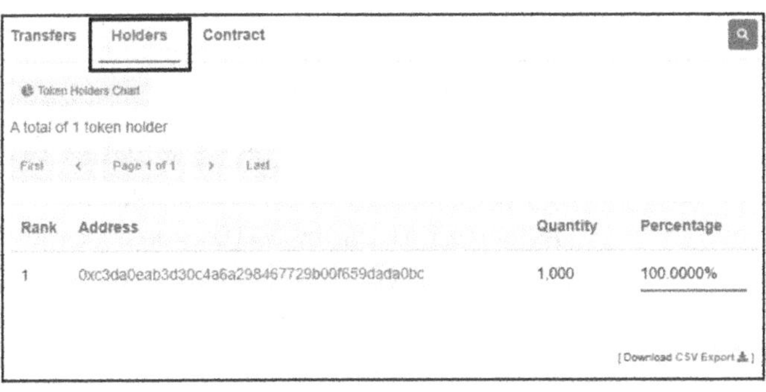

FIGURE 13-10: `DEFIFD` token holders displayed under the Holders tab on the Etherscan's Token Tracker.

So far, just one token holder is holding 100 percent of the token supply (1,000 tokens). Notice that the displayed account address here, 0xC3Da0eaB3D30C4a6a298467729B00F659daDA0BC, corresponds to the founder account that I used to deploy the Crowdfund contract.

Funding Crowdfund

Now you can see what happens when you contribute funds to the Crowdfund contract account. To demonstrate, I use a separate account from the founder account that I used to deploy my Crowdfund contract in the previous section. Specifically:

- My founder account address is 0xC3Da0eaB3D30C4a6a298467729B00F659daDA0BC.
- I've created a separate account, whose address is 0xE3C615a53481A69F118ecbe499CAe1f7DB350988, to send rETH to my Crowdfund contract account at 0xc325b0C0e7fC36e227C88b0a9e18cfA6809f68b6.

REMEMBER

To create a new account in your MetaMask wallet, simply click the colorful circle in the upper-right corner of the main MetaMask menu and select the + Create Account option from the drop-down menu that appears. Refer to the section about funding your account in Chapter 3 for a refresher on getting some ETH or test ETH for your account.

Follow these steps to contribute funds to the Crowdfund contract account and check the updated token stats for DEFIFD:

1. **Click the MetaMask fox icon in your browser's toolbar, and sign in to your account.**
2. **Select your desired account, and make sure you're on the appropriate network.**

   As for me, I'm using my DeFi User account, with account address beginning in 0xE3C; also, I'm connected to the Ropsten Testnet, as shown in Figure 13-11.
3. **Click the Send button, enter your Crowdfund contract address, specify how much rETH to send, and click the Next button.**

   I've opted to send 1 rETH, as shown in Figure 13-12.

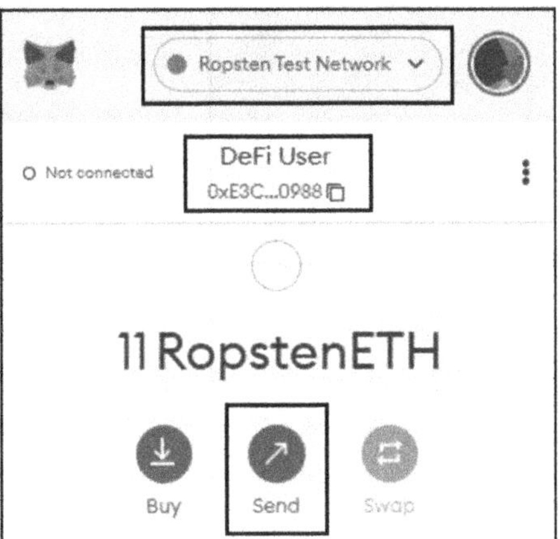

FIGURE 13-11: Initial balance of a separate account, named DeFi User, that will be used to contribute rETH to `Crowdfund`.

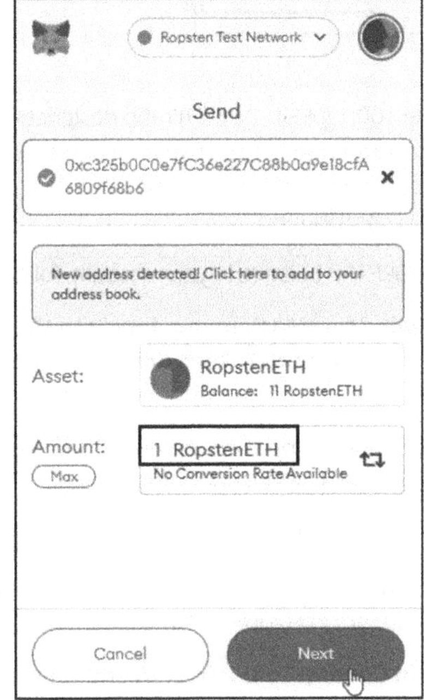

FIGURE 13-12: Sending 1 rETH from my DeFi User account to the `Crowdfund` contract account.

4. **Click the Confirm button on the following screen.**

   After your transaction is mined and completed, you can see that your account balance has decreased accordingly, as shown in Figure 13-13.

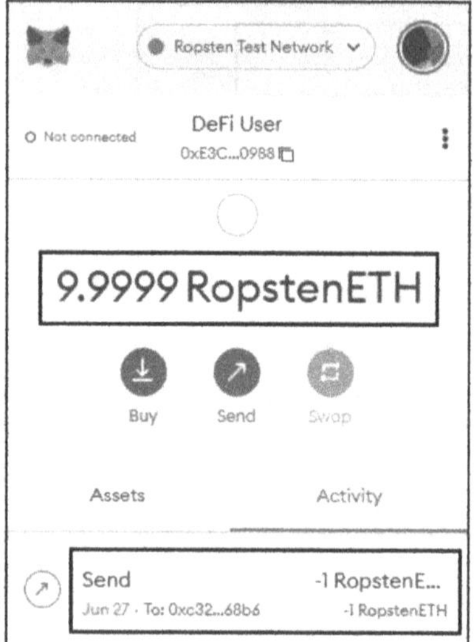

FIGURE 13-13. Updated balance of DeFi User account after sending 1 rETH to `Crowdfund`.

Based on the 100:1 (`DEFIFD`:rETH) ratio designated by the `Crowdfund` contract (see lines 10 and 19 of the `Crowdfund.sol` source code), I should receive 100 `DEFIFD` in exchange for my 1 rETH contribution.

To check the `DEFIFD` balance in your account, follow these steps:

5. **From the main MetaMask menu, toggle to the Assets tab and click the Import Tokens link, as shown in Figure 13-14.**

   A new screen appears, prompting you for information regarding the custom token you want to add.

6. **Enter your `Crowdfund` contract account address.**

   The Token Symbol and Token Decimal fields automatically populate, as shown in Figure 13-15.

7. **Click the Add Custom Token button and then click the Import Tokens button on the page that follows.**

   A new screen appears with your account's `DEFIFD` balance, as shown in Figure 13-16.

   Yay! As expected, my account has been credited 100 `DEFIFD`. Also, as of this step, you have the option to send `DEFIFD` to other accounts. You can return to this screen at any time from the Assets tab on the main MetaMask menu, as shown in Figure 13-17.

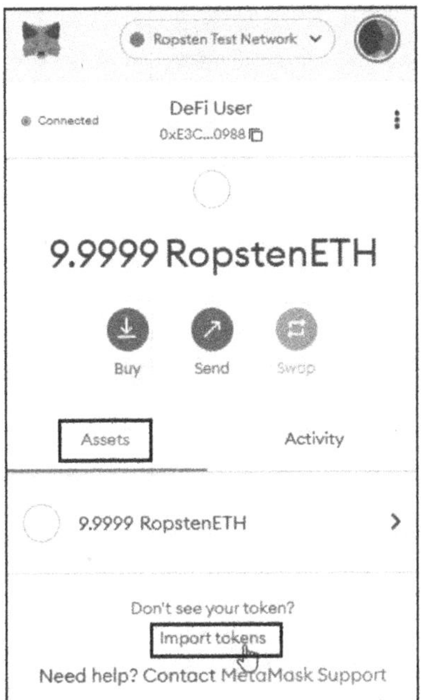

FIGURE 13-14. All token balances are displayed under the Assets tab on the main MetaMask menu.

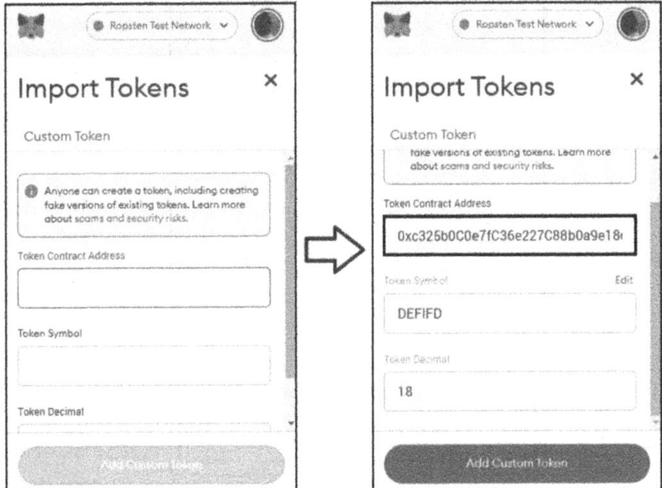

FIGURE 13-15: Adding a custom token to your MetaMask wallet.

For completeness, you can now view this information on the public block explorer.

8. **Return to the Token Tracker on the Etherscan block explorer.**

FIGURE 13-16: My DeFi User account's DEFIFD balance shown in my MetaMask wallet.

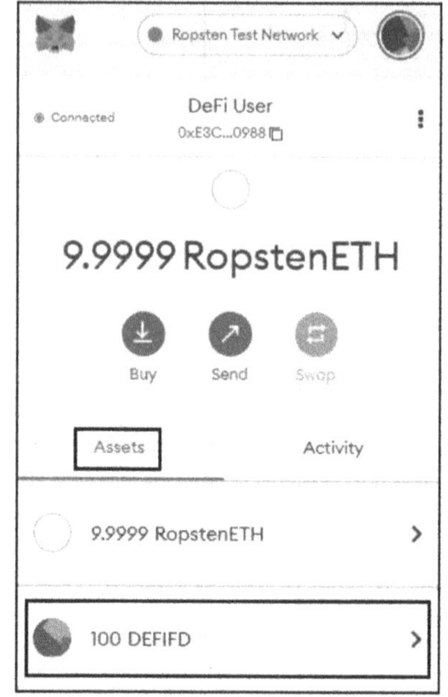

FIGURE 13-17: Accessing DEFIFD balance and option to send DEFIFD tokens from the Assets tab on the main MetaMask menu.

If you've already closed that browser tab, you can follow these steps to return:

a. **Go to** `https://ropsten.etherscan.io/`.

b. **Paste your** `Crowdfund` **contract address into the search bar.**

You can see that the `Crowdfund` contract account now holds a balance of 1 rETH, as shown in Figure 13-18. (Recall that I sent 1 rETH to my `Crowdfund` contract account in Step 3 of this step list.)

c. **Click your hyperlinked token name** — DeFi For Dummies (DEFIFD) **— to access the token-tracker mode.**

Ta-da! You're now back on the `DEFIFD` Token Tracker, as shown in Figure 13-19.

The total token supply is now 1,100 `DEFIFD`, and there are two token holders. (Recall from Figure 13-9, the `DeFi For Dummies` token began with a token supply of 1,000 `DEFIFD` with just one token holder.)

FIGURE 13-18: The updated `Crowdfund` contract account balance shown on the Etherscan block explorer.

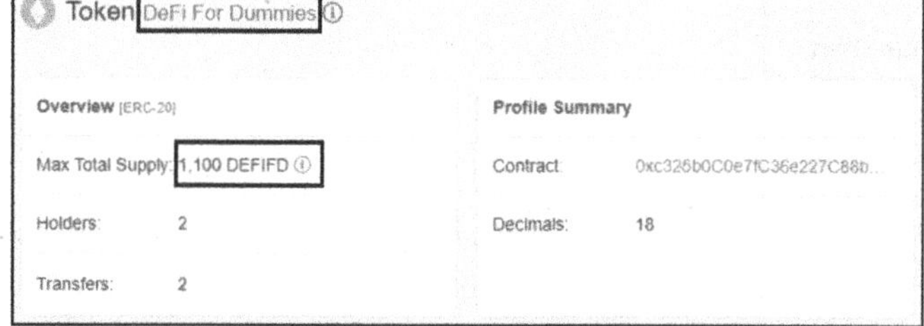

FIGURE 13-19: The updated token supply for `DEFIFD` shown on Etherscan's Token Tracker.

9. **Toggle to the Holders tab.**

A page appears displaying the updated list of `DEFIFD` token holders, as shown in Figure 13-20.

You can also click the Token Holders Chart button for an automatically generated pie chart, as shown in Figure 13-21.

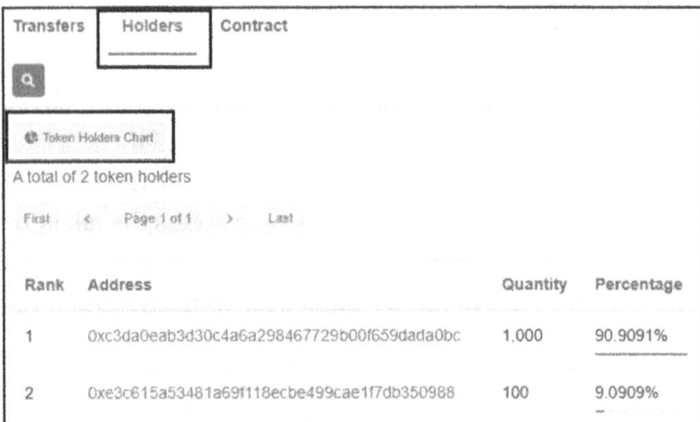
Transfers
Holders
Contract
Token Holders Chart
A total of 2 token holders
First < Page 1 of 1 > Last

Rank	Address	Quantity	Percentage
1	0xc3da0eab3d30c4a6a298467729b00f659dada0bc	1,000	90.9091%
2	0xe3c615a53481a69f118ecbe499cae1f7db350988	100	9.0909%

FIGURE 13-20: The updated `DEFIFD` token-holder information under the Holders tab.

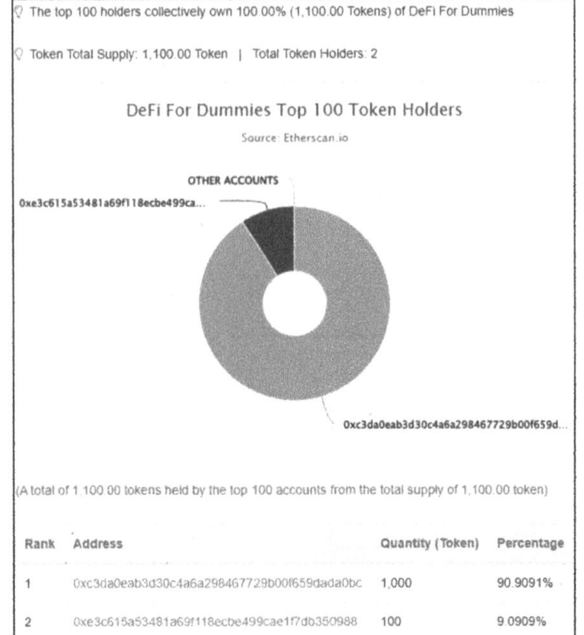

Rank	Address	Quantity (Token)	Percentage
1	0xc3da0eab3d30c4a6a298467729b00f659dada0bc	1,000	90.9091%
2	0xe3c615a53481a69f118ecbe499cae1f7db350988	100	9.0909%

FIGURE 13-21: A pie chart of `DEFIFD` token ownership provided by Etherscan's Token Tracker.

Verifying your `Crowdfund` contract

Finally, to maintain the openness and transparency necessary for a well-functioning DeFi world, follow the steps below to verify and publish your `Crowdfund` contract code.

If you've gone through this process before in Chapter 11 or Chapter 12, you'll notice that the process this time around requires a few extra steps because the `Crowdfund` contract inherits from several other contracts. Specifically, you need to create a flattened file that consolidates the source code across all inherited contracts. Thankfully, Remix has a prebuilt plugin that will do the flattening for you.

Follow these steps to create a flattened file:

1. **Return to your Remix browser tab and click the Home tab from the main Remix browser pane on the right.**
2. **From the home page, click the More button located under the Featured Plugins section, as shown in Figure 13-22.**

   The Remix Plugin Manager appears in the left browser pane, as shown in Figure 13-23.

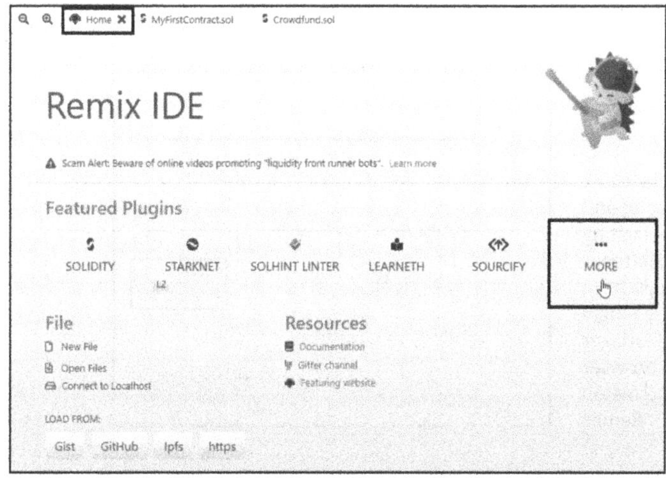

FIGURE 13-22: Accessing additional plugins from the Remix home page.

3. **From the Plugin Manager browser pane, type** flattener **in the search bar.**

   The Flattener plugin appears under the search bar, as shown in Figure 13-24.

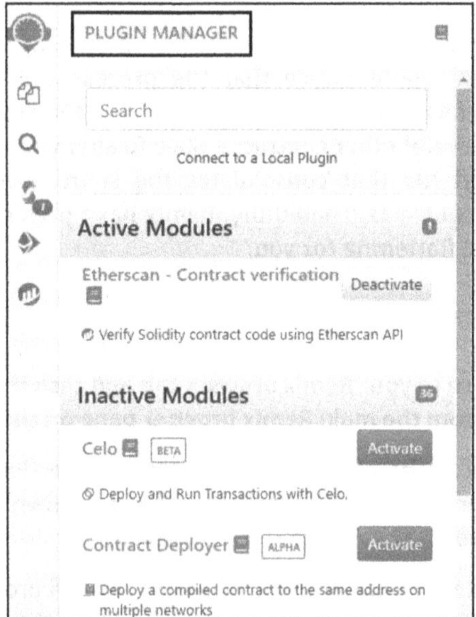

FIGURE 13-23: The Plugin Manager browser pane on Remix.

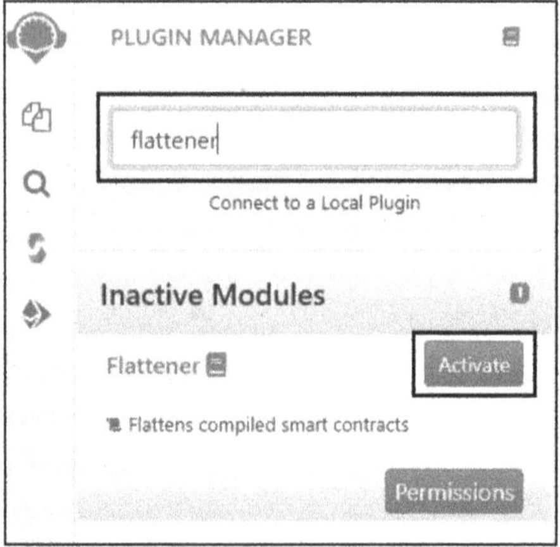

FIGURE 13-24: Locating and activating the Flattener plugin from the Plugin Manager browser pane on Remix.

4. **Click the Activate button.**

   The Flattener plugin's status changes to Active, and a new icon for this plugin appears in the Remix navigation toolbar located to the far left, as shown in Figure 13-25.

5. **Click this new Flattener plugin icon (in the navigation toolbar on the far left).**

   The Flattener page appears in the left browser pane, as shown in Figure 13-26.

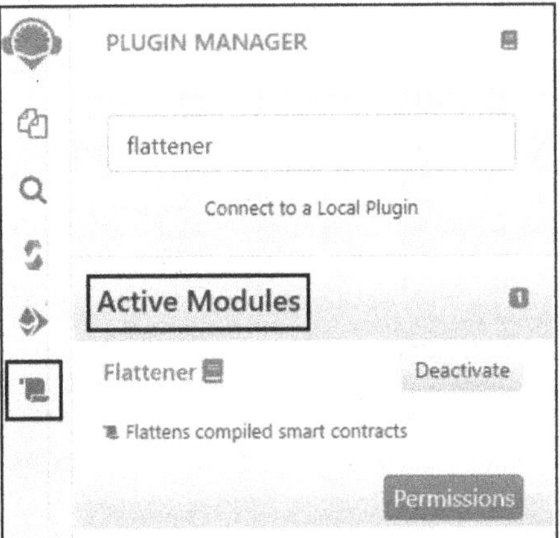

FIGURE 13-25: The activated Flattener plugin with corresponding icon added to the navigation toolbar on Remix.

6. **Click the Flatten Crowdfund.sol button.**

   The label on the button below the Flatten Crowdfund.sol button updates to say Save Crowfund_flat.sol, as shown in Figure 13-26.

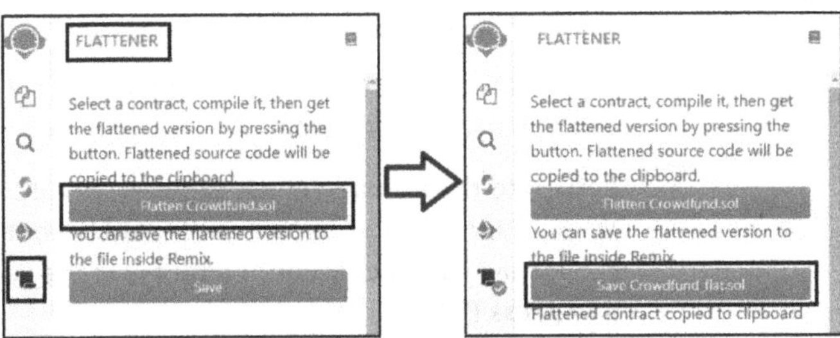

FIGURE 13-26: Flattener browser pane on Remix.

7. **Click the Save Crowdfund_flat.sol button; then click the Accept button on the pop-up window that appears, as shown in Figure 13-27.**
8. **Click the double-page icon in the navigation toolbar (located to the far left) to return to the File Explorer browser pane.**

   A new file, `Crowdfund_flat.sol`, is added to your workspace, as shown in Figure 13-28.

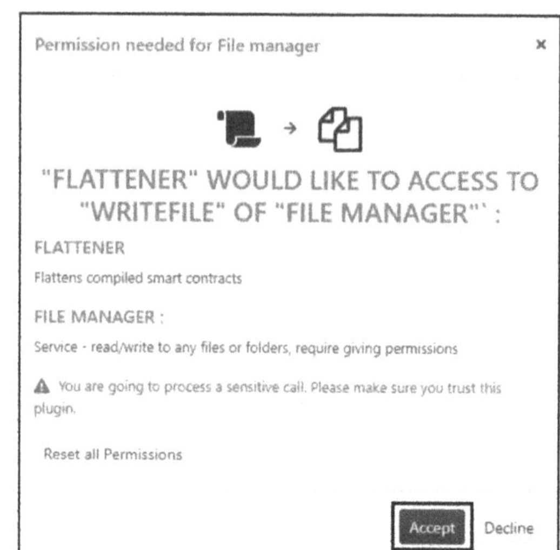

FIGURE 13-27: A pop-up window requesting permission to save the flattened file to your Remix workspace.

9. **Click to open the** `Crowdfund_flat.sol` **file and then copy the source code.**

TIP

You can also access a copy of this flattened file at `https://www.seoyoungkim.com/DEFIFD/Crowdfund_flat.sol`.

Great work; now you're ready to submit your code for verification on Etherscan!

10. **Return to the Ropsten block explorer, accessed at** `https://ropsten.etherescan.io`**, enter your** `Crowdfund` **contract account address in the search bar, and press Enter.**

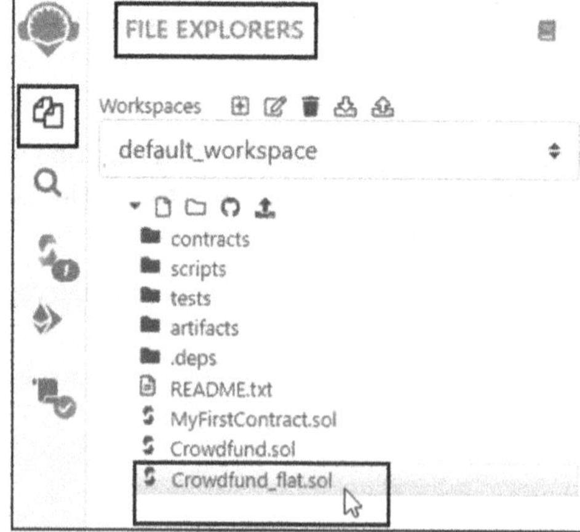

FIGURE 13-28: The newly flattened file in the File Explorer browser pane on Remix.

11. **From the main information page for your `Crowdfund` contract, click to toggle to the Contract tab.**

TIP

If you copied my `Crowdfund` contract code verbatim (from the earlier section called "Entering your code"), you'll likely see that this contract code has already been verified and published, as shown in Figure 13-29. If this is the case, you can skip the rest of this step list.

12. **On the Contract tab, click the Verify and Publish hyperlink.**

    A new page appears with an initial form to complete.

13. **Make the following selections and then click the Continue button:**

    - Verify your `Crowdfund` contract account address, which in my case is:
      `0xc325b0C0e7fC36e227C88b0a9e18cfA6809f68b6`
    - For Compiler Type, select: Solidity (Single file)
    - For Compiler Version, select: v0.8.14+commit.80d49f37
    - For Open Source License Type, select: 3) MIT License

    A new page appears, prompting you to enter your Solidity Contract Code.

14. **Paste in the exact code from the flattened `Crowdfund_flat.sol` source file, and then scroll down to click the Verify and Publish button. (You can ignore the rest of the items on this page.)**

    After your source code has been compiled, a new Compiler Output tab appears, providing the final details.

15. **Click the hyperlinked address to your contract account to return to your `Crowdfund` contract details on the Ropsten block explorer.**

    The Solidity source code is now included under the Contract tab, as shown in Figure 13-29.

FIGURE 13-29: Crowdfund source code now available under the Contract tab.

Yay, you've now successfully verified and published your `Crowdfund` source code! From here, you can toggle to Read Contract or Write Contract modes by clicking the respective buttons under the Contract tab, which provide convenient interfaces to interact with your `Crowdfund` contract.

However, you may notice that the user experience leaves much to be desired, particularly for newbies. For instance, when querying the `DEFIFD` balance of a particular account, as shown in Figure 13-30, the user would have to take into account that `decimals` is set to 18, which means that the displayed `balanceOf` needs to be divided by 10^{18} to arrive at a more meaningful metric of 1,000,000,000,000,000,000,000 / 10^{18} = 1,000 `DEFID`.

So far, this chapter has covered how to deploy and publish your `Crowdfund` contract and `DEFIFD` token on Etherscan. The next section takes a break from the blockchain side and works on the front-end web application for your dApp.

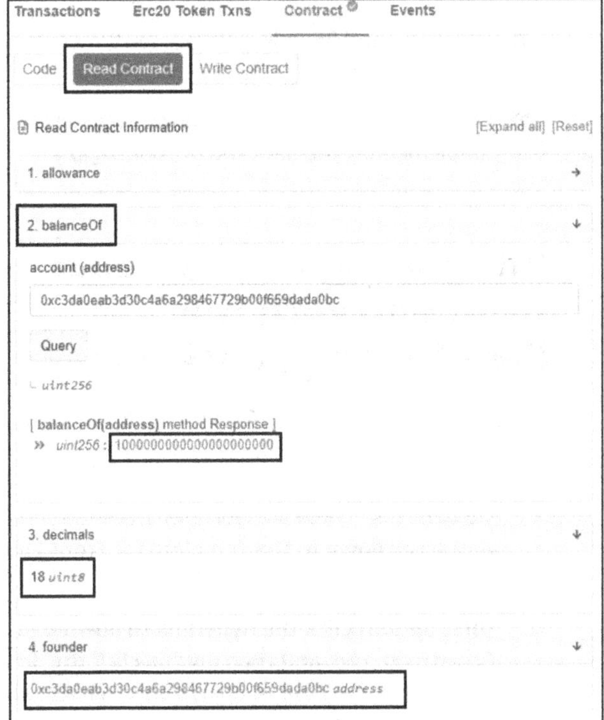

FIGURE 13-30: Viewing values stored in various state variables housed in the `Crowdfund` contract account.

Creating the Front-End User Interface

This section walks you through how to modify the provided template to create a simple front-end web application that is integrated with your `Crowdfund` contract.

I've chosen to proceed in R, which is an open-source language with a robust library of prebuilt packages that allow you to easily implement more complex solutions with minimal programming experience.

REMEMBER

I assume that you have already done the following:

» Created an Etherscan account and API Key Token (see the earlier section "Setting up necessary accounts")

- Installed R and RStudio Desktop (see the earlier section "Setting up necessary IDEs")
- Deployed your `Crowdfund` contract (see the earlier section "Implementing the Back End of Your DApp")

Integrating the friendlier front end with the (less friendly) back end

Follow these steps to download, tweak, and connect your own custom dApp:

1. **Go to** `https://www.seoyoungkim.com/defifdcode.html` **and scroll down to the Template for Front-End Web Application.**
2. **(first option) Click the hyperlink to download** `Crowdfund.rmd`**, and then double-click the downloaded file on your desktop to open it through RStudio.**

   If you're unable to download the hyperlinked file from this Step 2, follow the alternative instructions for Step 2:
3. **(alternative) Open the RStudio Desktop application.**
   a. **Click the New File icon in the RStudio toolbar; then select the R Markdown option from the drop-down menu that appears, as shown in Figure 13-31.**

      A pop-up window appears, prompting you for details of your new R Markdown document, as shown Figure 13-32.

   b. **Click the Create Empty Document button in the lower-left corner of this New R Markdown pop-up window.**

      A blank R Markdown document appears.

   c. **Paste the code from** `https://www.seoyoungkim.com/DeFiFD/Crowdfund.rmd` **into this blank R Markdown document.**

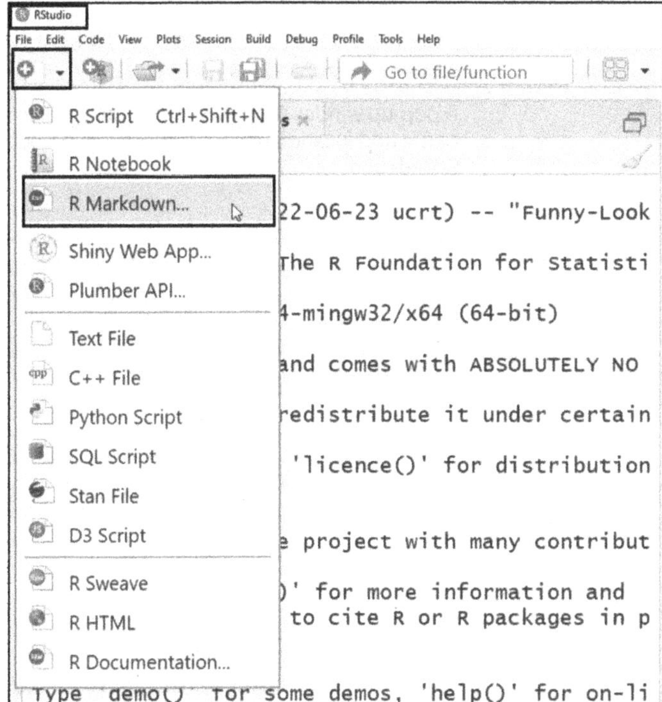

FIGURE 13-31: The drop-down menu to create a new file in RStudio.

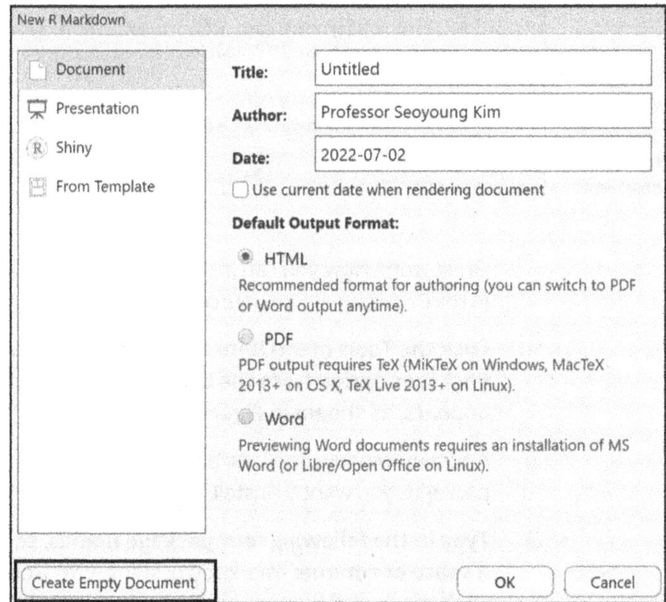

FIGURE 13-32: A pop-up window with specifications for your new R Markdown document.

d. Click the disk icon in the toolbar to save your file, as shown in Figure 13-33.

A pop-up window appears, prompting you to provide the name and location to save this file. I've named my file `Crowdfund.rmd`.

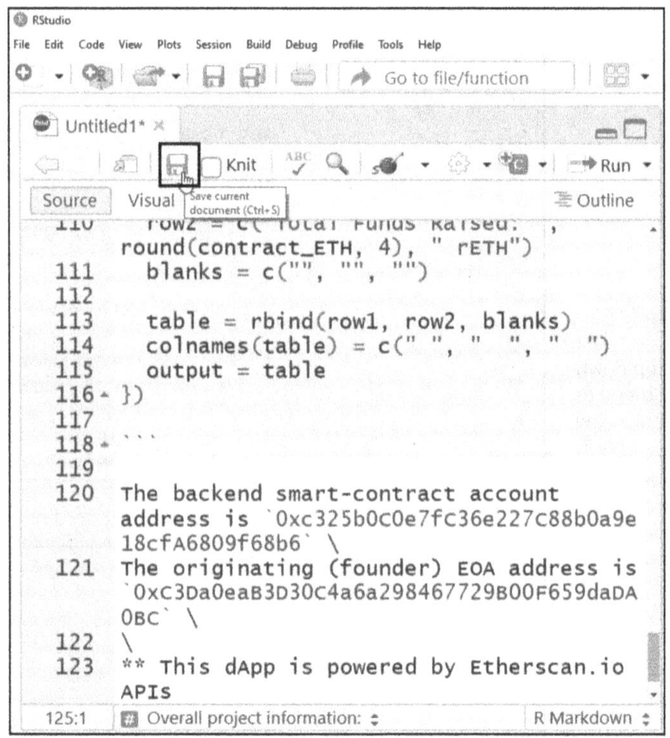

FIGURE 13-33: Saving your new R Markdown document.

Great work! Now you can install the prebuilt packages used in the `Crowdfund.rmd` source code.

4. **Click the Tools menu item and then select the Install Packages option from the drop-down menu that appears, as shown in Figure 13-34.**

   A pop-up window appears, prompting you to list the packages you want to install.

5. **Type in the following four package names, separated by a space or comma:** rmarkdown, shiny, httr, jsonlite**; then click the Install button, as shown in Figure 13-35.**

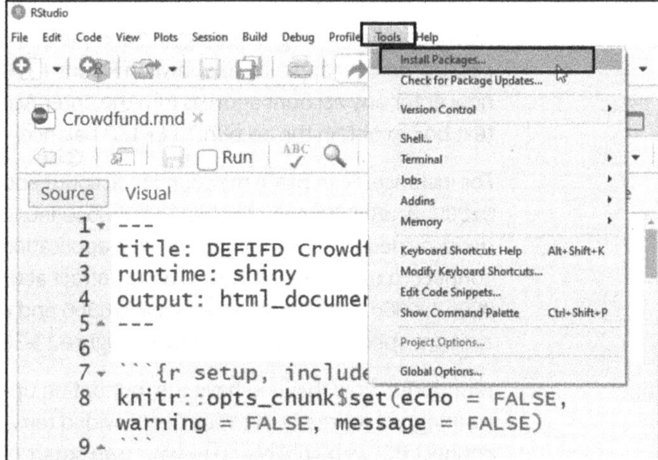

FIGURE 13-34: The Tools drop-down menu on RStudio.

You see a flurry of activity as RStudio works to download and install these packages along with other packages necessary for these to function.

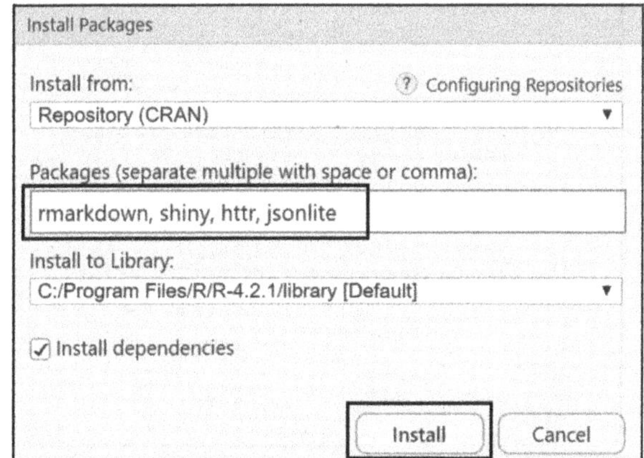

FIGURE 13-35: The Install Packages pop-up window on RStudio.

6. **Click the Run Document play-button icon in the toolbar, as shown in Figure 13-36.**

WARNING

You must compile the code using the Run Document play-button and *not* the Knit button. Compiling your code with the Knit button won't allow you to send HTTPS requests to communicate with Etherscan's server.

After compilation and rendering are complete, a new interactive pop-up window appears, as shown in Figure 13-37. You can now enter any account address into the Enter Account Address text box to obtain the account's `DEFIFD` balance.

For instance, I can paste my `founder` account address, `0xC3Da0eaB3D30C4a6a298467729B00F659daDA0BC`, into the provided text prompt and the web application will connect to my deployed `Crowdfund` contract at `0xc325b-0C0e7fC36e227C88b0a9e18cfA6809f68b6` and update the account-specific metrics, as shown in Figure 13-38.

Wonderful, now that you have the foundation up and running, you're ready to tweak the provided template to connect the web application to your own smart contract.

Crowdfund.rmd ×

Run | Run | Source | Visual | Outline

```
---
title: DEFIFD Crowdfund DApp
runtime: shiny
output: html_document
---

```{r setup, include=FALSE}
knitr::opts_chunk$set(echo = FALSE,
warning = FALSE, message = FALSE)
```

```{r}
library(shiny)
library(httr)
library(jsonlite)
```

\

Want to contribute?
```

125:1 | Overall project information: | R Markdown

FIGURE 13-36: Running `Crowdfund.rmd` on RStudio.

7. **Go to lines 20, 41, 84, and 120 of the code in the** `Crowdfund.rmd` **source file to replace my** `Crowdfund` **contract address,** `0xc325b0C0e7f-C36e227C88b0a9e18cfA6809f68b6`, with yours.

TIP

Line 20 corresponds to the instructional text on the web page; lines 41 and 84 correspond to actual calls to the contract; and line 120 corresponds to informational text presented on the web page.

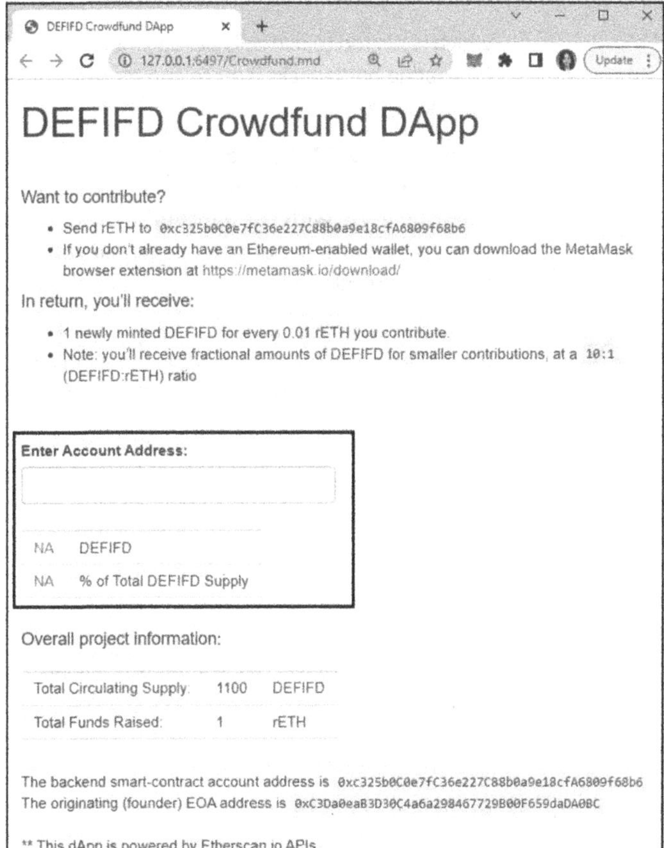

FIGURE 13-37: DEFIFD Crowdfund DApp.

Enter Account Address:

0xC3Da0eaB3D30C4a6a298467729B00F65

1000	DEFIFD
90.9091	% of Total DEFIFD Supply

FIGURE 13-38: Updated account-specific metrics on the DEFIFD Crowdfund DApp.

8. **Go to lines 40 and 83 of the code to replace my Etherscan API Key (beginning in A8BJX) with yours.**

WARNING

The code will still work properly with your `Crowdfund` contract address even if you don't update lines 40 and 83 with your Etherscan API Key. However, using the same complimentary API Key that I created for this exercise, which is limited to five calls per second, is sure to create frustrating bottlenecks if more and more readers simply use my API Key!

9. **Go to lines 45, 57, 87, and 98 of the code to replace the portion of the** `sub1` **string,** `https://api-ropsten.etherscan.io`**, with the appropriate URL for your chosen network (where you deployed your** `Crowdfund` **smart contract).**

WARNING

If you don't edit your code accordingly, the API endpoints won't connect to the correct server and you won't be able to access information about your particular smart contract.

Specifically, the endpoint URLs in your code for Mainnet and the various testnet explorers should begin as follows:

- Mainnet: `https://api.etherscan.io`
- Goerli: `https://api-goerli.etherscan.io`
- Kovan: `https://api-kovan.etherscan.io`
- Rinkeby: `https://api-rinkeby.etherscan.io`
- Ropsten: `https://api-ropsten.etherscan.io`
- Sepolia: `https://api-sepolia.etherscan.io`

10. **Go to line 121 of the code to replace my founder account address,** `0xC3Da0eaB3D30C4a6a298467729B00F-659daDA0BC`, with yours.

TIP

This edit corresponds to a purely cosmetic change to the instructional text presented on the web page.

11. **Click the disk icon in the toolbar to save your file; then click the Run Document play-button icon in the toolbar.**

Lovely; you have now integrated a simple front-end web application with your own back-end smart contract!

Nurturing your dApp

As a final note, your dApp is now like a living organism that is not self-contained in a static and closed system that's under your control. Given the API calls that are critical to the functioning of your front-end interface, you need to monitor and adjust your dApp regularly to ensure that the current specs for the API endpoints haven't changed.

For instance, line 49 (of the `Crowdfund.rmd` code) forms the URL with the current specs to send a request to the Etherscan API endpoint to obtain the `DEFIFD` balance of a given account. Because of the reliance on other systems and the communication protocol required by those systems, you can imagine that your dApp's functionality may change even if (or, especially if!) you keep everything untouched on your end.

With all that said, ta-da! You are now a full-stack developer. Yay!

4 The Part of Tens

IN THIS PART . . .

Discover the ten most-used DeFi applications.

Explore the top ten smart-contract platforms for building tokens, dApps, and DAOs.

IN THIS CHAPTER

» Presenting the ten most used DeFi applications

» Examining use cases of the most popular dApps

Chapter 14
Top Ten DeFi Applications

DeFi activity has exploded in recent years, and in this chapter I cover the top ten dApps by *total value locked* (TVL), as shown in Figure 14-1. As discussed in Chapter 2, the TVL provides a better sense of the actual usage of a given dApp than metrics such as the total market cap or trading volume of the dApp's associated governance token.

You'll notice most of the dApps on this top ten list operate on Ethereum. You'll also notice that dApps running on Ethereum are often deployed on other EVM-compatible platforms as well. If you've gone through the instructional guides in both Chapters 11 and 12, you've experienced firsthand the ease of deploying a smart contract on any EVM-compatible platform after you've done so on Ethereum. Behold the flexibility and power of EVM compatibility!

REMEMBER

As you flip through this chapter, keep in mind that the metrics presented are from August 1, 2022.

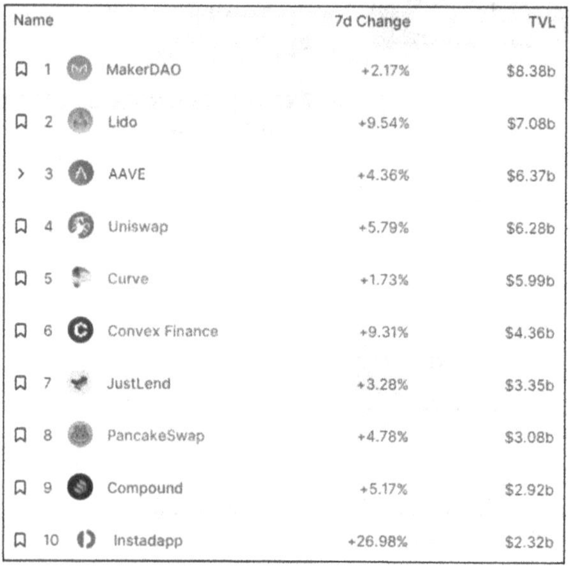

Name		7d Change	TVL
1	MakerDAO	+2.17%	$8.38b
2	Lido	+9.54%	$7.08b
3	AAVE	+4.36%	$6.37b
4	Uniswap	+5.79%	$6.28b
5	Curve	+1.73%	$5.99b
6	Convex Finance	+9.31%	$4.36b
7	JustLend	+3.28%	$3.35b
8	PancakeSwap	+4.78%	$3.08b
9	Compound	+5.17%	$2.92b
10	Instadapp	+26.98%	$2.32b

FIGURE 14-1: The top ten DeFi protocols by TVL from the DefiLlama dashboard, accessed on August 1, 2022.

Instadapp (INST)

Instadapp, which operates on the Ethereum platform (in addition to other EVM-compatible platforms), begins this chapter's list as the tenth most used dApp with a TVL of $2.32 billion (1.44 million ETH). This protocol, which you can access at `https://defi.instadapp.io/`, integrates popular Ethereum-based dApps such as MakerDAO, Compound, Aave, and Uniswap.

The Instadapp dashboard allows users to seamlessly track and move positions in and out of these individual dApps from one location. Instadapp doesn't yet charge a supplementary fee to use the interface to migrate positions across supported dApps on Ethereum (though, of course, users must pay for the gas required to execute these transactions). Instadapp also allows users to migrate their positions across blockchains for dApps that also operate on a related L2 platform, which does incur an additional fee on top of the gas required to execute the transaction.

The associated governance token, INST, is currently valued at $1.015 with a total market cap of approximately $18.4 million.

Compound (COMP)

Compound, a lending protocol operating on the Ethereum platform, comes in at ninth place with a TVL of $2.92 billion (1.79 million ETH).

This protocol, which you can access at `https://app.compound.finance/`, allows users to borrow and lend Ethereum-compliant tokens. The Compound dashboard allows users to track their collateral against their liabilities. Lenders earn a yield on the tokens supplied, and borrowers pay interest on the tokens borrowed. Borrowers must be careful to post additional collateral if the value of their collateral decreases or the value of what they owe increases.

The associated governance token, COMP, is currently valued at $58.82 with a total market cap of approximately $423 million.

PancakeSwap (CAKE)

PancakeSwap, a decentralized exchange operating on the Binance Smart Chain, comes in at eighth place, with a TVL of $3.08 billion (10.95 million BNB).

This protocol, accessed at `https://pancakeswap.finance/swap`, allows users to swap BSC-compliant tokens or to serve as liquidity providers by locking up tokens in any of the liquidity pools. Users who initiate a swap must pay a fee (in addition to the underlying network's transaction fee), and liquidity providers earn a fee for locking up their tokens.

The associated governance token, CAKE, is currently valued at $3.83 with a total market cap of approximately $548 million.

JustLend (JST)

JustLend, a lending protocol operating on the TRON platform, comes in at seventh place in the top ten most used apps, with a TVL of $3.35 billion (48.16 billion TRON).

This protocol, accessed at `https://justlend.just.network/`, allows users to borrow and lend TRON-compliant tokens or to serve as liquidity providers. Like other collateralized lending protocols, borrowers must monitor the value of their collateral against their liabilities and post additional collateral accordingly.

The associated governance token, JST, is currently valued at $0.032 with a total market cap of approximately $287 million.

Convex Finance (CVX)

Convex Finance, a Curve-focused staking protocol operating on the Ethereum platform, comes in at sixth place, with a TVL of $4.36 billion (2.69 million ETH). Curve is a decentralized trading protocol that ranks fifth on this top ten list.

Convex Finance, accessed at `https://www.convexfinance.com/stake`, provides a streamlined way for users to stake their CRV and Curve LP tokens to earn boosted yields on the collective pool. CRV is the governance token associated with the Curve protocol. Curve LP tokens are generated and given to liquidity providers on Curve for each token they stake in any of Curve's liquidity pools.

The associated governance token, CVX, is currently valued at $7.20 with a total market cap of approximately $476 million.

Curve (CRV)

Curve, a decentralized exchange known for trading stablecoins, comes in at fifth place with a combined TVL of $5.99 billion (3.66 million ETH) across ten smart-contract platforms, including Ethereum ($5.65 billion TVL), Polygon ($118 million TVL), and Avalanche ($92 million TVL).

This protocol, which can be accessed at `https://curve.fi/`, allows users to select one of ten networks where the Curve protocol has been deployed. From there, users can swap tokens compatible to that network or opt to serve as liquidity providers by locking tokens in a liquidity pool.

Like other decentralized exchanges, users who initiate a swap must pay a fee (in addition to the transaction fee required by the underlying smart-contract platform), and liquidity providers earn a fee. One unique feature of Curve relative to other decentralized exchanges is that the Curve protocol stakes unused liquidity on the Compound lending protocol to generate additional income for liquidity providers.

The associated governance token, CRV, is currently valued at $1.31 with a total market cap of approximately $682 million.

Uniswap (UNI)

Uniswap, the first widespread and successfully deployed automated market maker, comes in at fourth place with a combined TVL of $6.28 billion (3.8 million ETH) across five smart-contract platforms, including Ethereum ($6.27 billion TVL), Polygon ($82 million TVL), and Artbitrum ($76 million TVL).

This protocol, accessed at `https://app.uniswap.org/`, allows users to select one of five networks where they can either swap compatible tokens or lock up tokens to provide liquidity.

The associated governance token, UNI, is currently valued at $8.38 with a total market cap of approximately $6.2 billion.

Aave (AAVE)

Aave, a lending protocol that was the first to implement flash loans, is the third most used DeFi application, with a combined TVL of $6.37 billion across two active versions:

- Aave V2, which has a combined TVL of $5.21 billion (3.18 million ETH) across Ethereum, Polygon, and Avalanche
- Aave V3, which has a combined TVL of $1.16 billion (49.2 million AVAX) across Avalanche, Optimism, Polygon, Arbitrum, Fantom, and Harmony

This protocol, accessed at `https://app.aave.com/`, allows users to borrow and lend on the selected network.

The associated governance token, AAVE, is currently valued at $96.90 with a total market cap of approximately $1.35 billion.

Lido (LDO)

Lido comes in at second place with a combined TVL of $7.08 billion (4.38 million ETH) across Ethereum, Solana, Kusama, Polygon, and Polkadot.

This protocol, accessed at `https://stake.lido.fi/`, allows users to stake a supported native token (ETH, SOL, KSM, MATIC, and DOT). Users earn a yield on staked tokens and also receive corresponding staking tokens that can then be lent or staked to earn further yields.

The associated governance token, LDO, is currently valued at $2.08 with a total market cap of approximately $651 million.

Maker (MKR)

Finally, number one on the list is the Maker Protocol, a lending protocol operating on Ethereum with a TVL of $8.38 billion (5.17 million ETH).

This protocol allows users to borrow funds, in the form of DAI (an algorithmic stablecoin), by creating and depositing supported collateral in a Maker Vault. To retrieve the collateral, the DAI must be repaid along with a stability fee. Oasis, accessed at `https://oasis.app/`, provides a simple user interface to deploy and collateralize a Maker Vault contract. Oasis also facilitates leveraged positions and leveraged yield farming by automatically redeploying the borrowed DAI.

The associated governance token, MKR, is currently valued at $1,065.75 with a total market cap of approximately $1.08 billion.

IN THIS CHAPTER

» Exploring the ten most active smart-contract platforms

» Presenting additional measures of DeFi activity

Chapter 15

Top Ten Smart-Contract Platforms

In this chapter, I cover the top ten smart-contract platforms by *total value locked* (TVL), as shown in Figure 15-1. As discussed in Chapter 2, a platform's TVL provides a better sense of the actual DeFi activity on the platform than metrics such as the total market cap or trading volume of the platform's native token. I also provide the number of active DeFi applications built on each of these platforms along with the market cap of the native token for each platform.

Unsurprisingly, you'll notice that the vast majority of platforms on this list are EVM-compatible, and a few layer-2 protocols have made the list. See Chapter 10 for more details on layer-1 versus layer-2 platforms.

At the time of this top ten snapshot, all the platforms, except for Ethereum, were secured by proof-of-stake consensus protocols. As of September 15, 2022, Ethereum underwent a process known as The Merge, effectively transitioning from a proof-of-work to proof-of-stake consensus protocol. See Chapter 9 for more details on consensus mechanisms.

Name		Protocols	7d Change	1m Change	TVL
1	Ethereum (ETH)	526	+3.79%	+24.89%	$57.11b
2	BSC (BNB)	434	+2.93%	+12.02%	$6.72b
3	Tron (TRON)	10	+1.55%	+50.00%	$5.86b
4	Avalanche (AVAX)	239	-9.03%	+4.78%	$2.76b
5	Solana (SOL)	73	+1.38%	+14.53%	$2.71b
6	Polygon (MATIC)	279	-0.25%	+15.18%	$1.85b
7	Cronos (CRO)	73	+3.09%	+11.20%	$1.29b
8	Fantom (FTM)	253	-1.07%	+4.80%	$890.05m
9	Arbitrum	107	+13.52%	+14.64%	$842.74m
10	Optimism	60	+36.11%	+114%	$592.55m

FIGURE 15-1: Top ten smart-contract platforms by TVL from the DefiLlama dashboard accessed on August 1, 2022.

REMEMBER

As you flip through this chapter, keep in mind that the metrics presented are from August 1, 2022.

Optimism (OP)

Based on a combined TVL of $593 million across 60 dApps, Optimism starts off this chapter's list as the tenth most active smart-contract platform.

Optimism is an EVM-compatible blockchain, which allows developers to easily port over smart contracts developed for Ethereum onto Optimism. Moreover, as a layer-2 rollup (see Chapter 10), transactions on Optimism are both faster and cheaper than on Ethereum. Here are a few of its most active protocols:

- Aave V3, a lending protocol that has also been deployed on Avalanche, Polygon, Arbitrum, Fantom, and Harmony.
- Synthetix, a synthetic liquidity protocol that issues derivative tokens designed to track and provide payoffs based on how another asset performs. Synthetix has also been deployed on Ethereum.
- Velodrome, a decentralized exchange.

» Uniswap, a decentralized exchange that has also been deployed on Ethereum, Polygon, Arbitrum, and Celo.

OP, the native token of Optimism, is currently valued at $1.52, which puts the total market cap at approximately $367 million.

Arbitrum (N/A)

Aribitrum, another EVM-compatible blockchain, comes in at ninth place with a combined TVL of $843 million across 107 dApps. Like Optimism, Arbitrum is also a layer-2 rollup, providing cheaper and faster executions than Ethereum.

A few of its most active protocols are

» GMC, a decentralized exchange that has also been deployed on Avalanche

» Radiant, a lending protocol that aims to add cross-chain interoperability over time

» Sushiswap, a decentralized exchange that has also been deployed on 14 other platforms (including Ethereum, Polygon, and Avalanche, to name a few)

» Curve, a decentralized exchange that has also been deployed on nine other platforms (including Ethereum, Polygon, and Avalanche, to name a few)

Arbitrum doesn't have its own native token. Instead, ETH and other Ethereum-compliant tokens are deposited in a bridge contract on Ethereum, and corresponding tokens are minted for use on Arbitrum.

Fantom (FTM)

Fantom, which is also EVM-compatible, is in eighth place with a combined TVL of $890 million across 253 dApps. Unlike Optimism and Arbitrum, Fantom operates independently as a separate layer-1 protocol.

A few of its most active protocols are

- SpookySwap, a decentralized exchange
- Beethoveen X, another decentralized exchange
- Geist, a lending protocol

FTM, the native token of Fantom, is currently valued at $0.34, which puts the total market cap at approximately $874 million.

Cronos (CRO)

Cronos, another EVM-compatible layer-1 protocol, comes in at seventh place with a combined TVL of $1.3 billion across 73 dApps. A few of its most active protocols are

- VVS Finance, a decentralized exchange
- Tectonic, a lending protocol
- Ferro, a decentralized exchange specializing in stablecoin swaps

CRO, the native token of Cronos, is currently valued at $0.14, which puts the total market cap at approximately $3.5 billion.

Polygon (MATIC)

Polygon, an EVM-compatible layer-2 plasma chain, is the sixth most active smart-contract platform with a combined TVL of $1.85 billion across 279 dApps. A few of its most active protocols are

- Aave V2, a lending protocol that has also been deployed on Ethereum and Avalanche
- Quickswap, a decentralized exchange

- Curve, a decentralized exchange specializing in stablecoins that has also been deployed on nine other platforms (including Ethereum, Avalanche, and Arbitrum, to name a few)

MATIC, the native token of Polygon, is currently valued at $0.89, which puts the total market cap at approximately $7.2 billion.

Solana (SOL)

Solana ranks as the fifth most active platform with a combined TVL of $2.71 billion across 73 dApps. Unlike most of the platforms on this list, Solana is not EVM-compatible. Yet, the platform is already buzzing with DeFi activity.

A few of its most active protocols are

- Marinade, a protocol that allows users to stake SOL to earn a yield as well as receive corresponding staking tokens that can then be lent or staked to earn further yields
- Solend, a lending protocol
- Serum, a decentralized exchange

SOL, the native token of Solana, is currently valued at $41.79, which puts the total market cap at approximately $14.5 billion.

Avalanche (AVAX)

Avalanche, another EVM-compatible layer-1 protocol, comes in at fourth place with a combined TVL of $2.76 billion across 239 dApps. A few of its most active protocols are

- Aave V3, a lending protocol that has also been deployed on Optimism, Polygon, Arbitrum, Fantom, and Harmony
- BENQI, a lending protocol

- Trader Joe, a self-proclaimed one-stop shop for trading, lending, staking, pooling, and yield farming

AVAX, the native token of Avalanche, is currently valued at $23.66, which puts the total market cap at approximately $6.7 billion.

TRON (TRON)

TRON is in third place as a smart-contract platform with a combined TVL of $5.86 billion across 10 dApps. TRON is mostly EVM-compatible, which eases the learning curve for developers familiar with Ethereum. However, TRON has a few key differences from Ethereum, making it incompatible with MetaMask, as discussed in Chapter 10.

A few of its most active protocols are

- JustLend, a lending protocol
- SunSwap, a decentralized exchange
- JustStable, a protocol that allows users to borrow funds in the form of USDJ (an algorithmic stablecoin) by creating and maintaining collateralized debt positions

TRON, the native token of TRON, is currently valued at $0.07, which puts the total market cap at approximately $6.5 billion.

Binance Smart Chain (BNB)

The second-place platform is Binance Smart Chain, another EVM-compatible layer-1 protocol, with a combined TVL of $6.72 billion across 434 dApps. A few of its most active protocols are

- PancakeSwap, a decentralized exchange.

- Venus, a protocol that allows users to borrow funds in the form of VAI (an algorithmic stablecoin) by creating and maintaining collateralized debt positions.
- Alpaca Finance, a lending protocol that facilitates leveraged yield farming by redeploying borrowed tokens. Alpaca Finance has also been deployed on Fantom.

BNB, the native token of Binance Smart Chain, is currently valued at $283.54, which puts the total market cap at approximately $45.75 billion.

Ethereum (ETH)

Finally, number one on the list (of course!) is Ethereum, with a combined TVL of $57 billion across 526 dApps. A few of its most active protocols are

- Maker, a protocol that allows users to borrow funds in the form of DAI (an algorithmic stablecoin) by creating and maintaining collateralized debt positions
- Lido, a liquid staking protocol that has also been deployed on Solana, Kusama, Polygon, and Polkadot
- Uniswap, a decentralized exchange that has also been deployed on Polygon, Arbitrum, Optimism, and Celo
- Curve, a decentralized exchange specializing in stablecoins that has also been deployed on nine other platforms (including Polygon, Avalanche, and Arbitrum, to name a few)
- Aave V2, a lending protocol that has also been deployed on Polygon and Avalanche

ETH, the native token of Ethereum, is currently valued at $1,635.20, which puts the total market cap at approximately $199 billion.

Index

C

D

E

F

G

H

I

J

K

L

M

P

Q

R

S

T

U

V

W

X

Y

Z

About the Author

I enjoy reading, writing, ideating, staying up late, going down endless rabbit holes, and guiding the discourse in new and highly impactful areas. This book is the magical by-product of these core interests.

Dedication

This book is for Big Bird (a.k.a. `tlaurence2`), my beautiful friend and coauthor-in-crime, who held my hand through my first crypto transaction many years ago. And, of course, Mama Kim and Papa Kim. I love you guys. XXOO. ❤

Author's Acknowledgments

This book would not have been possible without the guidance and support of a generous and highly talented village.

Prefacing that order doesn't convey relative importance, I first thank the editorial team: Alex Cracraft (my technical editor) for lending his expertise and labor of love; Susan Christophersen (my project/copy editor) for keeping the production process on track and for her careful attention to detail; and Steve Hayes (my executive editor) for making this whole thing happen.

I am also most grateful and forever indebted to my Indian Mafia: Sanjiv Das, for bringing me to Silicon Valley; Seema Sarin, for promising me tenure; Atulya Sarin, for making it happen; and George Chacko, for his ongoing encouragement and astute judgment.

Finally, I thank: Chris Paisley, my very dear friend and lunch buddy, for providing a constant source of wisdom and comfort; Navah Statman, for always providing an open heart and open home; Meir Statman, my aspirational mentor, for lending his expert guidance in straddling the worlds of academic ("non-normal") and "normal" people; Dixie and Roman Wang, for providing a peaceful writing sanctuary; and Susan and Jim Cracraft for their troubleshooting support and for turning this journey into a heartwarming family affair.

Thank you, everyone!

Publisher's Acknowledgments

Executive Editor: Steve Hayes

Project and Copy Editor: Susan Christophersen

Technical Editor: Alex Cracraft

Production Editor: Mohammed Zafar Ali

Cover Image: © Yurchanka Siarhei/ Shutterstock